Development Prospects for North Korea

The contributors to this book explore the current situation of North Korea in various aspects and provide policy suggestions for North Korea to become part of the international community and achieve sustainable development.

Focusing on three key areas of economic development, namely, international sectors, agriculture and urban development, and energy and environment, this book lays out recommendations and prospects for North Korea. Authors assess the current situation of North Korea, explore preconditions for becoming a member of the international community, and suggest policies necessary for the sustainable development of North Korea. They cover a wide range of areas including reforestation, WTO accession, and the potential for economic integration with South Korea. These evaluations draw on both what is understood about the current situation in North Korea and comparisons with other countries and territories.

This book will be a valuable resource for scholars and policy planners who focus on North Korea.

Tae Yong Jung is Director of the Research Center for Global Sustainability at the Institute for Global Engagement and Empowerment and a professor in the Graduate School of International Studies, at Yonsei University, South Korea.

Sung Jin Kang is Professor in the Department of Economics and Graduate School of Energy and Environment at Korea University, South Korea.

Routledge Advances in Korean Studies

38 **Strategic, Policy and Social Innovation for a Post-Industrial Korea**
Beyond the Miracle
Joon Nak Choi, Yong Suk Lee and Gi-Wook Shin

39 **North Korea's Foreign Policy**
The DPRK Part on the International Scene and Its Audiences
Lenka Caisova

40 **Public Management in Korea**
Performance Evaluation and Public Institutions
Edited by Soonae Park

41 **Megacity Seoul**
Urbanization and the Development of Modern South Korea
Yu-Min Joo

42 **Korean Adoptees and Transnational Adoption**
Embodiment and Emotion
Jessica Walton

43 **Digital Development in Korea, Second Edition**
Lessons for a Sustainable World
Myung Oh and James F. Larson

44 **The State, Class and Developmentalism in South Korea**
Development as Fetish
Hae-Yung Song

45 **Development Prospects for North Korea**
Edited by Tae Yong Jung and Sung Jin Kang

For more information about this series, please visit: www.routledge.com/asianstudies/series/SE0505

Development Prospects for North Korea

Edited by Tae Yong Jung and Sung Jin Kang

Routledge
Taylor & Francis Group
LONDON AND NEW YORK

First published 2021
by Routledge
2 Park Square, Milton Park, Abingdon, Oxon OX14 4RN

and by Routledge
605 Third Avenue, New York, NY 10017

First issued in paperback 2022

Routledge is an imprint of the Taylor & Francis Group, an informa business

Publisher's Note
The publisher has gone to great lengths to ensure the quality of this reprint but points out that some imperfections in the original copies may be apparent.

British Library Cataloguing-in-Publication Data
A catalogue record for this book is available from the British Library

Library of Congress Cataloging-in-Publication Data
A catalog record for this book has been requested

ISBN 13: 978-0-367-56944-0 (pbk)
ISBN 13: 978-0-367-56943-3 (hbk)
ISBN 13: 978-1-003-10001-0 (ebk)

DOI: 10.4324/9781003100010

Typeset in Times New Roman
by Apex CoVantage, LLC

Contents

Preface

This volume is an edited collection of studies by several experts in the field of North Korea. In these pages, the reader will find academic studies aimed at aiding North Korea in achieving sustainable development.

These authors' careful analyses of topics run the gamut from the marketization occurring under Kim Jong-un; suggestions on new reforms, openness, and other policies; joining the international community in organizations like the World Trade Organization; North Korea's accomplishments and failures dealing with climate change under the Paris Agreement; and even comprehensive strategies to end and reverse the degradation of forests in North Korea.

This book is unified by the aim of driving North Korean policies in a direction as yet unseen in the "hermit kingdom." This book is directed to multiple audiences, from experts studying North Korea's economy or inter-Korea cooperation, to policy practitioners developing tomorrow's strategies, it is hoped that there is something for everyone. The authors of this book earnestly hope that readers will find something of use in this book to further their ardent search for a better tomorrow for the Korean Peninsula and international community.

Figures

Tables

Abbreviations, acronyms, symbols, and units

Abbreviations and acronyms

ADB	Asian Development Bank
AREP	Agricultural Recovery and Environment Protection
ASEAN	Association of Southeast Asian Nations
AWE	agricultural water equilibrium
BAU	business as usual
BOA	Bank of America
C2C	city to city
CBD	Central Business Districts
CDM	Clean Development Mechanism
CER	Certified Emission Reduction
CGE	computable generable equilibrium
CI	carbon intensity
CO2	carbon dioxide
COP	Conference of Parties
CRI	Climate Risk Index
CTCN	Climate Technology and Center Network
DM	German mark
DMZ	demilitarized zone
EDZ	economic development zone
EI	energy intensity of energy
ET	emission trading
ETS	emission trading system
EU	European Union
FAO	Food and Agriculture Organization
FDI	foreign direct investment
Fe	iron ores
FETZ	free economic and trade zone
FTA	Free Trade Agreement
GATT	General Agreement on Tariffs and Trade
GDP	gross domestic product
GEF	Global Environment Fund

GHG	greenhouse gas
GIC	Gaeseong Industrial Complex
GNI	gross national income
GSP	General System of Preferences
GTAP DB	Global Trade Analysis Project Database
GVSP	Gross Value of Social Product
HDB	Housing Development Board
IBK	Industrial Bank of Korea
ICBM	intercontinental ballistic missile
IMF	International Monetary Fund
INDC	intended nationally determined contribution
IT	information technology
ITMO	internationally transferred mitigation outcome
IUCN	International Union for Conservation of Nature and Natural Resources
JCM	Joint Crediting Mechanism
JI	joint implementation
K-ETS	Korea's Emission Trading Scheme
KDB	Korea Development Bank
KIEP	Korea Institute for International Economic Policy
KIET	Korea Institute for Industrial Economics and Trade
KNDA	Korea National Diplomatic Academy
KORUS FTA	The Korea-US Free Trade Agreement
KOSIS	Korean Statistical Information Service
KOTRA	Korea Trade-Investment Promotion Agency
KP	Kyoto Protocol
KRW	Korean won
LMDI	Logarithmic Mean Divisia Index
MFN	most favored nations
MFTR	Memorandum on Foreign Trade Regime
MgO	Magnesite
MoLEP	Ministry of Land and Environment Protection
NDC	nationally determined contributions
NGO	nongovernmental organization
NEP	net ecosystem production
NSTM	new sub-work team management
NT	national treatment
NTR	normal trade relations
ODA	official development assistance
OECD	Organisation for Economic Co-operation and Development
PA	The Paris Agreement
POP	persistent organic pollutant
PPP	public-private partnership
REDD+	reducing emissions from deforestation and forest degradation

RUB	Russian ruble
SD	sustainable development
SDGs	sustainable development goals
SDM	sustainable development mechanism
SEZ	special economic zone
SGD	Singapore dollar
SMG	Seoul Metropolitan Government
SOC	social overhead costs
STRI	Service Trade Restrictiveness Index
SWIID	Standardized World Income Inequality Database
TEC	Technology Executive Committee
TFC	total final energy consumption
TiSA	Trade in Service Agreements
TOE	tonne of oil equivalent
TPES	total primary energy supply
TPP	Trans-Pacific Partnership
UN	United Nations
UNDP	United Nations Development Program
UNEP	United Nations Environment Program
UNFCCC	United Nations Framework Convention on Climate Change
UNSCR	United Nations Security Council Resolution
URA	Urban Redevelopment Authority
US	United States
USD	United States dollar
USSR	Union of Soviet Socialist Republics
WFP	World Food Programme
WTO	World Trade Organization

Symbols and units

°	degree
Gt CO_2eq	gigatonnes carbon dioxide equivalent
ha	hectare
kg	kilogram
km^2	square kilometer
kWh	kilowatt-hour
m	meter
$MtCO_2$	metric tonnes carbon dioxide equivalent
tCO_2	tonne of carbon dioxide equivalent
TWh	terawatt-hour

Contributors

Shijun Cao is an assistant professor at the College of Economics, and Management, Yanbian University. He was a researcher at the Institute for Sustainable Development, Korea University. His current research interests are economic reform and sustainable growth of economic transition economies. He holds a BA and an MS from Yanbian University and a PhD from Korea University.

Sung Taek Cho is an associate research fellow at the Division of Coprosperity and Balanced Development, Gyeonggi Research Institute. He was a research professor at Korea University. His research interests are international trade and investment and the North Korean economy. He holds a BA from Konkuk University and an MS and PhD from Korea University.

Cheon Woon Choi is a professor at The Institute for Far Eastern Studies, Kyungnam University. He was a team leader and research fellow at Korea Foundation for Advanced Studies, a senior researcher at State-owned Property Management Office, and a deputy director and expert advisor at the Presidential Committee for Unification Preparation in Korea. His research interest is real estate policy in the Korean Peninsula. He holds a BL from Korea Aerospace University and an MRED and PhD from Dankook University.

Hyun-Ah Choi is a research professor at Ojeong Resilience Institute, Korea University. She was a senior researcher at Hanns Seidel Foundation Korea Office, researcher at Division of Natural Resources Conservation, Korea Environment Institute and vising research fellow at River Basin Research Centre, Gifu University. Her research interests are biodiversity and ecosystem services, vulnerability assessment of ecosystem using GIS, and emission reduction from deforestation and forest degradation. She holds a BA from Chonbuk National University and an MA and PhD from Korea University.

Yoonhee Ha is a professor for Special Affairs at KU-KIST Green School. She was a senior policy analyst and advisor at the Yeouido Institute, National Assembly of the Republic of Korea, and an independent executive director at KEPCO KPS. Her research interests are energy and environmental policy in the context of sustainable development, institutional governance for green infrastructure, carbon markets, and political economy of climate change. She holds a BA from

Ewha Womens University, an MA from Seoul National University, and a PhD from the University of Delaware.

Tae Yong Jung is a professor at the Graduate School of International Studies and a director of the Research Center for Global Sustainability, Yonsei University. He is currently a director of sustainable development program at Ban Ki-moon Foundation for a Better Future. He was a professor at the KDI School, principal climate change specialist at the Asian Development Bank, a deputy executive director of the Global Green Growth Institute, and a senior energy economist at the World Bank. He was a project leader in Climate Policy at the Institute for Global Environmental Strategies of Japan and senior fellow at Korea Energy Economics Institute. He holds a BA from Seoul National University and an MA and PhD from Rutgers, the State University of New Jersey.

Dahyun Kang is a PhD candidate at the Graduate School of International Studies and a researcher at the Research Center for Global Sustainability, Yonsei University. Her research interests are renewable energy systems and the economic development of developing countries including North Korea in the context of sustainable growth. She holds a BA from University of California, Davis and an MA from Yonsei University.

Sung Jin Kang is a professor at the Department of Economics, an adjunct professor at KU-KIST Green School, and a director of the Institute for Economic Research, Korea University. His main fields of research are issues on sustainable development such as green growth, climate change, and economic development, including foreign direct investment, poverty reduction, and foreign aid. He has published several articles and books on international economics and the field of development economics. He holds a BA and MA from Korea University and a PhD from Stanford University.

Tae Soo Kang is an adjunct professor at Economic Department at Korea University and external board member at Samsung Card Co. He was a senior research fellow at Korea Institute for International Economic Policy, Secretary General at National Economic Advisory Council to the President, a distinguished resident fellow at School of Advanced International Studies, Johns Hopkins University, Deputy Governor at Bank of Korea, a professor at Korea Banking Institute, and a research fellow and consultant at the World Bank. His research area is the financial market in Asian countries. He holds a BA from Sungkyunkwan University and an MAcc and PhD from the University of Missouri-Columbia.

Donghun Kim is a professor at the Graduate School of International Studies, Yonsei University. He was an associate dean of academic affairs at Yonsei University, an associate editor at the *Journal of Korean Economic Association* and the *Korean Journal of Industrial Organization*, an assistant professor at the University of Connecticut, and an economist at Bank of Korea. His research field is industrial organization. He holds a BA and an MA from Yonsei University and a PhD from Cornell University.

Young-hoon Kim is a senior researcher at Korea Rural Economic Institute. He joined the Korea Rural Economic Institute as a Researcher in 1987 and researches issues related to the agricultural system in North Korea. He is also interested in topics related to agricultural cooperation between North and South Korea. He holds a BA, MA, and PhD from Korea University.

Hongshik Lee is a professor at the Department of Economics, Korea University. He was an associate professor at Inha University and a head of the FTA Research Team at the Department of Trade and Investment Policy, Korea Institute for International Economic Policy. His research fields are international trade and foreign direct investment. He holds a BA from Korea University and an MA and PhD from the University of Texas at Austin.

Hong Soo Lee is a senior urban specialist at the Asian Development Bank. He was an executive director at Office for Urban Development, Seoul Housing and Communities Corporation, a director at the Urban Regeneration Division, Ministry of Land, Infrastructure, and Transport, and an executive architect at the Urban Redevelopment Authority in Singapore. His research interests are urban redevelopment and regeneration. He holds a BA from Inha University and an MA from the University of Pennsylvania and Harvard University.

Sle-gee Lee is a PhD candidate and researcher at Environmental GIS/RS Laboratory, Korea University. He was a researcher at Biogeography Laboratory, Kyunghee University and Division of Forest Biodiversity and Herbarium, Korea National Arboretum. His research interests are the assessment of climate change vulnerability and restoration of degraded land in North Korea. He holds a BA and an MA from Kyunghee University.

Woo-Kyun Lee is a professor at the College of Life and Environmental Sciences and a director at the Ojeong Eco-Resilience Institute and at the Environmental GIS/RS Center, Korea University. He was a visiting professor at University of Göttingen and Yanbian University and a research fellow at the Korea Rural Economic Institute. His research interests are forest management planning using GIS and RS, tree measurement and forest survey, forest growth and yield models, and climate change. He holds a BS and an MS from Korea University and a PhD from University of Göttingen.

Jongwoo Moon is a PhD candidate at the Graduate School of International Studies and a researcher at the Research Center for Global Sustainability, Yonsei University. He was a researcher at the Institute for Sustainable Development, Korea University, and a research assistant at the US-Korea Institute at Johns Hopkins University. His research interests are renewable energy policies and carbon pricing schemes. He holds a BA from Korea University, and an MA from the School of Advanced International Studies, Johns Hopkins University.

Hyo Chan Oh is a researcher at the Division for Environmental Economy, Sustainability Strategy, Korea Environment Institute. He was a researcher at the Research Center for Global Sustainability, Yonsei University. His research interests are environmental sustainability and the sustainability nexus. He holds a BA from Keimyung University and an MA from Yonsei University.

Zhenan Quan is a professor and dean at the College of Economics and Management, Yanbian University. He was a visiting professor at Fukui Prefectural University and an associate professor and assistant professor at the College of Economics and Management, Yanbian University. His research interest is the economic development of North Korea and China. He holds a BA from Yanbian University and an MA and PhD from Tokyo Keizai University.

Hankyoung Sung is an associate dean at the College of Public Affairs and Economics and an associate professor at the School of Economics, University of Seoul. He was an assistant professor at Kookmin University and an associate research fellow at the Korea Institute for International Economic Policy. His teaching and research areas are experimental economics, political economy, and international trade using a computable general equilibrium model. He holds a BA and an MA from Sogang University and an MA and PhD from The Ohio State University.

Moon-soo Yang is a vice president for academic affairs and professor at the University of North Korean Studies. He was a research fellow at the LG Economic Research Institute and a reporter at the *Maeil Economic Daily Newspaper*. His research interests are the North Korean economy, inter-Korean economic cooperation, and the economic integration of the Korean Peninsula. He holds a BA from Seoul National University and an MA and PhD from the University of Tokyo.

Acknowledgement

We sincerely appreciate the support of the Research Center for Global Sustainability, the Institute for Global Engagement & Empowerment (IGEE) at Yonsei University, the Institute of Economics Research (IER) and OJEong Resilience Institute (OJERI) at Korea University, and the Korea Peace Foundation. We also want to express our appreciation for the editorial support of Dahyun Kang, YoungJu Han, Hye Rin Bang, Dafydd N. Phillips, and Je Hee Um of the Graduate School of International School, Yonsei University, and Stephen J. Malinosky.

Part I

Macroeconomic perspective

1 Reformation open-door policy and development proposals for North Korea

Sung Jin Kang and Tae Yong Jung

1 Introduction

Recently, studies have been actively conducted on which country's development strategy will be the benchmark of North Korea if North Korea implements a transition policy through a full-scale reformation open-door policy. Excluding the possibility of transition through unification as enacted by East and West Germany, the strategy North Korea is likely to pursue can be largely divided into two types (Kang and Jung 2017). The first possible strategy is the one that was pursued by Eastern European countries after the collapse of the Soviet Union, where they reformed their political systems into democratic ones and reformed their economic systems into capitalist open market systems. The second strategy is referred to as the East Asian model, which, as pursued by China, Vietnam, and others, reformed the economic system into a capitalistic market system but maintained their political structure.

Determining a transition strategy is critical for North Korea to achieve realizing an autonomous and sustainable development. This is because while the transition progresses, the specific reformation open-door policies the country implements are realized in various ways. Even among the former Soviet Union countries, the implemented policies and the pace of implementation varied by country. For instance, while processing privatization of state-owned enterprise, countries varied their policies in terms of target companies, privatization pace, method, etc. (Kang and Jung 2017). Moreover, in cases where North Korea implements specific transition policies and achieves North-South or international cooperation, the economic effect will also vary, as will the costs and benefits for not only North Korea but also partner countries.

Previous research has mainly discussed the required cost for unification and has not covered, in-depth, the measures of supplying the financial resources needed for unification. As a result, unification seems as though it would be a burden to the South Korean people because South Korea and its citizens would have to bear all costs of unification or the cost of any plan of economic cooperation. Realistically, however, if North Korea joins the international community and proceeds with an economic development strategy that is acknowledged internationally, the necessary resources will be shouldered not only by South Korea but also by the international community. The main sources of funding that could be utilized for economic development in North Korea are ODA (Official Development Assistance) or FDI (Foreign Direct Investment) (Kang 2019).

In order for investment resources to flow into North Korea, the economic and institutional environment of North Korea should aim to provide infrastructures and conditions with the goal that foreign lenders find investment attractive. For example, labor and wage contracts, profit remittance, exchange rate stabilization, investment incentives, etc. should be established to suit the global standard. This is one of the reasons why it is important for North Korea to determine a specific transition strategy as a precondition.

This chapter assumes that North Korea will follow the East Asian transition model as a realistic alternative if it implements a full-scale reformation open-door policy. It examines the transition strategies of these countries and discusses necessary preconditions for North Korea to proceed with a development strategy. In addition, several contributors of this book recommend North Korea to adopt an export-driven economic development strategy based on aggressive marketization policies to achieve economic development. Furthermore, to successfully process this strategy, contributors propose that North Korea establish clear and concrete infrastructures and systems such as exchange rate reformation, inflation stabilization, reliable statistics infra establishment, statistics accessibility enhancement, etc.

This edited book is composed of two parts. The chapters in Part I propose economic development prospects for North Korea on a macro-level. The chapters in Part II suggest specific strategies for major sectors, including financing, industrial development, agricultural development, WTO accession, and urban development strategies. Part II also contains energy, climate change response, and forest degradation recovery strategies. The policy recommendations made by each of the contributors are summarized by chapter in this section.

2 Concept transition (system transformation) and outcome/ performance

2.1 Concept of transition

Transition generally implies conversion of political economic systems into reformation open-door systems. Political system transition refers to a transformation from a communist system, where only one party is admitted, to a multiparty democratic system. Economic system transition refers to a transformation from a socialist system, where every economic decision is determined by the planned economy of the central government, to a capitalistic market system, where economic decisions are decided by market mechanisms.

In reality, however, it is not easy to clearly distinguish which form the transitions are following. Nevertheless, as shown in Table 1.1, much of the existing literature classifies the transition type of countries into three types: Perfect Union, Former Soviet Union, and East Asian (Kang and Jung 2017; Kang 2019).

Table 1.1 Transition countries' type, year, and description

	Year	*Country*	*Description*
Perfect Unification Type	1990	Germany	Two countries with completely different systems unify as one country (both political and economic integration)
East Asian Type	1978	China	Each country maintains its one-party communist system but transforms economically into capitalistic market systems
	1986	Laos, Vietnam	
	1990	Cambodia	
Former Soviet Union Type	1990	Macedonia, Croatia, Hungary, Poland, Slovakia, Slovenia, Mongolia	Each country transforms not only economically into a capitalistic market system but also politically into a multiparty system
	1991	Albania, Bulgari, Turkey, Cyprus, Rumania, Czech Republic	
	1992	Baltic States (Estonia, Latvia, Lithuania), Armenia, Azerbaijan, Republic of Belarus, Georgia, Moldova, Ukraine, Russia, Kazakhstan, Kyrgyz Republic, Tajikistan, Uzbekistan, Turkmenistan	
	1996	Bosnia Hercegovina	
	2002	Serbia, Montenegro	
	2012	Kosova	

Source: Kang 2019

First, the German type is the typical transition where two completely different systems unify into one type. It is this type that East and West Germany, which differed politically and economically, used to unify their territories, and at the same time, interactively integrate political and economic structures.

Second, Former Soviet Union type is a transition of political and economic systems into democratic and capitalistic market systems, respectively. It generally refers to countries that transitioned after, and owing to, the collapse of the Soviet Union, which was the suzerain (dominant state) of the communist regime. It includes Eastern European countries and countries that once belonged to Soviet Union.

Third, the East Asian transition type includes China, Vietnam, Cambodia, and Laos. These countries transformed their economic systems into capitalistic market systems through reform and opening up, however, they maintained their one-party communist system. This type is often what is referred to when discussing economic transition.

Considering these various transition types, discussion is required over which type would make the most sense for North Korea. Many existing studies argue North-South Korea unification on the premise that it follows the German type transition. On the other hand, some studies argue North-South Korea unification on the premise that it follows the Former Soviet Union type, where both political and economic systems are converted.

It isn't realistic to assume that North Korea will choose a transition type such as the German or Former Soviet Union types, however, especially after observing policy failures and regime collapse during the Soviet Union's transition. The most realistic development strategy North Korea could choose, considering its political and economic situation, is the East Asian transition model. This is because North Korea, under this model, will not have to abandon political domination of their existing one-party communist system. That is, economically, North Korea will switch to a capitalistic market system, while, politically, their system will remain unchanged. This type of transition might be the logical choice given the interest North Korea showed in Vietnamese reform and opening-up policy at the inter-Korean summit in April 2018.

The four East Asian countries never underwent a transition like the Former Soviet Union where their regimes collapsed due to a combination of internal and external problems. They implemented a capitalistic market system focusing on a price function in order to supplement the weaknesses of their centrally planned socialist economy system. China, for instance, started a full-scale reformation open-door policy in 1978, and Doi Moi in Vietnam and the New Economic Mechanism in Laos both started in 1986, etc. On the other hand, politically, they maintained a one-party communist system and did not implement multiparty systems that are emphasized in a democracy.

2.2 Comparison of economic performances of transition countries

This subsection examines the economic successes and failures of the three transition groups classified earlier by comparing the change in per capita GDP, inflation, and Gini Index. Economic outcome after transition has already been compared using various indicators, focusing on the Former Soviet Union in the 1990s (Fischer et al. 1996; de Melo et al. 1997). However, previous studies have compared only twenty years' worth of transition outcomes. Nevertheless there is hardly any research that has systematically compared long-term outcomes of the various countries' transitions – including East Asian countries.

The World Development Indicator of the World Bank was utilized to measure per capita GDP (2010 baseline) and inflation. Inflation refers to increases in the

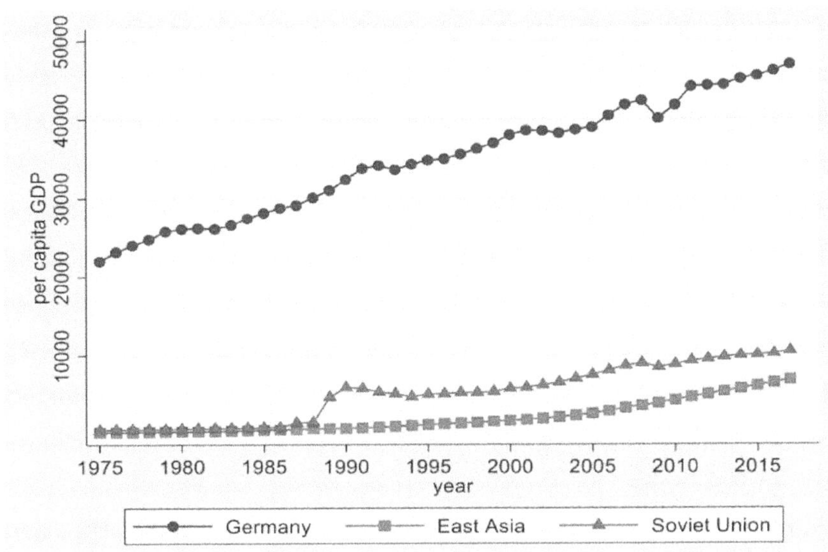

Figure 1.1 GDP per capita trend of transition countries

Source: Author created (World Bank 2019)

consumer price index. SWIID (Standardized World Income Inequality Database) by Solt (2019) was utilized to measure the Gini Index. Per capita real GDP is measured by adding up the real GDP of each group and then dividing by the total population of each group, so it differs from the simple average of per capita real GDP of each country. Two other indicators are additionally measured by calculating an arithmetic average.

The trend of per capita real GDP is presented in Figure 1.1. For the German type, as Germany was unified by the West absorbing the East, the per capita real GDP of Germany increased steadily along with the level of West Germany, which had already joined the ranks of advanced countries. For the Former Soviet Union types, around 1990, when they underwent their transition their per capita real GDP rapidly increased, then showed a gradually increasing trend. Similarly, the per capita real GDP of East Asian countries increased gradually after undergoing their transitions after the 1980s. However, these two groups of countries have remained at a very low level of per capita real GDP compared to the German type.

Figure 1.2 displays the trend of inflation. German and East Asian types are maintaining a stable level on average. However, in the case of the Former Soviet Union types, they experienced very high inflation rates before and after the collapse of the Soviet Union. In the mid-1980s, just before the collapse of the Soviet Union, the average inflation rate had already reached a level of over 400 percent,

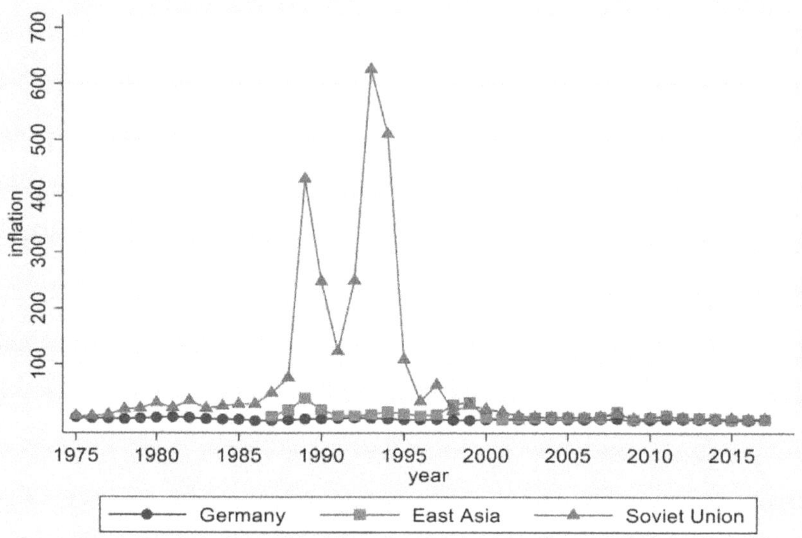

Figure 1.2 Inflation trend of transition countries

Source: Author created (World Bank 2019)

forewarning that the Soviet Union was collapsing. Moreover, in the early 1990s, just after the transition of the Soviet Union, the average inflation rate reached over 600 percent, and this implies that Former Soviet Union types faced higher price instability than the other transition countries. Since the mid-1990s, a stable inflation rate has been maintained.

Figure 1.3 shows the state of income distribution using the Gini coefficient, where the higher the value, the worse the income distribution. Just after the transition, income distribution had deteriorated, but after a certain period, this deterioration stopped. Still, these countries are not recovering to the state that they were in before the transition.

Comparing these three types, East Asian countries had the lowest income distribution compared to other two types at the start of the transition phase, and only became worse during the transition process. Although they have stabilized since the middle of the first decade of the 21st century, they have not recovered from the state of their early transition periods. The Former Soviet Union types have showed a deteriorating trend since the early 1990s when their transitions occurred, however, they have improved in the first decade of the new millennium. On the contrary, the German type has shown an aggravating trend in the early 2000s, and more in-depth research is required into whether the transition policy is a main factor of this phenomenon or not.

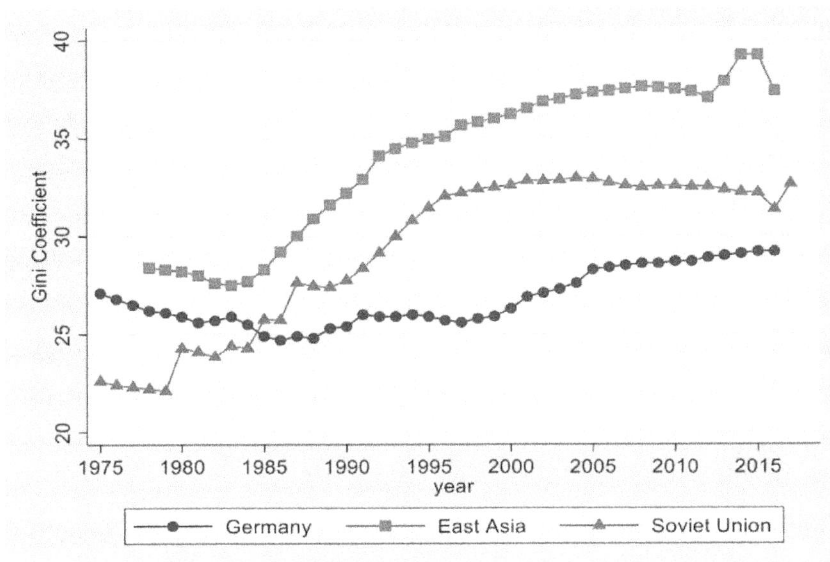

Figure 1.3 Gini index trend of transition countries

Source: Author created (World Bank 2019)

2.3 Economic outcomes of East Asian transition countries

This subsection compares the major economic indices (per capita GDP, inflation, Gini Index) of the four East Asian countries that North Korea is likely to pursue as a benchmark.

Figure 1.4 shows the per capita real GDP of four countries. In China, which shows the most rapid improvement, the per capita real GDP has increased rapidly since 1978 as it started a full-scale transition from below $1,000 in the 1970s to over $7,000 in 2017. On the other hand, the other three countries' per capita real GDPs have remained at a low level. Since the mid-1980s when these countries started their transitions, their per capita real GDP growths have been flatlined to such a degree that they are still under the $2,000 level as of 2017. This implies that the gap between these countries and China became wider, indicating that the East Asian type transition does not always result in a high economic growth rate.

Figure 1.5 displays the inflation trends of the four East Asian countries under discussion. The previous subsection mentioned that the Former Soviet Union countries had shown a very high inflation rate before and after their transition periods. The Four East Asian countries have shown stable inflation on average, though Laos showed an unstable inflation trend in the late-1990s.

Figure 1.6 shows the trend of the Gini coefficient of the four East Asian countries. To be more specific, China experienced rapid growth, but the income distribution showed a steadily deteriorating trend until the early 2000s. Afterwards, the

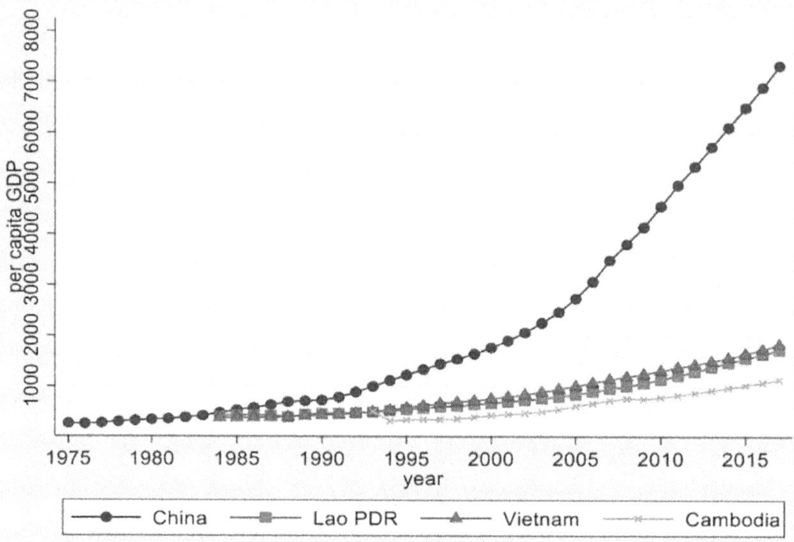

Figure 1.4 Real GDP per capita trend of four East Asian transition countries

Source: Author created (World Bank 2019)

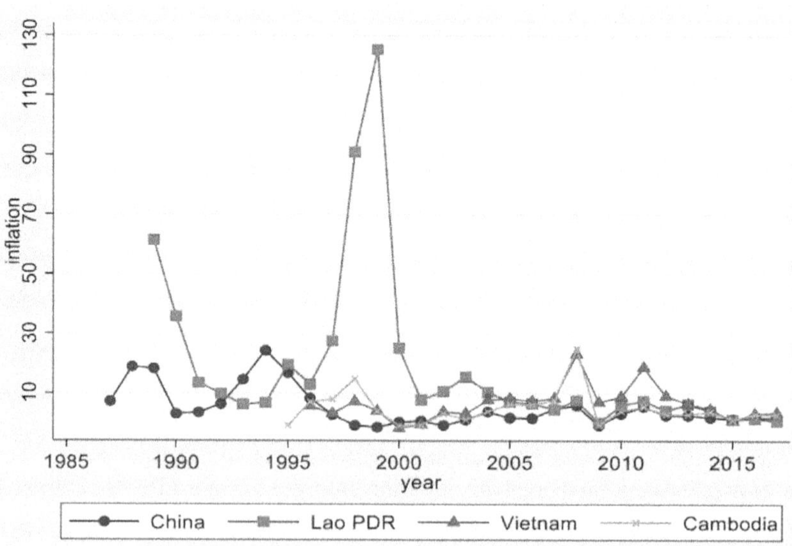

Figure 1.5 Inflation trend of four East Asian transition countries

Source: Author created (World Bank 2019)

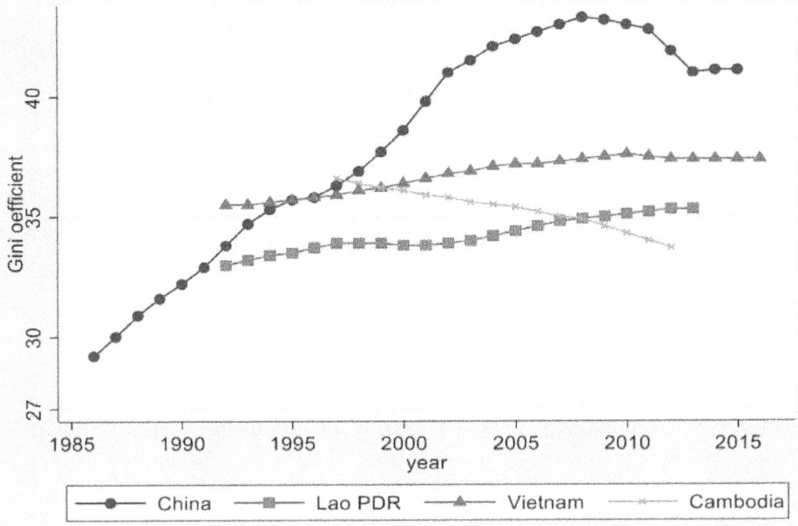

Figure 1.6 Gini Index trend of four East Asian transition countries

Source: Author created (World Bank 2019)

income distribution improved, though it has not recovered from the state of the early transition period in the 1980s. Similarly, the income distribution of the other two countries (Vietnam, Laos) are showing that they have experienced a consistently worsening trend. However, the income distribution of Cambodia is showing a consistently improving trend in contrast to the trend of the other countries.

As shown in the trend of per capita real GDP and the trend of inflation, not every change of the economic indicators of the East Asian countries shows the same pattern after the transition. China can be seen as a very successful transition country in terms of economic growth, while the other three countries still remain underdeveloped. Notably, Laos experienced an extreme rate of inflation during its transition.

Most of these countries experienced a deterioration of their income distribution during the transition. However, it is overinterpretation to argue that the transition policy itself had failed or was unnecessary. This is because the per capita income increased, leading to an improvement in standards of living. Most countries underwent this trend as their economic development progressed from developing countries to developed countries. Currently developed countries also at one time or another went through this experience, though when economic development reached a certain level, income distribution started to improve as governments implemented income redistribution policy and enhanced social welfare policies (Kang 2018).

3 Reform toward an open-door policy for North Korea and its prospects

3.1 Existing research on economic effects and limitations

Existing studies on the effects of economic cooperation between North and South Korea have been conducted from various perspectives.

First, in the past, research has actively been done on the amount of investment cost that would be required to achieve aimed for economic growth rates or income levels during a certain period, on the premise that North and South Korea will reunify. In these studies, estimated values of unification costs show quite large deviations depending on the target economic development stages or vary by a particular author's scenario. Depending on the type of unification, estimation method, target income level, etc., the range is widely estimated from ten billion to up to five trillion US dollars.

Kang (2009) argued that from 31.3 to 42 billion dollars, depending on various assumptions on economic growth rate, is required to achieve a per capita GNI of $3,000 in North Korea within ten years. This type of research outcome shapes a view that reunification is a cost, laying a burden upon the shoulders of the South Korean people, leading to a negative impression on reunification. Thus, in addition to the existing studies that only emphasize the unification cost under the premise of unification, the benefits that could be generated from reunification should also be considered at the same time.

An even higher estimate, Hyundai Research Institute (2010) calculated that about $157 billion is required to achieve a per capita income of $3,000 in North Korea within 10 years (2010–2018) of the date of reunification. Other scenarios estimated that about $4,710 and $7,065 billion are required to achieve a per capita income of $7,000 and $10,000, respectively. This study assumed that North Korea will follow the economic growth rate trends of South Korea in the 1970–1980s, and defined reunification cost as well as required resources to achieve the target income.

Second, recent studies are investigating the spillover effect on South Korea that would occur if North Korea expands its reform open-door policy. That is to say that along with the expansion in investment in North Korea, and the economic cooperation with neighboring countries, North Korean market reform will positively affect the economic growth not only of North Korea but also of South Korea. These aforementioned studies assume reunification as a precondition like the previous studies, but some studies assume inter-Korean economic cooperation as a precondition instead, which is more realistic.

Representative studies include Sung (2014) and Choi and Kim (2017). These studies investigated the impact of investment in economic growth in North Korea by varying the amount of investment, however, they not only considered the investment cost, but also considered the positive effects such as economic growth. Further, they examined the benefits that can be generated North Korea if North-South Korean cooperation or multinational cooperation are carried out.

A study by Sung (2014) showed various outcomes depending on different scenarios, but it argued that if North and South Korea succeeded in economic integration, after twenty years the real GDP of North Korea and South Korea would increase by 4.3–110.6 percent, and 1.7–3 percent, respectively. If they expanded the participating countries and proceeded with six-party talks, then the GDP of the US and Japan could also increase due to the impact of the TPP (Trans-Pacific Partnership) and North-South Korean economic integration. It is also shown in this research that China and Russia could partially ease the tensions and predicted that among the analyzed countries, Japan would benefit the most from the North-South Korean economic integration. Choi and Kim (2017) examined the current status of North-South Korean economic cooperation and reached the conclusion that if this cooperation continues to expand, it will bring benefits to both countries.

3.2 Comprehensive direction for reform and the opening up of North Korea's economy

Previous research has taken as a premise that North Korea's achievement of reform and opening up would attract ODA and FDI from the outside. Indeed, the reason that North Korea should promote this political economic environment is because it is the most basic precondition for foreign aid like ODA and FDI to enter North Korea. If such an environment is not formed, North Korea will not be able to receive any resources from outside and the economic effect of economic cooperation that the study is suggesting would not be practically realized.

This study expects that the direction of reform opening up of North Korea will follow the East Asian type transition and not the Former Soviet Union type that a lot of existing studies are suggesting. Also, most of the contributors of this book recommend foreign open-door development strategy as a specific transition method for North Korea rather than establishing a self-reliant national economy that is based on a planned economy system. Realistically, given its situation, North Korea will not go ahead with a full-scale and radical reform open-door policy. Therefore, like the special economic zone of China, North Korea should implement a progressive policy focusing on developing certain areas from scarce resources. The study suggests specific policy direction to North Korea proposing the steps as in the following (Kang 2019).

The first stage is economic aid-driven development strategy. Specifically, the Kaesong Industrial Complex project, the Mt. Geumgang tour project, etc. are included. At this stage, the purpose is not to maximize the benefit from the North-South Korean economic cooperation, but rather it is a form of assistance from South Korea. In the case of the Kaesong Industrial Complex project, the South Korean firms and multinational companies are unable to freely invest in this project since it is not in a general SEZ (special economic zone) stage. For instance, labor and wage contracts must be made with the North Korean government, and not directly with the workers. Moreover, there is a restriction in free transfer of the profits made by the investments.

Going beyond the simple economic aid-driven development strategy, the second stage is implementing specific area-based development strategy through the SEZ policy. This can prevent any chaos that could arise if the external funds or human resources come in too rapidly were North Korea to develop in an unrestrained, unregulated manner. Especially, given that the development infrastructure has not yet been matured to where it needs to be in North Korea, and that North Korea is unable to fund its development by itself, the most realistic strategy would be to focus on developing specific areas. Not only China, but also Vietnam, Cambodia, and Laos chose to implement similar policies. At this stage, like other countries, North Korea should create various investment environment improvements such as incentives on FDI, worker employment, wage agreements, wire transfers, etc. to attract foreign investors.

The third stage, in the long run, will be implementing full-scale reform open-door policy in North Korea like the other East Asian transition countries. At this stage, employment and wage contracts are made directly between the investors and workers, profit transfer is enabled almost freely, and the exchange rates can be determined flexibly by the market. Through this process, North Korea will ultimately be enabled to join international organizations such as the WTO.

There is another important issue besides the preconditions on the direction and content of reform open-door policy of North Korea. Previous research estimated the cost of required resources to achieve economic growth and development of North Korea, but it failed to make clear exactly who would bear this cost. Concerns that South Korea would bear all the costs have appeared as an obstacle to North-South Korean cooperation. As we can see from the research summary of Chapter 4, not only South Korea but also other countries and various international organizations will share the burden of providing financial resources to assist North Korea's reform open-door policy and to enable North Korea to join the international community.

4 Economic policy recommendations

This edited book is composed of two parts. First, it proposes the economic development prospects of North Korea on a macro-level. Second, it suggests specific strategies for major sectors including financing strategies, industrial development strategies, agricultural development strategies, WTO accession strategies, and urban development strategies. Finally, it contains energy and climate change response strategies, and forest degradation recovery strategies. The policy recommendations by each of the contributors are summarized in this section.

In Chapter 2, the authors point out that North Korea has two options for economic development. The first is the direction of development that North Korea has pursued so far, focusing on the construction of a self-reliant national economy based on the planned economic system, and complementing it by expanding external economic cooperation. The second is the policy direction of establishing a gradual market-based system through the implementation of export-driven economic development strategies and active external opening and marketization policies at the national strategic level. For instance, the special economic zone and the economic development zone fit with this policy direction. It is desirable to adopt an export-driven economic development strategy by implementing aggressive open-economy policies. If such policy were moving forward, it would be a stepping-stone for strengthening multilateral economic cooperation among the five Northeast Asian countries, including China, Russia, and Mongolia, as well as between the two Koreas. The global community also emphasizes the need for active cooperation in order to maximize the benefits of economic cooperation by implementing North Korea's aggressive open-economy policy.

In Chapter 3, the author points out the importance of marketization in North Korea. It leads to the virtual collapse of the planned economy, which alleviates the fiscal shortages in all sectors, including the party, the military, and the cabinet. However, it is also worthwhile to note that North Korea's marketization has some limitations in the areas of self-motivation and self-expansion. North Korea's market system is proceeding in the context of immature internal and external political conditions. Meanwhile, the North Korean government's policy toward the market is ambivalent. It can serve as a deterrent as well as a facilitator of marketization. Even if the authorities step up and put the brakes on the market, how much effect they can have is questionable. If North Korea's denuclearization progresses in the future, the international community's sanctions against North Korea will be eased and lifted, expanding the material foundation for the North's marketization, and expanding both market demand and supply. On the other hand, if North Korea's denuclearization is delayed and the sanctions on them continue, it is likely that the demand and supply for the market will decrease, leading it to shrink and retreat.

In Chapter 4, the author shows that, in the case of economic integration between the two Koreas or between North Korea and other participating countries, not only North Korea but also the other countries participating in economic integration can benefit. Under a variety of assumptions, it has been shown that, in the case of official development assistance (ODA) or foreign direct investment (FDI) in North Korea, the participating countries may take cost burdens, but they can also benefit from economic spillover effects. Assuming ultra-fast growth, this research has shown that North Korea's per capita GDP could reach 65 percent of South Korea's in 2050.

The author of Chapter 5 suggests and predicts outcomes based on North Korea's open-industrialization strategy and leapfrogging developmental strategy. It is critical to secure initial investment capital as a prerequisite for implementing these strategies. Since North Korea has a skillful labor force, the research proposes to foster light industry such as the textile industry and the software-oriented IT industry. In order to foster these industries, incentive systems to attract foreign capital through special economic zones should be well established. North Korea is located in a geopolitically advantageous position for capital inflow and market acquisition because South Korea and China are adjacent. Therefore, if both the current economic sanctions were resolved through the resolution of the North Korean nuclear issues, and the inter-Korean relations were improved, it would be expected that economic cooperation with the global community would foster comparatively advantageous industries in North Korea in a short time frame.

In Chapter 6, the authors suggest the following two stages of attaining financing. The first is to finance the public sector through international organizations such as the International Monetary Fund (IMF) and the World Bank. The second is attracting FDI from the global community, including South Korea. The authors argue that the following prerequisites must be met in order to attract investment. First, a dual banking system in which market functions can operate must be established. Second, prerequisites such as a reform of the exchange rate system, stabilization of inflation, and access to the global payment network should be met. These prerequisites depend primarily on efforts to build a reliable North Korean statistical infrastructure and strengthen access to statistics.

In Chapter 7, the authors point out that North Korea will only have truly integrated into the global economy by joining the World Trade Organization (WTO). The most important prerequisite for joining the WTO, the authors argue, is that North Korea should reorganize its policy-making process to be transparent and predictable. In addition, the pricing and financial system that has thus far been carried out under the planned economic system should be reformed so as to occur in an open market-based system, and laws and systems conforming to international standards should be prepared. The authors also point out that inter-Korean economic cooperation will play a pivotal role in institutional preparation. North Korea could learn international trade norms through inter-Korean economic cooperation and accumulate trade experience through economic integration such as regional trade agreements with South Korea. It is also suggested that there be a way to recognize the specificity of economic cooperation between the two Koreas when joining the WTO and to recognize the economic cooperation between the two Koreas as an exception to the most favored nation (MFN) rule.

The authors of Chapter 8 propose promotion of agricultural development programs centering on the special economic zones in order to solve the food shortage in North Korea, which could become a new model for international cooperation in the agricultural sector. Inter-Korean cooperation is essential to develop such programs. Agricultural cooperation between the two Koreas should be promoted through agricultural cooperation projects by nongovernmental organizations (NGOs) and infrastructure development and other cooperative projects encouraged by the public sector. Commercial trade and investment cooperation projects should be led by private companies.

The authors of Chapter 9 present the following four points. First, the concept of city to city (C2C), rather than South Korea and North Korea, is to be introduced to promote closer exchange and cooperation between cities rather than nations (e.g. "Seoul-Pyongyang"). Second, in order to increase the sustainability of urban development projects, it is necessary to include plans to improve living conditions for the residential sector in the humanitarian cooperation projects. Third, it is necessary for South Korea to share its experience and know-how on state-owned urban development with financing techniques. Fourth, it is necessary to introduce the concept of land swapping as performed by Singapore and Malaysia.

The authors of Chapter 10 make policy proposals on the premise that North Korea eventually becomes a member of the global community through North Korea's sincere denuclearization efforts, and the process of creating and implementing concrete programs. In order to implement the policies set out in the Nationally Determined Contributions (NDC) submitted to the United Nations Framework Convention on Climate Change (UNFCCC) and effectively achieve their goals, the global community helps North Korea in implementing NDC by developing concrete financial and technical assistance programs. It is assumed that North Korea will prioritize climate adaptation plans at the national and local levels by utilizing internationally available support programs for developing countries.

The author of Chapter 11 emphasizes that the Paris Agreement under the UNFCCC guarantees a variety of support measures for adaptation, reduction, and capacity building in developing countries. As a result, North Korea, which faces various socioeconomic problems due to climate change, could find opportunities to solve environmental, energy, and economic problems through the support of the global community. The author points out that the carbon market mechanism under Article 6(2) of the Paris Agreement will be especially useful as a channel of cooperation between the two Koreas.

The book ends with the authors of Chapter 12 making the following suggestions on repairing the ecology of North Korea. First, North Korea's deforestation is directly and indirectly linked to international issues such as poverty due to food shortages, threats to basic human rights due to water and energy shortages, and destruction of environmental resilience. Therefore, in order to cope with these issues, it is necessary to promote multilateral cooperation projects through international organizations that both North and South Korea have joined. Second, it is necessary to follow the "strategic framework for cooperation between the United Nations and North Korea," which provides a comprehensive direction for UN organizations to consider when working in North Korea. In order to restore the degraded forests of North Korea, it is necessary to promote international cooperation measures that utilize the priorities and strategies suggested by this framework. Lastly, forestation projects between the two Koreas need to be promoted simultaneously. As a first step, a recovery plan and project guidelines for combating deforestation in North Korea are prepared. In order to develop further such concrete plans and guidelines, the formation of a joint investigation and planning group for the identification and restoration plan of the North Korean wasteland, is proposed.

References

Choi, Jang Ho, and Beom Hwan Kim. 2017. "Developing Analysis Model and Analyzing Growth Effect of South and North Korea Economic Integration." *Long-term Trade Strategies Study Series* 17 (1).

de Melo, Martha, Cevedet Denizer, Alan Gelb, and Stoyan Tenev. 1997. "Circumstance and Choice: The Role of Initial Conditions and Policies in Transition Economies." *The World Bank Economic Review* 15 (1): 1–31.

Fischer, Stanley, Ratna Sahay, and Carlos Vegh. 1996. "Stabilization and Growth in Transition Economies: The Early Experience." *Journal of Economic Perspectives* 10 (2): 45–66.

Hyundai Research Institute. 2010. "South and North Korea Reunification, Benefits Outweigh Costs—Estimation and Implication of Reunification Costs and Benefits." *Economic Review* 422: 10–42.

Kang, Sung Jin. 2009. *North Korea's Economic Growth Potential and Precondition to Achieve $3,000 Income*. Paju: Nanam.

Kang, Sung Jin. 2018. *Theory of Economic Development*. Seoul: Parkyoungsa.

Kang, Sung Jin. 2019. *North Korea's Successful Economic Transition*. 21cbooks.

Kang, Sung Jin, and Tae Yong Jung. 2017. *Economic Transition and North Korea: In Perspective of Sustainable Development*. Seoul: Korea University Press.

Solt, Frederick. 2019. "Estimate of Gini Index of Inequality in Equivalenced (square root scale) Household Disposable (post-tax, post-transfer) Income." *The Standardized World Income Inequality Database* 8. Accessed July 7. https://dataverse.harvard.edu/dataset.xhtml?persistentId=doi:10.7910/DVN/LM4OWF.

Sung, Han Kyung. 2014. "Effects of South and North Korea Economic Integration." *Long-term Trade Strategies Study Series* 14 (5).

World Bank. 2019. "World Development Indicators (WDI)." Accessed July 7. https://datacatalog.worldbank.org/dataset/world-development-indicators.

2 Economic characteristics and prospects for economic development of North Korea

Zhenan Quan and Shijun Cao

1 Introduction

North Korea experienced a change in leadership after Chairman Kim Jong-il passed away in December 2011 and Kim Jong-un became the new head of state. Chairman Kim Jong-un implemented an "economic management system in our own style," referred to as the 6.28 Policy, in June 2012, signaling economic reform (Hong 2017, 61). He further expressed that he placed more importance on economic construction than on the "military-first politics" of Chairman Kim Jong-il by selecting "line on carrying out economic construction and the building of nuclear-armed forces simultaneously" in the plenary meeting hosted by the Central Committee of the Workers' Party of North Korea on March 2013.

Therefore, Chairman Kim Jong-un launched a policy that aimed to develop nuclear and ballistic weaponry, while also taking a series of actions such as state-owned (collective) economic reform and the expansion of the market economy and foreign economy in order to enhance economic growth and national living standards. However, North Korea faced tightened economic sanctions from the international community and underwent tremendous difficulties from late 2016. Under these circumstances, in April 2018, North Korea held the third plenary meeting of Seventh Central Committee of the Workers' Party of North Korea and declared the completion of the historical mission of "line on carrying out the economic construction and the building of nuclear-armed forces simultaneously." Also, the agreement of implementing an "economic construction-centered route," to which all people would be devoted and that would be utilized to build the socialist economy, was concluded. Simultaneously, improvement in international relations began actively with the New Year's address in 2018 delivered by Chairman Kim Jong-un. As a result, the economic characteristics of North Korea and the attention on its future development are attracting focus from around the world. Therefore, this study aims to introduce various characteristics of the North Korean economy and forecast its development.

This chapter consists of the following: Section 2 describes the conditions and characteristics of North Korea's endowed resources. Section 3 presents the basic characteristics of the economy. Section 4 foresees a shift in the development route and economic development. Section 5 concludes with suggestions.

2 Endowed resource conditions and characteristics of North Korea

The characteristics of endowed resources in North Korea have significant impacts on its economic growth. The territory accounts for 123,000 km^2 and houses a population of nearly 24.9 million people (in 2016).[1] Its nominal GDP turned out 24.5 billion USD and 26.1 billion USD in 2013 and 2014, respectively, which classifies it as a typical small economy.[2] Mountains and highlands account for 80 percent of the total territory and agricultural production conditions are inadequate. No petroleum or bituminous coal are produced, even though these and other mineral resources are abundant. Accordingly, foreign economic exchange and cooperation are indispensable if North Korea wants to achieve constant economic growth.

2.1 Agricultural resources

The agricultural production conditions in North Korea are very poor. Mountains and highlands account for 80 percent of its entire territory, and agricultural land area is only about 1.6 million hectares, with the majority – 64 percent of it – mainly in mountainous areas. Crops are also centered on the production of corn and rice for self-sufficiency and consumption, and the cultivation area of economic crops is very small (Quan 2013, 51). Thus, it is necessary to rely on imports not only because of the difficulty of self-sufficiency of food, but also due to the lack of most raw materials used in light industries such as wheat flour, plant oil, sugar, and cotton.

2.2 Mineral resources

Although mineral resources in North Korea generally offer advantageous conditions for economic growth, some of the demand should inevitably rely on foreign resources. There are a variety of mineral resources produced in North Korea. Nearly 300 types of mineral resources were identified and nearly 200 types were found useful in industry. Some reserves are massive: coal (20.5 billion tons) and iron ores (Fe 50 percent, five billion tons) ranked sixth in the world, Magnesite (MgO 45 percent, six billion tons) ranked as third, tungsten (metal, 246,000 tons) ranked as fourth, and, notably, graphite was ranked as the largest reserve in the world. Rare-earth element concentrations also ranked high compared to global quantities. In addition, North Korea has an abundance of lead, zinc, and copper (Jung 2015, 16; KDB Bank 2015). These mineral resources provide not only adequate amounts of raw materials for its industrial development, but also favorable conditions for foreign exchange earnings by exports.

Nevertheless, since petroleum and bituminous coal are not produced in North Korea, it entirely relies on imports. The plunge of petroleum imports since the 1990s caused serious energy depletion, having adverse impacts on its vulnerable petrochemical industry. At the same time, a dramatic drop in the quantity of imported bituminous coal is cited as one of the causes of the long-term depression in the steel industry. In light of this, North Korea must inevitably increase the imports of petroleum and bituminous coal for its economic recovery.

2.3 Hydroelectric resources

North Korea's hydroelectric resources are plentiful. Therefore, North Korea has concentrated on establishing electric power industry development policies based on its abundant hydroelectric resources and its coal resources and has been expanding both hydroelectric and thermal power developments. However, since the early 1990s, the utilization rate of power generation facilities, especially that of thermal power facilities, significantly plunged due to the deterioration of facilities, lack of components, and shortages of fuel supplies such as heavy oil and high-quality coal. Thus, electric power generation problems occurred, and the power generation structure has since been shifted into hydroelectric power generation (Quan 2018a, 49–51).

North Korea has four clear seasons, as it is located in the temperate region. The amount of hydroelectric power is dramatically reduced during the dry season. Therefore, power outputs vary considerably according to seasonal changes, as thermal power outputs cannot complement the shortage of hydroelectricity production. Furthermore, electric power loss rates reach nearly 30 percent in the process of power transmission and distribution due to insufficient materials in the power grid, such as insulated wire and coated wire as well as deteriorated power transmission wiring (JETRO 2015, 130). Electric shortage problems thus remain unsolved in spite of the active efforts to combat these challenges.

2.4 Human resources

The North Korean government put emphasis on national education and has implemented a four-year compulsory education program since 1956 and an extended ten-year obligatory education since 1972. This has led to the relative enhancement of the basic educational level. However, more advanced educational levels are comparatively lower due to long-term national isolation. The development of advanced education programs and higher industrial technological levels appears urgent. Therefore, international exchanges and imports of educational resources from foreign countries are required.

The working age population (15–64 years old) of North Korea was 17.32 million people in 2016, accounting for 69.6 percent; while the aging rate (the demographic percentage of people 65 years and older) is as low as 11.6 percent (KOSIS 2019). In addition, North Korea labor has significantly low wages, with monthly average wages of Gaeseong Industrial Complex (GIC) workers at 127 USD in 2014,[3] and a monthly average wage in the Rason SEZ of 94 USD (Quan and Li 2018, 24–25). Its low wage is seen as appropriate for the labor-intensive industry. However, this competitively low-wage workforce is likely to be insufficient due to small absolute numbers of laborers if economic growth is fully launched.

2.5 Geographic location

North Korea is geographically located at the center of the Northeast Asia region. Thus, it holds an advantageous geographical position in terms of international economic exchange and cooperation.

If the economic sanctions imposed on North Korea are lifted, active opening and domestic market reform are implemented, and the bilateral (North-South) relationship becomes rosy, this country can be connected with South Korea, northeastern parts of China, far eastern parts of Russia, and Mongolia by road using land-based transportation systems such as railroads. In addition, one-day market zones will be formed in these regions if new infrastructure such as high-speed railroads and expressways are constructed, thereby creating a large new international market (Quan 2018b, 29). Moreover, Japan can gain access to the northeastern parts of China and Mongolia with the shortest distances by using the port cities on the east North Korea coastline such as Rajin, Chongjin, and Wonsan.

Currently, comparative advantages such as the labor force and natural resources in investing regions as well as the regional market size, activation degree, and long-term development potential are considered crucial in terms of capital investment. Accordingly, the formation of an international market depending on the implementation of its opening up and marketization reform will serve as an important element for investment and trade activation.

As articulated earlier, North Korea retains a cheap and comparatively skilled workforce and plentiful mineral resources. Moreover, it holds geographical advantages in its possible connections with international economies. Therefore, it has tremendous economic growth potential. However, due to limited endowed resources, it requires constant exchange and cooperation with international economies for accomplishing constant economic growth.

3 Basic characteristics of the economy in North Korea

North Korea has carried out economic development strategies focusing on the development of heavy industries, particularly the defense industry. This has been a top priority based on the planned economy as well as due to constant national isolation and self-rehabilitation since the late 1950s.

North Korea's foreign economic relations primarily leaned toward trade with, or aid from, socialist countries, and economic relations with capitalist countries were almost completely cut off until the late 1960s. However, in the 1970s, the North Korean government attempted to introduce plants from Western countries due to a sense of crisis caused by the economic growth seen in South Korea. The sluggish economy and recession that started in the 1980s caused North Korea to adopt a partial opening up as well as marketization policies.

Observing the process of North Korea's opening up and marketization policies since the 1980s shows that it has never made a clear long-term decision on opening up or on marketization policies in terms of a national development strategy. North Korea has recognized the implementation of opening up and marketization policies and maintenance of domestic political system as paradoxical and difficult for integration, thereby rifting them and prioritizing the maintenance of its political system. Therefore, it has fluctuated, at different times, between opening up and marketization on the one hand and national isolation and self-rehabilitation on the other. Ultimately however, it did not carry out active opening up and marketization policies.

Accordingly, its attempts to introduce foreign investment have failed repeatedly due to the inconsistency of domestic and overseas policies and a loss of credit (Quan 2013, 51). This has triggered a continuing economic crisis, putting the national economy in jeopardy and trapping it in a vicious cycle: low production → low export → lack of foreign currency → low import → low production.

3.1 Vulnerable drives for economic growth

According to statistics released by North Korea, nominal GDP in 2013 and 2014 were 25.0 billion USD and 26.13 billion USD, respectively, and the growth rate of the GDP in 2014 was 4.5 percent.[4] However, statistics released by the Bank of Korea (in South Korea) showed that the growth rate of the GNI in North Korea in 2014 was 1.0 percent, which is 3.5 percentage point lower than shown in data released by North Korea (Bank of Korea 2019). According to statistics estimated by the Bank of Korea, from 2011 to 2015, growth rates of North Korea's GNI annually are shown as 0.8 percent, 1.3 percent, 1.1 percent, 1.0 percent, and −1.1 percent, respectively, with outcomes approximately around 1 percent. However, it rose significantly to 3.9 percent in 2016. As the FAO estimated, North Korea's growth rate of crop production between 2012 and 2016 were 3.9 percent, 5.7 percent, 2.2 percent, 1.0 percent, and −5.5 percent, respectively (FAO 2015, 2016; FAO and WFP 2010, 2011). In addition, the growth rates of North Korea's external trade between 2011 and 2016, as estimated by the KOTRA, were found as 51.3 percent, 7.1 percent, 7.8 percent, 3.6 percent, −18 percent, and 4.7 percent, respectively (KOTRA 2017). Given these statistics, it can be said that the economic growth rates of North Korea estimated by the Bank of Korea were underestimated. Considering the actual economic conditions of North Korea along with these factors, it is believed that the true economic growth rate of North Korea (except for 2015) has remained around 4 percent in recent years.

However, since North Korea's economic size is extremely small, any increase in total quantities brought by a 4-percent economic growth rate is trivial. Considering the economic growth potential discussed earlier, the economic growth rate is still insignificant and the economic growth drive is also weak when compared to its great potential. The fundamental cause lies in the economic development strategy that focuses on heavy industries, particularly defense industries, based on the planned economy, as well as its long-standing national isolationism and goals of self-rehabilitation. If North Korea does not take measures to improve its international environment, address economic sanctions posed by the international community, turn to an export-oriented economic development strategy, and implement active opening up and marketization policies, it will be difficult for it to achieve its economic growth potential.

3.2 Formation of dual economic structures

A dual economic structure where both a planned economy and a market economy coexist was formed in North Korea due to the augmenting market activities that occurred after the economic crisis. However, contrary to other socialist countries such as China or Vietnam, instead of the government actively implementing opening up and marketization policies from the top down, North Korea's dual economic structure was created by residents who were unable to sustain themselves without market activities, leading to the government ignoring its black-market activities, regulating them afterwards, and finally approving them as lawful. This is the unique characteristic of North Korea's dual economic structure.

Under these circumstances, in which North Korea did not, and as of yet does not pursue active opening up and marketization policies, the planned economy and the market economy of North Korea maintain a complementary and confrontational relationship. The planned economic part not only absorbs any economic surplus generated from the market economy to supplement an inadequate national budget, but also the state sustains the operation of the state-owned economy by utilizing market economy. The market economy is also expanded by taking advantage of resources in the planned economy. However, the market economy is continuously expanded through continuous capital accumulation, while the material basis of the planned economy is eroded due to the diverting activities in the market economy and the continuous loss of resources. At the same time, with the expansion of the market economy, the awareness of the market economy, individualism, and money-oriented idea spreading, the gap between rich and poor is widening, in turn weakening the political system base of North Korea.

When the late Kim Jong-il was the leader, North Korea took advantage of the market economy or took contrary measures (strict control) depending on variations in both domestic and overseas political and economic situations. This demonstrates that what this country wants is the use of a controllable market economy, not the constant expansion of market economy. More observation is needed regarding Chairman Kim Jong-un's trend of marketization policy.

3.3 High external economic dependency

In order for North Korea to realize continuous economic growth, international economic exchange and cooperation needs to be augmented. Although a variety of small industrial sectors were made in North Korea under the long-term planned economic system, it shows an inefficient economy, poor technical skill level, and low industrial competitiveness. To make it worse, continuous economic crises occurring from the 1990s until present have triggered the destruction and deterioration of industrial facilities and caused a shortage of energy, crops, machinery, and raw materials. Furthermore, the national economy cannot function without importing these items.

Due to these problems, North Korea's need for external economic dependency is still considerable. In addition, North Korea has performed measures on the diversification and variety of external trade proposed by the late Kim Il-sung.[5] Nevertheless, North Korea is completely dependent on China in terms of external trade due to sanctions posed by the United Nations, Japan, South Korea, and the United States. This is in contrast to its attempted policy of the diversification of external trade that North Korea has pursued.

4 Transition of development routes and prospects for economic development of North Korea

After North Korea determined to achieve the policy of "line on carrying out the economic construction and the building of nuclear armed forces simultaneously" and launched nuclear and missile development into high gear, it has faced tightened economic sanctions from the international community and as a result has undergone tremendous difficulties since late 2016. In April 2018, North Korea held the third plenary meeting of Seventh Central Committee of the Workers' Party of North Korea and declared the completion of the historical mission of "line on carrying out the economic construction and the building of nuclear armed forces simultaneously" and came to agreement on implementing an "economic construction-centered route" in which all competences of parties and people are devoted and proceed to build the socialist economy. Simultaneously, with the New Year's address in 2018 delivered by Chairman Kim Jong-un, it has started to improve international relations.

4.1 Background on the transition of development routes

The background of North Korea's decision to implement the "economic construction-centered route" is outlined as follows.

The fundamental administrative objective pursued by North Korea's leadership is the maintenance of the political system and economic development, among which the former was adopted as the top priority. The purpose of carrying out nuclear and missile development in the face of strong opposition from the international community was and is to maintain the political system.

The rapid change of socialist countries in Eastern Europe in the late 1980s; the dissolution of the Soviet Union; the diplomatic tie and rapid development of political and economic relations between Russia, China, and South Korea in the 1990s; armed subversion of the Hussein government in Iraq by Western countries led by the United States in 2003; and the subversion of the Gaddafi regime in Libya in 2011 triggered a pending crisis of leadership North Korea. These events have provoked North Korea to speed up its nuclear and missile development. It can be said that developing nuclear weapons is assumed to be a "reasonable" choice with relatively fewer investments and stronger restraints under the present circumstance in which it is unable to compete with the US-South Korea military alliance in terms of economy or technology.

More stringent economic sanctions against North Korea by the international community since December 2016 have further weakened its external economy from 2017. Significant foreign exchange earnings, moreover, have all been prohibited due to the export ban, including mineral products, aquatic products, textile products, and labor. Thus, North Korea's foreign exchange earnings dramatically reduced, and capacity to make foreign currency payments fell, resulting in decreasing imports. At the same time, the mining industry and fishery industry have inevitably also met the same fate. Sanctions such as the bans on exporting machinery to North Korea, exporting petroleum and petroleum products to North Korea, and managing foreign-invested enterprises in North Korea have considerable negative impacts on North Korea's economy. Also, these bans and sanctions have a severe impact on North Korea's trade and the trust placed in the country by foreign investors. This plays a huge role in North Korea's foreign economic exchanges and cooperation.

North Korea's six nuclear tests secured a certain level of nuclear deterrence. However, it is hard to deny the fact that its nuclear capability and established military force are utterly inferior to that of the US-South Korea military alliance. The nuclear development by North Korea, then, aims to maintain the political system internally, not to provoke wars externally. Additionally, it is a suitable option for North Korea to continuously bring the United States to the negotiating table by using nuclear weapons and missiles as a negotiation card.

If Chairman Kim Jong-un attains sustained economic growth and improves national living standards, he has a high possibility of long-term governance. Thus, if the political system maintenance is guaranteed, it would be a strategic choice for him to further improve international relations by addressing nuclear issues, which would trigger a lifting of the economic sanctions against North Korea, extend foreign economic exchange and cooperation, and likely cause continuous economic growth. Indeed, Chairman Kim Jong-un has come to normalize state control in the years since assuming leadership, striving to enhance national living standards, and he has pursued opening up and marketization policies including the "field responsibility system," state-owned enterprise reform, and the establishment of economic development zones and SEZs. Based on this, Chairman Kim Jong-un is likely to continue to implement active opening up and marketization policies, thereby promoting a rapid economic recovery and growth.

In particular, the improvement of bilateral relations launched by South Korea's President Moon Jae-in and the movement for joint prosperity provide a good environment for North Korea to change the course of its development route.

The key is the trend of the relationship between North Korea and the United States. There is no reason why North Korea should not seek a fundamental solution to the nuclear issue if both North Korea and the United States resolve the mutual distrust and if the security of the North Korean regime is secured.

4.2 Two aspects of economic construction of North Korea

There are two aspects in the economic construction of North Korea. If North Korea launches economic construction under the principle of an "Economic construction-centered route," it will attempt to (1) reinforce the building of self-reliance and an independent national economy and (2) extend international economic exchange and cooperation.

The first aspect is to strengthen the construction of self-reliance and independent national economy. North Korea has aimed to build up its national independent economic system by encouraging self-rehabilitation that relies on the wisdom and power of its people, taking advantage of sufficient domestic resources, and thus boosting the economy.

In the Seventh Central Committee of the Workers' Party of North Korea held in 2016, Chairman Kim Jong-un reemphasized the importance of self-reliance and building up that self-reliance through an independent economic system, and asked to realize the localization of raw materials, fuels, and facilities, and address energy, electricity, and food shortage problems as a top priority. Furthermore, as a means of realizing this, he decided to establish a process of production technology that guarantees strategic fuel and supplies by using domestic resources through the innovation of science and technology and produce technical equipment such as advanced (high-tech) equipment to fit the national situation.

In addition, the third plenary meeting of the Seventh Central Committee of the Workers' Party of North Korea held in April 2018 decided to focus all the capabilities of the party and the nation on socialist economic construction and called for the mobilization of the full potential of the nation's human and material capabilities and technologies to enhance self-reliance and increase production.

The focus of North Korea's science and technological innovation is implemented as an objective of building a self-reliant and independent national economy. It shows fruitful outcomes in superior agricultural species, biological pesticides, aquaculture technology, the extraction of petroleum by using coal, the development of chemical fertilizer production technology, the establishment of the Juche iron production system, and the production of Computerized Numerical Control (CNC) machine tools. However, the speed of building this self-reliance and independent national economy is slowed by restrained foreign economic development and poor-level industrial development.

The second aspect is to extend international economic exchange and cooperation. North Korea has consistently adhered to signing economic relations with other countries and developing foreign trade based on the construction of an independent national economy. North Korea's principle of allowing foreign trade lies in the diversification and variety of trade.

For continuous economic growth in North Korea, it is necessary to expand international economic exchange and cooperation. However, its foreign economic exchange and collaboration have faced difficulties due to vigorous economic sanctions against North Korea since late 2016. The top priorities are thus to address its nuclear and missile issues with the international community and enhance the general international environment and in so doing lift international sanctions.

With Chairman Kim Jong-un's New Year's speech in 2018, North Korea actively launched to improve international relations and held a series of events such as the North Korea-China summit, the North-South Korean summit, and the North Korea -US summit. As a result of these events, inter-Korean relations have remarkably improved, and negotiations between North Korea and the United States are underway. An improved relationship with the United States is required for North Korea to reduce or remove UN sanctions likely continue to make strenuous efforts to attain it. What is important for the international community is for it to cooperate with and guide North Korea to an active opening up and marketization. The economic stability and development of North Korea are beneficial to economic cooperation, peace, and development on the Korean Peninsula and beyond in the Northeast Asian region.

4.3 Prospects for economic development of North Korea

The international community has a keen interest in the matter of where North Korea's economy will head as its development direction can tremendously affect its economic growth as well as the economic exchange in the Northeast Asian region and further activation of economic cooperation.

There are two major possible paths the economic development direction of North Korea may take. One possibility is that it will concentrate on the construction of self-reliance and independent national economy based on the planned economic system and complement it by extending foreign economic cooperation. This is the development direction that North Korea has long pursued. Internally, it aims to contribute to the recovery and development of a planned economic system and state-owned economy through self-rehabilitation, promote production by utilizing domestic resources and technologies, and enhance economic efficiency and make an active economy by implementing partial marketization policies. Simultaneously, it aims for a partial opening as an external policy, through which it seeks to obtain foreign investment, build SEZs and development zones, and promote the development of export industries. It also aims to further exports and develop an international tourism industry, increasing foreign currency inflows, thereby expanding imports of energy, crops, raw materials, and the machinery needed in the construction of an independent national economy.

The other possibility is for North Korea to implement an export-oriented economic development strategy and utilize the active opening up and marketization policies in order to gradually establish a market economic system in terms of national development strategy. Internally, the government will push for systematic economic reform and gradually establish a market economy system. The aim of building special economic zones and development zones is not merely to develop export industries and increase foreign investments but also to serve as all- encompassing test spots for reform and opening up, a unity that connects national economy with the international economy, and nurturing human capital specialized in the market economy. Externally, the government will promote the specialization and development of industries utilizing the international division of labor system.

It is desirable for North Korea to take an export-oriented economic development strategy and carry out active opening up and marketization policies, gradually moving to the establishment of a market economic system in the eyes of the international community. This path is advantageous not only for realizing the enormous economic growth potential of North Korea, but also for the development of inter-Korean cooperation and because it furthers the development of multilateral economic cooperation in the Northeast Asian region. North Korea is geographically situated at the center of the Northeast Asian region and holds advantageous conditions for various connections with international economies and the development of international logistics. Also, it retains a relatively excellent workforce that is low cost compared to other Northeast Asian labor sources. Finally, plentiful mineral resources as well as tourism resources are to be found there in abundance. To sum up, North Korea has tremendous potential for economic development. Accordingly, if North Korea implements an export-oriented economic development strategy and active opening up as well as marketization policies, it can achieve rapid economic growth.

The Northeast Asian region possesses substantial productive factors such as resources, workforce, capital, and skill due to geographical adjacency, economic development levels, and its endowment with rich resource conditions, as well as economic factors needed for multilateral economic cooperation such as an enormous market size and development potential. Nonetheless, the remaining Cold War structure embedded in the Northeast Asian region is a significant cause of stagnated multilateral economic cooperation. The essence of this structure absolutely lies in the North-South Korean conflict.

If North Korea implements active measures such as opening up and marketization policies and progresses inter-Korean economic cooperation by improving inter-Korean relations, China, Russia, Mongolia, North Korea, and South Korea can be connected by road. If high-speed rail and expressways are built, a one-day economic zone and the massive market that would follow can be formed. Currently, not only comparative advantages such as traditional resources and labor force but also the degree of local market activation and the size of development potential are considered more important in terms of capital investment. Therefore, if multilateral economic cooperation joined by Northeast Asian countries such as China, Russia, North Korea, South Korea, and Mongolia is reinforced, Japan will have no choice but to participate in this organization for its economic growth. The change of North Korea and the strengthening of inter-Korean cooperation will spark the activation of multilateral economic cooperation in the Northeast Asian region.

North Korea's active opening up and its marketization policies and economic stability and development are beneficial to the stability and development of the Korean Peninsula and even to the Northeast Asian region as a whole. The international community is essential in creating conditions for North Korea's active opening up and marketization policies by strengthening cooperation and encouraging North Korea to implement these measures.

5 Conclusion

This study outlines the characteristics of the North Korean economy and predicts economic development. From the characteristics of its endowed resources, North Korea retains a comparatively skilled workforce and plentiful mineral resources. Moreover, it holds geographical advantages in connection with international economies. Therefore, it has tremendous economic growth potential. However, due to limited access to its endowed resources, it requires constant exchange and cooperation with international economies in order to accomplish constant economic growth.

Due to the limitations of development strategies, opening up, and marketization policies, North Korea has wavered over solutions between isolation and self-rehabilitation and opening up and marketization policies. As a result, policies have not been continuous, and the investment environment has not improved, ultimately failing to attract foreign investment and failing to escape its economic crisis. This indicates that North Korea has not implemented active opening up and marketization policies in terms of the national development strategy; as its leaders have recognized, active opening up and marketization policies and the maintenance of the domestic political system are unharmonious conflicting entities, and therefore it has alternatively prioritized the maintenance of the domestic political system. From the basic characteristics of the North Korean economy, we see a weaker growth drive and dual economic structure where the planned economy and market economy exist, which creates considerable external dependence.

There will be two major possibilities for the economic development directions of North Korea. One possibility is to concentrate on the construction of self-reliance and independent national economy based on the planned economic system and to complement it by extending foreign economic cooperation. This is the development direction that the country has long pursued. The other possibility is to implement an export-oriented economic development strategy and active opening and marketization policies in order to gradually establish the market economic system in terms of the national development strategy.

North Korea's active opening and marketization policies and its economic stability and development are both beneficial to the stability and development of the Korean Peninsula and of the Northeast Asian areas. The Northeast Asian region, in particular, has the economic factors necessary for multilateral economic cooperation. Despite this, the remaining Cold War structure in the Northeast Asian region centered on South-North Korean relations is a significant reason for the sluggishness of multilateral economic cooperation.

Therefore, it is desirable for the international community to create conditions for North Korea's active opening up and marketization policies to succeed by strengthening cooperation as well as by inducing and encouraging North Korea to implement these measures.

Notes

1 According to the second demographic consensus survey conducted in 2008 by North Korea, it has a population of 24.05 million people. And, demographic statistics in North Korea estimated by Statistics Korea (in South Korea) showed 23.93 and 24.9 million people in 2008 and 2016, respectively (KOSIS 2019). Both statistics match the population in 2008.
2 The statistics were released by Professor Lee Ki-sung (Academy of Social Sciences of North Korea) at an academic forum held at College of Economics and Management of Yanbian University (China) on April 26, 2016.
3 Wages for workers from North Korea increase 5% every year according to the bilateral agreement.
4 The statistics were released by Professor Lee Ki-sung (Academy of Social Sciences of North Korea) at an academic forum held at School of Economics and Management of Yanbian University (China) on April 26, 2016.
5 The late Chairman Kim Il-sung pointed out in a speech called "Concerning the Diversification and Variety of External Trade" at the Trade Sector Council on March 1978 that one-way trade with socialist countries in external trade is eliminated and valiantly jump into the capital market. The diversification of external trade refers to business aiming at increasing participant units and expanding its external market to many countries and regions in the world. The variety of external trade is a business for trade with a variety of merchandise, styles, and methods. Both are closely associated (Jin and Quan 2015, 74).

References

Bank of Korea. 2019. "GDP Estimates for North Korea." Accessed June 20. www.bok.or.kr/por-tal/maiu/couteuts.do?weuuNo=200091.

Food and Agriculture Organization of the United Nations (FAO). 2015. "GIEWS Update: The Democratic People's Republic of Korea Outlook for Food Supply and Demand in 2014/15 (November/October)—Democratic People's Republic of Korea." *ReliefWeb*, February 3. https://reliefweb.int/report/democratic-peoples-republic-korea/giews-update-democratic-people-s-republic-korea-outlook.

Food and Agriculture Organization of the United Nations (FAO). 2016. "GIEWS Update: The Democratic People's Republic of Korea; Outlook for Food Supply and Demand in 2015/16 (November/October)." *ReliefWeb*, April 27. https://reliefweb.int/report/democratic-peoples-republic-korea/giews-update-democratic-peoples-republic-korea-outlook-food.

Food and Agriculture Organization of the United Nations (FAO) and United Nations World Food Programme (WFP). 2010. "FAO/WFP Crop and Food Security Assessment Mission to the Democratic People's Republic of Korea." *Special Report*, November 16. www.fao.org/3/al968e/al968e00.htm.

Food and Agriculture Organization of the United Nations (FAO) and United Nations World Food Programme (WFP). 2011. "FAO/WFP Crop and Food Security Assessment Mission to the Democratic People's Republic of Korea." *Special Report*, November 12. www.fao.org/3/al994e/al994e00.pdf.

Hong, Jea Hwan. 2017. "North Korean Economy in the Kim Jong-un Regime." *KINU Study Series*: 17–18. Seoul: Korea Institute for National Unification.

Japan External Trade Organization (JETRO). 2015. "Survey on the Recent North Korean Economy in 2014." Accessed February 2. www.jetro.go.jp/en/.

Jin, Mingzhe, and Zhenan Quan. 2015. "The Current Situation of North Korea's Foreign Economic Relations and Several Issues to Be Solved." *Dongjiang Journal* 32 (3): 73–78.

Jung, Hwa Soon. 2015. *Understanding the Democratic People's Republic of Korea (Economy)*. Pyongyang: Foreign Languages Publishing House.

Korea Development Bank. 2015. "North Korea's Industry: KDB." https://ebook.kdb.co.kr/PublicContentDetail.kdb?menuseq=164&conseq=517&listmode=thumb.

Korea Trade Investment Promotion Agency (KOTRA). 2017. "2016 North Korea's Foreign Trade Trends." *KOCHI 17–011*. http://openknowledge.kotra.or.kr/handle/2014.oak/9954.

Korean Statistical Information Service (KOSIS). 2019. "North Korea Statistics Portal." Accessed February 26. http://kosis.kr/bukhan/index.jsp.

Quan, Zhenan. 2013. "North Korea's Food Shortage Problem and Its Solution Prospects." *Contemporary International Relations* 1: 47–53.

Quan, Zhenan. 2018a. "The North Korean Power Shortage Problem and Solution." *Dongjiang Journal* 2: 47–52.

Quan, Zhenan. 2018b. "North Korea's Transportation Bottleneck." *World Affairs* 12: 28–29.

Quan, Zhenan, and Gengqian Li. 2018. "Advantages, Limitations, and Prospects of Development and Utilization of North Korean Labor Resources." *World Affairs* 23: 24–25.

3 North Korea's marketization in the Kim Jong-un era

Facts, evaluation, and outlook

Moon-soo Yang

1 Introduction

North Korea's economic crisis, which began in the early 1990s, has still not been resolved thirty years later. As a result, the North Korean economy changed in many ways, and this prolonged economic crisis changed its character to become inevitable and structural rather than accidental and temporary.

The representative example is the market. Prior to the economic crisis, the market was extremely limited and marginal, but its stature has tightened its grip on the entire North Korean economy in no time. Particularly, it plays an important role not only in the people's daily life, but also in the operation of the state-run sector. Now, the North Korean economy without a market would be beyond imagination. Since the start of the 21st century, marketization has been regarded as the second driving force for invigorating the North Korean economy, along with North Korea-China trade.

This chapter aims to diagnose the current status of North Korea's marketization in the Kim Jong-un era and to present prospects for the future. The structure of this chapter is as follows: First, we will look at how North Korea's marketization has been expanding in the Kim Jung-un era, then draw out the characteristics of North Korea's current marketization, and briefly examine the achievements and limitations of North Korea's marketization, and finally present an ideal future image of North Korea's marketization.

Before discussing marketization, it is first necessary to take a brief look at the concept of marketization. Marketization is a broad and comprehensive concept that can take place at various levels. It is often the case that people think of a market as places or spaces, for instance department stores and traditional markets, but in reality, such a market is a physical entity, which is only a part of a larger market system. The system of the market is more important rather than its aspects as a physical place. The so-called market, therefore, should be technically called a market mechanism.

Assuming marketization as a concept that contrasts with planning, it can be defined as the introduction and diffusion of market mechanisms. In this case, the price is determined by the interaction of supply and demand, and the information reflected by the price adjusts not only economic actions of different decision-making units such as households and businesses, but also the resource allocation of the entire macro economy.

2 Current status of marketization in the Kim Jong-un era

2.1 Expansion of existing markets

The expansion of the market complex in North Korea best demonstrates the progress of North Korea's marketization, especially the expansion of existing markets. According to an analysis of satellite images of North Korea conducted by the researchers at Johns Hopkins University in the United States, the number of market complexes has almost doubled from about 200 in 2010 to 396 in 2015. In addition, the number increased to 436 in 2017, which is an increase of forty market complexes per year.

It is also important to note the expansion of service sectors, particularly the transportation and transport service market. Transportation services in the public sector, including railways, have failed to function properly since the economic crisis, but the demand for private transportation has increased sharply. This has resulted in a substantial imbalance between supply and demand, and the private sector voluntarily developed a means of supplying transportation services in several ways to fill the gap in supply through transportation services provided by the public sector. In the early and mid-1990s, an illegal transportation service, called a "service car," which utilized former cargo trucks to transport people, became popular. Subsequently, new transportation services, such as city buses, intercity buses and taxis, emerged and developed in the 2000s and 2010s.

However, the private sector is responsible for most road transportation systems, including city buses, intercity buses, and taxis. That is, all management activities are carried out under the responsibility of private, non-state actors, including the purchase of used buses and taxis or new buses and taxis from China, the repair of these vehicles, supply of fuel, and even employment of the drivers by utilizing one's own money or private financing. Since the private ownership of such transportation means it is not allowed in North Korea, however, they package them as if they belonged to a specific state institution or enterprise. This, in other words, means that people borrow the name of an institution or enterprise, register the means of transportation officially to the state, and pay a portion of the income earned by doing business in return for the loan of the name. This is called an enterprise with a "socialist cap" or "red cap." This phenomenon indicates that the private ownership of transportation, which used to be regarded as illegal, is now considered as half-legal activity.

2.2 The creation and expansion of new markets

While the private sector used to voluntarily create and expand new markets in North Korea, North Korean authorities have taken the initiative in the Kim Jong-un era. A case in point is the ownership of a mobile phone. The Ministry of Post and Telecommunications in North Korea established a joint venture with an Egyptian telecommunication company called Orascom and provides mobile phone sales and communication services.

Most of the mobile phones in North Korea are made in China. The Ministry of Post and Telecommunications in North Korea imports low-priced mobile phones from China and labels them made in North Korea. In North Korea, mobile phones sell at $200–300 for entry level models, $400–500 for middle market ones, and $600–700 for the most expensive. The North Korean government, along with Orascom, has actually emerged as an exclusive foreign importer and domestic supplier, driving the growth of the market by receiving monopoly profits arising from the enormous price gap between import prices and domestic sales prices. The North Korean government started the service in 2008, and the market has grown explosively, with more than 6 million subscribers as of the end of 2018, more than a decade later.

Another example of the creation and expansion of new markets in the Kim Jong-un era is the real estate market. The North Korean authorities promoted the growth of the real estate market by promoting the construction of large-scale apartment complexes at the national level and acquiescing to or actually encouraging apartment construction using private capital under the pretext of the "expansion of the construction of dwelling houses." Kim Jong-un completed the construction of Changjon Street, a high-rise apartment complex on Mansudae Street in June 2012, shortly after his inauguration, as part of the one thousandth construction project in Pyongyang City. This string of urban redevelopment projects, which began in 2008, has spearheaded a significant number of urban redevelopments and constructions, which include a new town, home to the Eunha Scientists Street, Kim Il-sung University's Science Apartment, Mirae Scientists Street, and Ryomyong New Town Street.

2.3 The expansion of private enterprise: progress in de facto privatization

In North Korea, the privatization of the means of production is not allowed by law, but in the real world, privatization of the means of production is in progress. Although primarily manifesting as small-scale companies, privatization is actually spreading as marketization begins to accelerate once again in Kim Jong-un's regime. In fact, private companies invested in and operated by individuals in North Korea are spreading not only in the service industry, but also in agriculture, fisheries, mining, trade, and even manufacturing sectors, especially in the construction industry such as the aforementioned apartment construction in the Kim Jung-un era.

However, there are no official statistics or reports on the size or level of these private companies. They can only be estimated from surveys of North Korean defectors at this point. This section examines the current trend of the private enterprises in North Korea by comparing three surveys of North Korean defectors, which were individually conducted in 2005, 2009 and 2015. These survey results are indeed subjective perceptions of the North Korean defectors on the private enterprises and may be biased due to the region, social stratum, or other background factors of the individual. The results, therefore, should be carefully interpreted.

Figures 3.1 through 3.6 present the survey results of six types of enterprises, namely, local industrial plants, central industries, state-owned stores, restaurants, personal service companies, and enterprises related to foreign currency earnings. As depicted in the figures, the proportion of companies that individuals invest in and operate in is significantly increasing in all but the central industry among these six categories, as shown in the 2005, 2009, and 2015 surveys. Comparing the survey results of 2005 and 2015, the increase is approximately 10 to 20 percent. This indicates that the number of private enterprises had a sharp increase between 2002 and 2015.

3 Characteristics and evaluation of North Korean marketization

3.1 Hierarchical structure of North Korean marketization

What is the driving force of marketization in North Korea? This is closely related to the nature of North Korean marketization. One view on the driving force is the so-called bottom-up marketization theory or spontaneous marketization theory. Another view is the theory of market forces or the hierarchical structure of marketization.

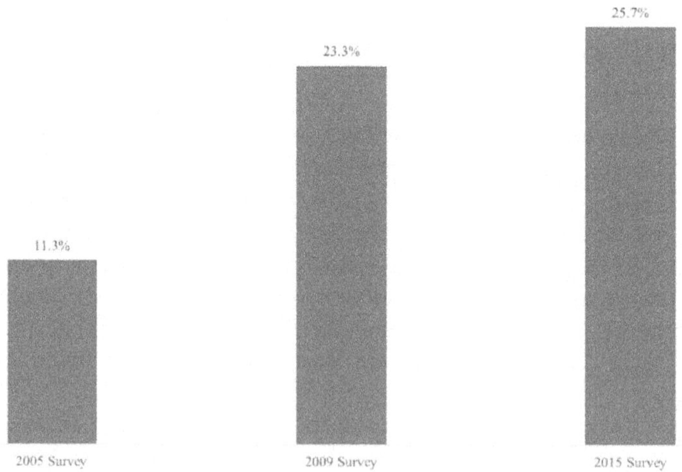

Figure 3.1 Share of local industrial plants invested in and operated by individuals

Source: Yang and Yoon 2016

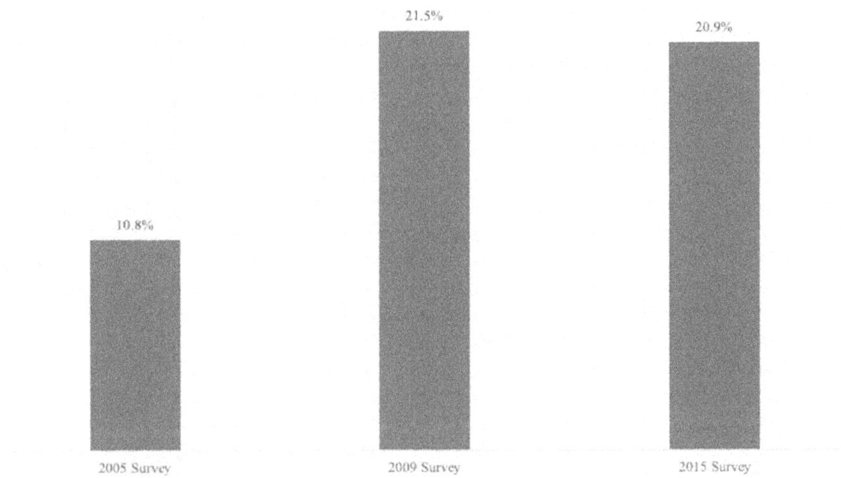

Figure 3.2 Share of central industries invested in and operated by individuals

Source: Yang and Yoon 2016

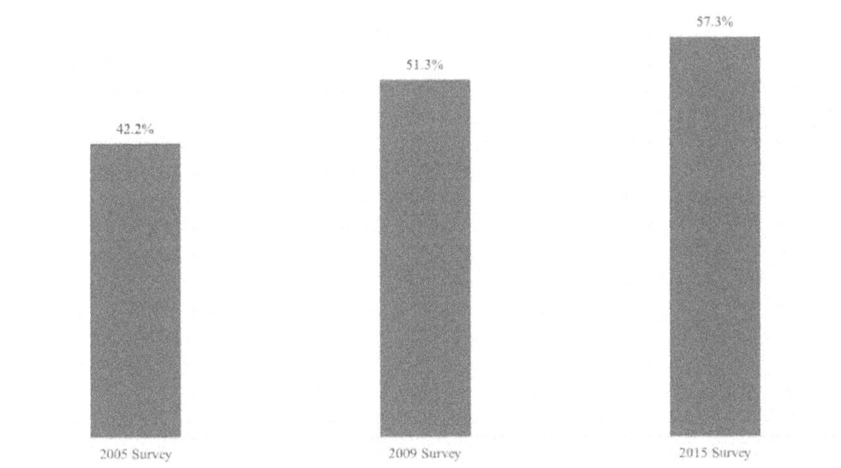

Figure 3.3 Share of state-owned stores invested in and operated by individuals

Source: Yang and Yoon 2016

"The theory of bottom-up marketization" or "spontaneous marketization" stresses the point that the marketization was initiated by bottom-line economic players such as businesses and households to rehabilitate themselves. The North Korean marketization after the 1990s can be defined as such a spontaneous marketization, meaning a natural expansion of commerce and personal

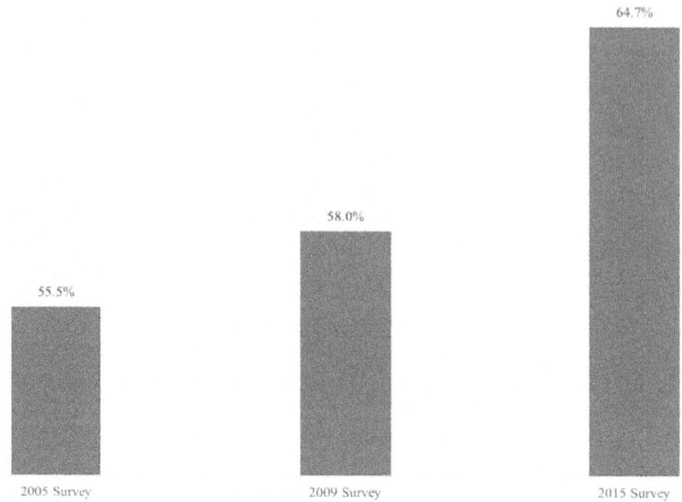

Figure 3.4 Share of restaurants invested in and operated by individuals
Source: Yang and Yoon 2016

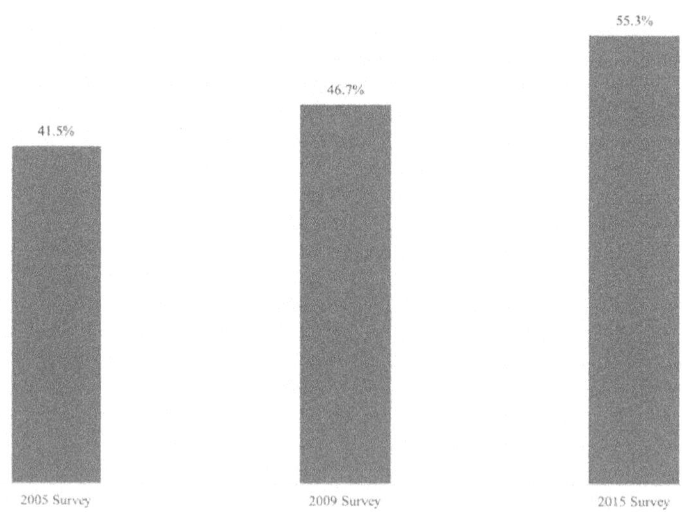

Figure 3.5 Share of personal services invested in and operated by individuals
Source: Yang and Yoon 2016

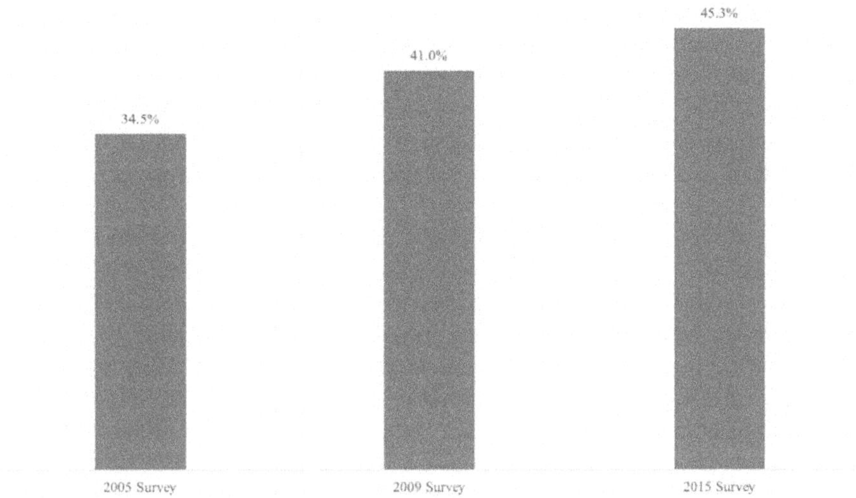

Figure 3.6 Share of enterprises for foreign currency earnings invested in and operated by individuals

Source: Yang and Yoon 2016

production by residents. This concept directly contrasts with state-led marketization and market introduction, which are commonly referred to as top-down marketization.

The so-called "theory of market force" is taking a somewhat different approach from this argument. In this theory, the main force driving marketization in North Korea comes from the omnidirectional development of foreign currency earning projects by "special units." The main players in North Korea's market development are individual merchants who are in collusion with the regime and its agency that enjoy a dominant position in the process of market expansion against the backdrop of the protection and special favors of power.

What is the relationship between the theory of market force and that of spontaneous marketization? In terms of contents, both deal with all activities related directly and indirectly to the marketplace (Jangmadang) and foreign trade on the marketization of North Korea. In general, spontaneous marketization mainly focuses on the marketplace, while the hierarchical structure of North Korean Marketization centers on foreign trade and the latter has a wider scope of coverage than that of the former. In terms of research history, the theory of bottom-up marketization (or spontaneous marketization) emerged in the early stages of the study of the North Korean market, especially in the mid- to late 2000s. The theory of market force (or the hierarchical structure of the North Korean marketization) appeared a little later in the 2010s. Therefore, both should be viewed as complementary rather than contradictory.

When divided into general population-led marketization and power-driven (foreign currency earnings) marketization are these two flows carried out in stages or in parallel? Or did it initially proceed separately and then merge into one at some point? While full-scale research is needed in the future, these two flows are now combined. Also, the more North Korea's marketization progresses, the more the hierarchical structural theory of the market gains explanatory power especially in the Kim Jong-un era.

From this point of view, the hierarchical structure of the market can be simply summarized as follows. At the top of the commodity flow pyramid of the market, there are trading companies affiliated with the state institution, under which there are huge financial backers in the private sector. In the middle of the pyramid, there are local power institutions and field workers, including provincial, municipal, and county offices, and several steps below there are export source extractors, producers, and marketplace (Jangmadang) retailers at the bottom of the pyramid. The main impetus behind the marketization in North Korea is that the "special units" in the privileged economy at the top of the pyramid, such as the Central Party's Office No 38 and 39, other special departments, each unit of the Ministry of the People's Armed Forces, People's Security Department, the State Security Department, and the Supreme Guard Command, are responsible for the omnidirectional expansion of foreign currency earning businesses. The key actor in the special units' foreign currency earning business here is the state-run trading company.

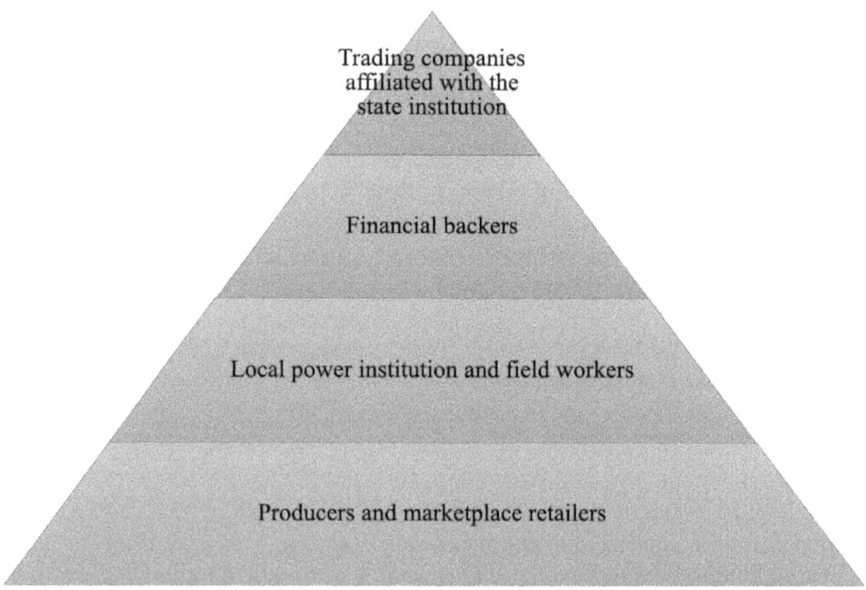

Figure 3.7 Hierarchical structure of marketization in North Korea

Source: Author created

Overall, it is necessary to note that the relationship between the financial backers and the trading company is basically vertical, not horizontal. In other words, the financial backers in the private sector are located below the trading companies in terms of economic and social structure.

3.2 Institutionalization and grey zone policy of North Korean marketization

Although North Korean Marketization is low in the level of institutionalization, it should be noted that from a perspective of nearly three decades of history, the policy of the North Korean authorities has moved to slowly raise the level of institutionalization of the market. Some have been completely legalized (White Zone), but many of them are a policy of imperfect legalization (Grey Zone).

For example, partial legitimacy was granted in the 2000s on Jangmadang (market complex) and Beul-e bus (especially intercity buses). In particular, the government provided a certain amount of space (land) for them to enter and engage in market economy activities. In other words, the authorities have gathered market economy actors within their physical control, granted partial legitimacy, while officially receiving de facto taxes.

In addition, although North Korea does not legally recognize the de facto private ownership of the means of production, such as restaurants, shops, small factories, small coal mines and buses, as they are officially incorporated under the umbrella of a particular state agency or state-run company, it nevertheless ensures maximum autonomy as a private business. In this way, it receives de facto taxes in return for granting them partial legitimacy by lending out the names of state institutions and corporations, that is, giving a "socialist cap." It is also to collect de facto taxes while registering state consumer goods that have the nature of production means such as mobile phones, bicycles, and motorcycles.

Then, directly or indirectly, marketization will help the operation of the state-run economy, and from an individual's perspective, a certain level of institutional protection is secured, thus allowing more stable market economy activities. To put it another way, we can think of the possibility that there is some sort of institutional compromise between the North Korean authorities and individuals (or the private sector) concerning the market, especially in the private ownership of the means of production. And these institutional compromises naturally contribute to the expansion and stabilization of marketization.

3.3 The emergence of domestic markets

Previously, North Korea's marketization was largely attributed to the development of distribution, especially foreign trade, rather than production, and therefore the development of the market in North Korea was characterized by not involving a significant increase in productivity. With domestic resources mostly exhausted and almost all of the nation's industrial connections destroyed, the effect of the market expansion stimulating domestic production was limited. Therefore, it was inconceivable that there was a domestic market in North Korea.

However, as marketization has progressed further in the Kim Jong-un era, slight changes have begun to occur in this trend. First of all, with the progress of marketization coupled with the increase in foreign trade, the private sector has been accumulating monetary assets little by little, creating and growing markets in North Korea, which can now be called the domestic market. With food and food processing at the center, domestic markets for clothing, cosmetics, medicine, and electronics are being formed. This formation of the domestic market is working to stimulate domestic production and restore some of the domestic industrial connections, while further advancing the marketization.

3.4 Expansion of linkage between state economy and marketization

With the continued progress of marketization, significant changes are also taking place in the state-run economy, especially in the mode of behavior and management patterns of state-owned enterprises. Such changes have been made mainly in unofficial areas since the outbreak of the economic crisis, but have been active in official areas since the 7.1 economic measures, and are spreading even further in the Kim Jong-Un era.

First, there has been an expansion of autonomy and authority of state-owned enterprises. State-owned enterprises utilize their greater autonomy and authority than ever before in a wide range of areas such as the preparation and implementation of the plan, namely the selection of production items, raw materials and financing, pricing and sales.

Second, there has been an increase in market economy activities of state-owned enterprises. State-owned companies are expanding their market-based management activities in a wide range of areas, including the selection of production items, raw materials and financing, and pricing and sales. In this regard, it is also noteworthy that the self-reliance belief system of state-owned enterprises is being strengthened and expanded through "8.3 Workers," "DuBeul-e" and "foreign currency earnings."

In addition, the link between state-owned companies and financial backers is also expanding significantly with the progress of marketization.

First, state-owned companies receive loan investments from financial backers. In this case, financial backers can make loan investments in cash or in kind, and can be repaid in cash or in kind as well. At this time, in case of repayment in kind, especially in goods, the person stores the goods and controls the timing of the sale of the goods for maximum profit. State-owned enterprises receive cash or in kind from financial backers and produce products designated by financial backers, handing them over to financial backers and receiving commissions, which fall into the category of foundry.

Second, a state-owned company lends to financial backers' various assets, that is, public assets, which can be of three types: (1) Lending only the state-owned company's name to the financial backers. (2) Lending the name and means of production (building and machinery) to the financial backers. (3) Lending only the means of production, not the name. Among them, (1) and (2) are the cases where a financial backer rents or acquires a part of an existing state-owned company or newly establishes a new company (start-up) and they are registered to the country as separate entities under a specific agency. This is often referred to as a company wearing a "Socialist cap" or a "Red cap."

What can't be left out as a change in North Korea's state-run sector during the Kim Jong-un era, meanwhile, is that the state-run sector is emerging in the market as a direct market economy actor. The distribution industry is a major area where this phenomenon is found. In other words, the state-run sector, which used to operate only as a planned economic system, has established a modern retailer (large retailer) that operates in a market economy style since Kim Jong-un took power. Apart from existing state-owned shops, department stores and foreign currency stores, an increasing number of state-owned units are setting up their own modern distribution facilities, including renovating and expanding existing department stores and building new facilities altogether.

Another case of North Korean authorities themselves starting to participate as direct market economy actors in the retail sector after Kim Jong-un took power is found in the oil sales industry, or gas stations. The main market sellers of petroleum products to consumers are state-owned trading companies (or their affiliated industries).

3.5 Evolution of North Korean authorities' perception of the market

The North Korean government's policy on the market fluctuated for more than two decades since the economic crisis had broken out in the early 1990s. In other words, they went back and forth with market-related policies with alternating repetitions of control and acquiescence in the 1990s, permission from the early 2000s, control from the mid-2000s, and permission again from May 2010.

However, the policies after the end of the Kim Jong-il regime and the launch of the Kim Jong-un regime have been quite different from those of the past, and this becomes more apparent with time. The North Korean government has been interfering with the market in various forms, incorporating the market into the official system, while also driving the growth of the market.

Changes in the North Korean government's attitude and position on marketization have been sufficiently detected. In the past, if the biggest concern was whether to eliminate or revive the market, now it is to acknowledge the market, and furthermore, to take advantage of the market and minimize the side effects instead. If, at a given time, what the North Korean government is aiming for is manageable marketization, it is to expand the scope and raise the level of manageable market, and if the current policy stance is compromise and coexistence with the market, it is to broaden its scope and increase its level.

In short, it is no longer a matter of whether it is a market or not. It has become important to know who is the main agent of the market economy activity, namely, the private sector or the state-run sector. This can be interpreted as the evolution of the North Korean leadership's perception of the market. This can be attributed to the firm recognition of the market's contribution to national finance and the income of those in power. In other words, the government receives various surpluses generated by the private sector's marketization through a wide range of taxes and quasi-taxes. This scale is by no means small, and thus marketization has been a great help to North Korean authorities struggling with financial difficulties

Table 3.1 Taxes and quasi-taxes from the North Korean market

		Direct Payer	*Tax, quasi-tax, and*	*Notes*
Official	Transaction revenue from factories, enterprises, and national corporate earnings	Factory, business and market linked form	Income (outside production and distribution), DuBeul-e bus, 8.3 Workers group, Liquid plan (cash plan)	
	Market Use Fees in the General Market, National Payments (also known as Marketplace)	Merchants in Market Complex	Sales of goods in the market complex	
	Service company's national payments.	(purchasing) shops, (consultative) service providers such as restaurants, baths, swimming pools, billiards, karaoke, and transportation.	General resident target, Service sale	
	Customs and State Payments of Trading Companies	Trading company	Domestic purchase of export goods, domestic sales of imported goods	
	Land Use Fee (the so-called land tax)	Small land, paddy field operator	Small land, paddy field	
	land and real estate fees	Institutions, businesses, cooperative organizations, individuals	Economic activities related to markets using national territory, such as land, housing, and buildings;	
Unofficial	Revolutionary Fund	Agencies of various levels and affiliated trading companies	All market-related economic activities associated with domestic and foreign trade	The receiver is the supreme leader.
	Policy tasks, social tasks	Institutions, enterprises, trading company	Market-linked economic activity	Financial resources invested in official economic activities
	Cash/donation, in kind, Giving rice in patriotism, etc.	Individual and financial backers (moneylenders)	Market-linked economic activity	Voluntary + involuntary
	Extra-tax burden	Institutions, businesses, individuals	Market-linked economic activity	Virtually involuntary

Source: Yang (2016)

(see Table 3.1). Otherwise, it may be due to the formation of confidence in the manageability of the market. To be specific, even if marketization has progressed, the government has been controlling the factors of systemic instability in their own way, so may have judged that there would be not much difficulty maintaining the system even if marketization continues to advance.

3.6 Characteristics and limitations of North Korean marketization

North Korea's marketization simultaneously has similarities and differences compared to those observed in the stage of economic reform or system transition stages of ordinary socialist countries. North Korea also has all of these components, if the components of marketization are demand (consumer), supply (supplier), market space, laws and institutions, products and currency. Moreover, if the progress of marketization entails the development of division of labor, formation of national markets through linkage of local markets, development of relevant laws and systems, development of transportation and communication, change of ownership, etc., then indeed North Korea's marketization also shows this aspect. In addition, in the case of the consumer goods market represented by the "Jangmadang," the generalization of North Korea's marketization can be found in that the connection with the market (marketization) is expanding not only among ordinary people and financial backers in private sector, but also by state-owned enterprises.

However, North Korea's marketization does not fully realize its potential and, therefore, its effect on economic growth has been somewhat limited. On the one hand, there are aspects that the North Korean authorities intended, and on the other hand, they are due to physical constraints (the absolute lack of resources in the country).

On a large scale, there are some issues that are attributable to the limitations of North Korea's marketization. Most importantly, North Korea's marketization is at a low level of institutionalization. In addition, the marketization of North Korea progresses mainly in the consumer goods and services markets, and the development of the production goods, capital and financial markets, and labor markets are lagging. Also, although North Korea's marketization is becoming more connected with state-run companies, there is still no change in supply that corresponds to the change in demand (i.e. the accumulation of monetary assets and the expansion of purchasing power in the North), especially the expansion of supply capacity (or production capacity). The economic difficulties of the early 1990s severely damaged and destroyed North Korea's industrial base (especially the manufacturing base) and resulted in only limited restoration despite efforts to recover in the 2000s.

4 Conclusion

It is necessary to first take a brief look at the factors promoting and inhibiting marketization in order to comprehensively evaluate the historical development process of North Korea's marketization.

The factors driving marketization are as follows. First, it is the breakdown of the physical and functional foundation of the planned economy. There are many reasons why the market has sprouted and developed in North Korea, but the biggest one is also the virtual collapse of the planned economy. It can be said that the market naturally filled the gap between supply and demand created by the shortfalls of the plan. Moreover, the authorities have made great efforts to curb the market since 2007 but failed in the end.

Second, the country's dependence on the market has increased greatly with the progress of marketization. The state relies on surpluses from the market in various forms to alleviate any fiscal shortage in all sectors, including the party, the military, and the cabinet. In other words, the nation is in a situation where survival is impossible without a market.

Third, a prolonged marketization is under way, with 29 years of market history. The market has already become indispensable in the operation of the North Korean economy, especially in the lives of its people. It can be seen that it is now becoming settled to some extent as a system.

On the other hand, factors that deter rapid downsizing in the planned economic sector should be considered. Put another way, it is a deterrent to marketization. If the state can directly control certain levels of resources (i.e., food, energy, etc.), it alone can prevent the planned economic area from shrinking below a certain level.

Another deterrent to marketization that should be considered is that, North Korea's marketization has some limitations on self-motivation and self-expansion. Other socialist countries also had some limitations on expansion of marketization, but North Korea has a greater limit. First of all, North Korea's marketization is proceeding under the assumption that the internal and external political conditions are immature. Above all, it is important to note that the conditions of domestic political leadership are invariable, especially considering the hereditary succession of three generations and unimproved external relations, particularly the relationship with the United States. In addition, surplus from the market economy is seized by the state in the form of various taxes and quasi-taxes, excessively, and also by leaders and middle-level officials in North Korea. Due to this, internal monetary accumulation is not easy.

Nevertheless, as marketization progresses, the material base of the planned economy becomes more vulnerable. Resources that the state can control are also slowly decreasing. This is because marketization in North Korea leads to the theft of national assets by individuals and companies, namely the erosion of the material base of the planned economy.

Meanwhile, the North Korean government's policy toward the market is ambivalent. It can serve as a deterrent as well as a facilitator to marketization. Even if the authorities step up and put the brakes on the market, how much effect they can have is questionable.

Overall, the factors for promoting and suppressing marketization still coexist. Therefore, even if marketization progresses in the future, it is uncertain whether the planned economy will erode completely.

Meanwhile, if North Korea's denuclearization progresses in the future, the international community's sanctions against North Korea will be eased and lifted in phases, expanding the material foundation for the North's marketization, and expanding both market demand and supply. Further progress in denuclearization will lift almost all sanctions against North Korea, and the international community's investment in North Korea will be in full swing. In addition, North Korea's reform and opening will expand significantly. Accordingly, the marketization of North Korea is expected to develop rapidly and contribute greatly to the growth of the North Korean economy. In particular, with the level of institutionalization of marketization significantly increasing, the boundary between marketization and economic reform is likely to disappear.

If North Korea's denuclearization is delayed and sanctions on them continue, however, it is likely that both the demand and supply for the market will decrease leading itself to shrink and retreat. Such signs have already begun to appear in 2018, and if sanctions on North Korea continue for the next two to three years, the contraction and recession of marketization is inevitable.

If sanctions on North Korea persist for a long enough period of time, there is a high possibility that the market will shrink and retreat, with decreased demand and supply for the market. Although the direct impact of a sharp drop in imports and exports to China is large, the indirect blows from a decline in domestic industrial production can never be ignored. However, the possibility of chaos to the extent of the past "March of distress" reappearing is not large for the time being.

References

Yang, Moon Soo. 2016. *5 Years of Kim Jong Un's Regime in Marketization Perspective: The Diagnosis of 5 years of Kim Jong Un's Regime*. Seoul: NeulPum.

Yang, Moon Soo, and In Joo Yoon. 2016. "De Facto Privatization of North Korean Enterprises—A Quantitative Approach on Level and Trend." *Korean Unification Studies* 21 (2): 45–88.

4 The economic effects of integration of South and North Korea

Hankyoung Sung

1 Introduction

Coinciding with the February 2018 Pyeongchang Winter Olympics, the world's largest winter sports event, the relationship between South and North Korea took a sharp U-turn from an extremely confrontational one to a friendlier one. Along with the two inter-Korean summits since then, the summit held between North Korea and the United States in May 2018 heightened the atmosphere of reconciliation between the two Koreas. Although the second round of talks between North Korea and the United States was not concluded successfully, both Koreas and the United States have continued to move forward to resume negotiations.

The relationship between the two Koreas has been affected by the status of domestic politics and diplomatic security in one way or the other. To maintain a steady relationship in a given circumstance of political and diplomatic interference, economic integration between the two Koreas is essential. Once an economic integration is established, any action causing a deterioration of the relations would damage the economy of both countries. Additionally, the countries sharing economic interests with an integrated Korean economy would increasingly support a friendly relationship between South and North Korea.

This study intends to analyze and compare studies by KIEP (2011) and Sung (2014) concerning the economic integration of South and North Korea. KIEP (2011) and Sung (2014) investigated the effects of an economic integration and the reunification of South and North Korea using a computable general equilibrium (CGE) model. Although both of their studies used the same model for analysis, they emphasized different aspects of economic integration due to different timing and analytical purpose. By reviewing these two studies, I try to derive meaningful implications that can be beneficial to the current efforts for building up a good relationship between the two Koreas.

2 The CGE model

KIEP (2011) and Sung (2014) utilized the CGE model based on actual data. The model is composed of equations that define the behaviors of each economic entity such as households, firms, and governments. The equations of the model are made up of major economic variables and behavioral parameters. For the analyses, the authors tried to capture the changes from an initial steady state to a new steady state as some shocks were given to the model.

The global CGE model used for both studies analyzes the ripple effect on countries around the world, not just on one country. The model is used to analyze the global effects of economic integrations such as the Uruguay Round, KORUS FTA (the Korea-US FTA), and TiSA (Trade in Service Agreements). This model is also used to estimate the effects of regulating carbon emissions under climate agreements like the Kyoto Protocol as well as ODA.

Among several global CGE models, the one most commonly used to measure the effects of economic integration or free trade is the standard Global Trade Analysis Project (GTAP) model. While KIEP (2011) used this standard model, Sung (2014) utilized the recursive dynamic GTAP model, which partially addresses the shortcomings of the standard model. The explanations on the dynamic model are from Ianchovichina (1998), based on the standard GTAP model, analyzes the economic effects that are derived through the accumulation of capital and wealth within the dynamic model frame. This process increases the reality of the model making it possible to estimate changes in economic effects over time. Although there are some advantages of the recursive dynamic GTAP, those two models come to similar conclusions.

The data used for their analyses is a GTAP database (DB) provided by GTAP Center at the Department of Agricultural Economics, Purdue University. GTAP DBs are collections of data including the global social accounting matrix (SAM), import and export, national accounts, industry-specific production, and customs rates. KIEP (2011) used GTAP DB Version 7.0, the latest available data at that time, in 2004, which covers global input-output based on data from 113 countries, fifty-seven industries, and five resources. Sung (2014) used GTAP DB Version 8.1, which was the most recent one in 2014. In the GTAP DB Version 8.1, the industrial classification and resource classification are the same as those of the GTAP DB 7.0, but the number of countries has been further expanded to 134. In particular, unlike GTAP DB 7.0, which classified North Korea, Mongolia, and Macau into the same category, it reclassified North Korea and Macau as one category (the rest of the East Asia) by separating Mongolia. This new classification has enabled the model to have more realistic information for North Korea. Although this DB was the latest available, there still exists a time gap between the time the database was acquired and the time of analysis. Therefore, relatively recent economic fluctuations have not been reflected in this analysis. To overcome this problem, Sung (2014), who used the recursive dynamic GTAP model, improved the model by having it reflect changes in the global economic environment such as GDP, population, and the labor supply. Despite the problem of the DB's age, many researchers dealing with this global CGE model still rely on GTAP DB, which makes it the most comprehensive and cross-validated data currently available.

3 Model setup and scenarios

3.1 KIEP (2011)

KIEP (2011) analyzed the effects of unification in the short- and long terms by using standard GTAP models. For analysis with the CGE model using GTAP data, country, industry, and resource should be classified and adjusted according to the research's purpose. In general, countries and industries of interest should be classified apart from other countries, and it is desirable to classify as simply as possible for reliable results.

Table 4.1 shows the classification of countries, industries, and production factors in KIEP (2011). Countries were classified as South Korea, North Korea, US, China, and Other. Since the data for North Korea was not available, its data was substituted with the data of Tanzania as among 113 countries of GTAP data Tanzania was the one the most similar to North Korea in terms of GDP and per capita GDP. Although Tanzania is an African country, that fact was considered insignificant since the GTAP DB does not account for geological location. The industry was divided and classified into eight categories: rice, grains, other agriculture, collecting, light manufacture, heavy manufacture, public service, and non-public service. The industry classification was a modification of a commonly used one for the analyses of free trade effects. For rice and grains, they were differently classified because their tariff rates were somewhat complicated and the sensitivity of the tariff rate reduction was high. In terms of production factors, natural resources were classified into land, and skilled and unskilled labor into labor. Land and natural resources are not mobile, but labor and capital was mobile within the country.

Table 4.2 shows the scenarios of long- and mid- term progressive unification in KIEP 2011. In the scenarios, tariff reductions comparable to FTA and the consequently increased domestic production were considered along with additional production related to capital accumulation, transfer of income from South Korea

Table 4.1 Classifications of countries, industries, production factors for KIEP (2011)

No.	*Country*	*Industry*	*Production factor*
1	South Korea	Rice	Land
2	North Korea (Tanzania)	Grains	Capital
3	US	Other agriculture	Labor
4	China	Collecting (fishery, forestry, coal, petroleum, gas, mineral)	
5	Rest of the world	Light manufacture	
6		Heavy manufacture	
7		Public service	
8		Non-public service	

Source: Adapted from KIEP 2011

Table 4.2 Long- and mid-term progressive unification scenarios

Promotion strategy in stages				
Unification stage	*Tariff*	*assistance*	*Self-financing*	*Economic system*
Economic community (2010–2040)	Eliminating tariffs on goods between South and North Korea	Financial assistance from South Korea to North Korea	Capital accumulation and increase in domestic production and Productivity enhancement in public services from tariff elimination	Keeping difference in economic system
Unification stage 1 (2041–2045)	Eliminated tariffs on goods between South and North Korea	Financial assistance from South Korea to North Korea	Capital accumulation and increase in domestic production and Productivity enhancement in light manufacture and public services from tariff elimination	Keeping difference in economic system
Unification stage 2 (2046–2050)	Eliminated tariffs on goods between South and North Korea	Financial assistance from South Korea to North Korea	Capital accumulation and increase in domestic production and Productivity enhancement in manufacture and public services from tariff elimination	Keeping difference in economic system

Source: Adapted from KIEP 2011

and related countries to North Korea, and increased productivity of industries in North Korea.

The long- and mid-term progressive scenario assumes that unification will take place in 2040 and that the unification process will be completed by 2050. In this scenario, it was assumed that unification would be achieved only with the support of South Korea and the increase in productivity of North Korea without any other assistance from foreign countries, as the economic community is formed for 30 years (2010–2040). During this period, it was assumed that tariffs on product between the two countries would be eliminated, South Korea's aid to North Korea would start, and productivity in North Korean public services would increase. In the first unification stage (2041–2045) starting with unification in 2040, the lack of any tariff is maintained and the productivity of public services in North Korea elevates with help of South Korea's aid that has been provided since the pre-unification period. In addition, the productivity of light manufacturing in North Korea increases because it is relatively easy to develop. In the second post -unification stage (2046–2050), it was assumed that the lack of any tariff would still be maintained and that the aid from South Korea would accumulate, leading to increased productivity not only in light industries but also in heavy manufacturing in North Korea. This scenario predicted that the GDP level per capita in North Korea would rise to about 65 percent of South Korea's by 2050 when the unification process is completed. In addition, the level of productivity increase was assumed to be 1.2 percent in the manufacturing sector, and 1 percent in the service sectors, referring to existing studies.

3.2 Sung (2014)

Sung (2014) analyzed the economic effects of integration of South and North Korea using the newer CGE model. As shown in Table 4.3, Sung (2014)

Table 4.3 Variation of four factors due to economic integration

Economic benefit		*Content*
Supply of production factors	Labor	Military reduction and growth in population with production ability
		Improved productivity of North Korean labor
		Based on labor productivity of Kaesong Industrial Complex and the experience of German reunification
		Assuming mobility of South-North Korean labor
	Capital	Increased degree of trust overseas due to declining North Korean risk; decline of interest expense for foreign debt
	Land	Change in the natural resource reserves of North Korea
		Increased North Korean land due to cultivation
		Land reclamation due to reduced military size
Market expansion		CEPA agreement between South and North Korea
		TPP entry by South and North Korea
		Expansion of South Korea FTA to include North Korea
Finance		Reduced military expenditure
		Northwards subsidies by South Korean government
Overseas trust		Change in military expenditure by the US, China, Russia, and Japan due to risk elimination on the Korean Peninsula

Source: Sung 2014

differed from the KIEP (2011) by taking into account (1) the supply of production factors, (2) market expansions, (3) finance, and (4) overseas trust. This is because the economic integration of South and North Korea is expected to increase the productivity of labor, capital, and the capacity to develop natural resources. The economic integration between the two Koreas will open up new export and import markets. In addition, from a South Korean point of view, it is possible to secure financial savings by reducing the defense cost that was incurred due to the confrontation between the two Koreas. Also, the easing of tensions between the two Koreas would improve overseas trust with North Korea and positively influence the countries participating in six-party talks as well.

Table 4.4 shows the classification of countries, industries, and resources. For this classification, South and North Korea were analyzed individually and countries participating in six-party talks – the US, China, Japan, and Russia – were classified individually. The EU was classified as one country. In order to be able to expand the analysis results, the ASEAN, South Asia, and Sub-Saharan Africa were separately classified. In addition, countries participating in TPP negotiation – Australia, New Zealand, Malaysia, Singapore, Vietnam, Brunei, Canada, Mexico, Chile, and Peru – were classified separately. Finally, the rest of the included countries were grouped as one country.

For industrial classification, rice, an exempted item of Korea's FTAs was classified individually and other primary industries were classified as agriculture. The coal industry, which is likely to be the basis for North Korea's future economic development, was separately classified. Manufactures were classified as light manufacturing or as heavy manufacturing, and service sectors were divided into public and non-public ones. For service sectors, STRI (service trade restrictiveness index) in OECD were added as trade equivalent. Production sectors were classified as land, capital, and labor.

Table 4.4 Classifications of countries, industries, production factors for Sung (2014)

No.	*Country*	*Industry*	*Production factor*
1	South Korea	Rice	Land
2	North Korea	Agriculture	Capital
3	US	Mining	Labor
4	China	Light manufacture	
5	Japan	Heavy manufacture	
6	Russia	Public service	
7	EU	Non-public service	
8	ASEAN		
9	South Asia		
10	Sub Sahar Africa		
11	Other TPP countries		
12	Rest of the world		

Source: Sung 2014

Sung (2014) considered two unification scenarios. While the first, scenario I, is a case in which unification is achieved only through inter-Korean activities, in the second, scenario II, countries participating in the six-party talks are involved in the unification process. Sung (2014) presented forecasts of future changes as intervals rather than reporting specific estimates for the various assumed economic benefits. Therefore, it was assumed that the estimated value could vary from 50 percent to 150 percent, marked as minimum and maximum.

For each scenario, application of the maximum or expected value to the model made the effect of unification unrealistic leading the author to consider five scenarios as realistic ones. However, this study only introduces the two scenarios that assume the smallest and the highest impacts among the scenarios, because the rest of the scenarios show the results between the two extremes. Table 4.5 compares the two extremes of each period, 1 and 5, at each extreme.

Unlike the static standard model, the dynamic CGE models used by Sung (2014) had baseline scenarios that were estimated regardless of the application of the unification scenario. As shown in Table 4.6, the baseline scenario included changes in the global economic environment such as GDP, population, and labor supply as well as major FTAs that Korea entered. Given the baseline scenario,

Table 4.5 Level of policy shocks in unification scenarios I-1, II-1, I-5, II-5

	1st period of unification ***(2016–2020)***	*2nd period of unification* ***(2021–2025)***	*3rd period of unification* ***(2026–2030)***
Unification scenario I-1, II-1	minimum	minimum	Minimum
Unification scenario I-5, II-5	minimum	maximum	Maximum

Source: Sung 2014

Table 4.6 Baseline scenarios

Unification period	*Baseline scenarios*
1st period of unification (2016–2020)	Changes in GDP, labor, population Entry in force of Korea-US FTA and Korea-EU FTA
2nd period of unification (2021–2025)	Changes in GDP, labor, population Korea-US FTA and Korea-EU FTA in effective Entry in force of Korea-China FTA
3rd period of unification (2026–2030)	Changes in GDP, labor, population Korea-US FTA, Korea-EU FTA, and Korea-China FTA in effective
4th period of unification (2031–2055)	Changes in GDP, labor, population Korea-US FTA, Korea-EU FTA, and Korea-China FTA in effective

Source: Sung 2014

when the integrated scenarios were applied at a certain point in time, new economic effects appeared. The application of unification scenarios estimates caused economic effects that modified the results of the base scenario. To study the pure effects of unification, it reported the differences in the effects between baseline and the unification scenarios.

4 Result of analyses

4.1 KIEP (2011)

KIEP (2011) analyzed the potential costs of unification as well as the resources to be utilized along with the benefits of unification. In KIEP 2011, the potential cost to South Korea included the amount of aid to North Korea as well as the cost generated by the contraction of domestic production due to the aid shown in Table 4.7. KIEP (2011) reported that all countries involved in reunification except North Korea would incur some level of damage as North Korea improves its productivity.

According to the long- and mid-term unification scenarios, the economy of North Korea is expected to grow at a rate of about 20 percent per year, which is a total of about 97.9 percent during stage I. Likewise the economy of North Korea is expected to grow at a rate of about 25 percent per year, which is about 125 percent during stage II. If such rapid growth is possible, it is expected that in 2050, ten

Table 4.7 Potential cost and finance required for unifications

Type of unification	*Potential cost of South Korea*	*Finance required*
Long- and mid-term progressive type	9.3 percent of its GDP	4 percent of its GDP

Source: Adapted from KIEP 2011

Table 4.8 Economic benefit of South and North Korea in the long- and mid-term progressive type

		Change in real GDP (Annual change)	*Change in welfare (Hundred thousand USD)*
South Korea	Unification stage 1 (2041–2045)	-1.18% (-0.23%)	-191.45
	Unification stage 2 (2046–2050)	-7.25% (-1.5%)	-492.48
North Korea	Unification stage 1 (2041–2045)	97.86% (20%)	392.19
	Unification stage 2 (2046–2050)	125.29% (25%)	3,261.69

Source: Adapted from KIEP 2011

years after reunification, the per capita GDP of North Korea would reach 65 percent that of South Korea's per capita GDP.

In stages I and II of the long- and mid-term unification scenarios, it was analyzed that both Koreas would benefit from the unification because the decrease in welfare of South Korea appears to be less than the increase in North Korea's welfare.

4.2 Sung (2014)

Figures 4.1 and 4.2 show the changes in real GDP based on unification scenarios I-1 and I-5. South Korea's real GDP in twenty years is expected to increase by

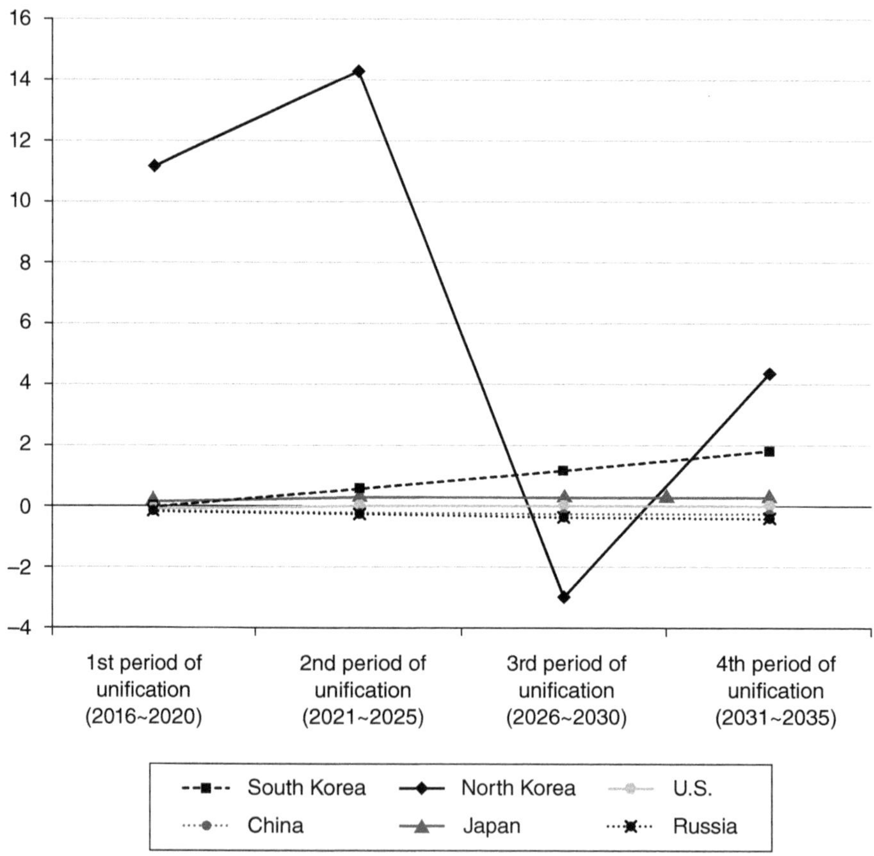

Figure 4.1 Changes in real GDP: unification scenario I-1

Source: Sung 2014

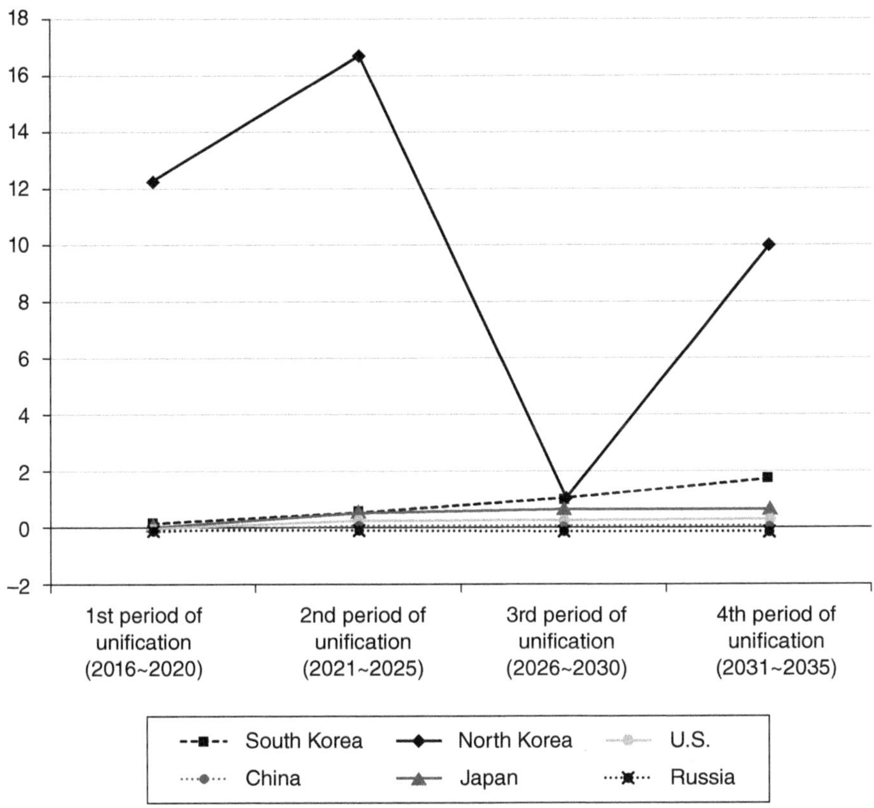

Figure 4.2 Changes in real GDP: unification scenario II-1

Source: Sung 2014

about 1.8 percent and 1.7 percent according to unification scenarios I-1 and II-1, respectively. In addition, North Korea's real GDP is expected to increase by about 4.4 percent and 10 percent, respectively. In both scenarios, the real GDP growth in the first and second period of unification increases, but its increase rates drop moving toward the transition period. If you compare unification scenario I-1, which does not consider international support in the unification process, with scenario II-1, which does consider international support, you see that the overall beneficial economic effects to both Koreas are greater in scenario II-1. In addition, the countries participating in six-party talks seem also to benefit more from scenario II-1. Interestingly, the resulting predicted increase of the real GDP in the US and Japan is larger than that of China and Russia due to two Koreas' participation in the TPP.

Figures 4.3 and 4.4 show the results of unification scenarios I-5 and II-5, respectively. Unification scenarios I-5 and II-5 were estimated by applying the real GDP figures to stage II and stage III, which makes scenarios I-5 and II-5 predict the largest change among the unification scenarios considered in the research of Sung (2014). According to scenarios I-5 and II-5, the real GDP of South Korea will increase by about 3.1 percent, and 2.9 percent, respectively, and that of North Korea will surge by about 86.5 percent, and 110.6 percent, respectively, by transition stage. In unification scenarios I-5 and II-5, unlike scenarios I-1 and II-1, the real GDPs of the United States and Japan will increase slightly, and the real GDPs of China and Russia will decrease, indicating that North Korea's radical growth may have some negative effects on neighboring countries.

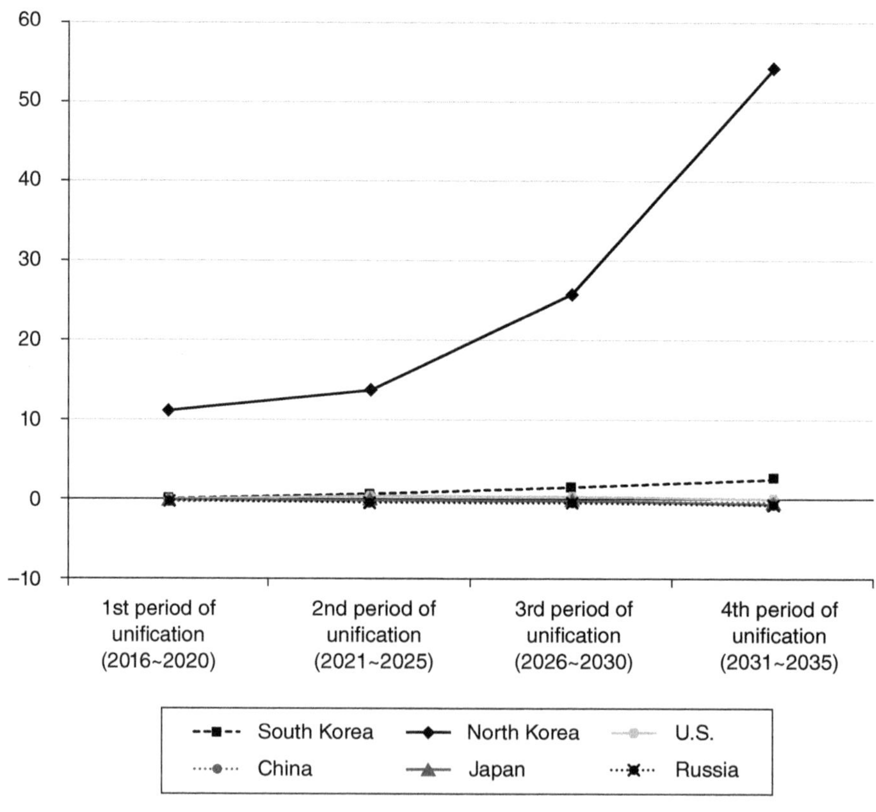

Figure 4.3 Changes in real GDP: unification scenario I-5

Source: Sung 2014

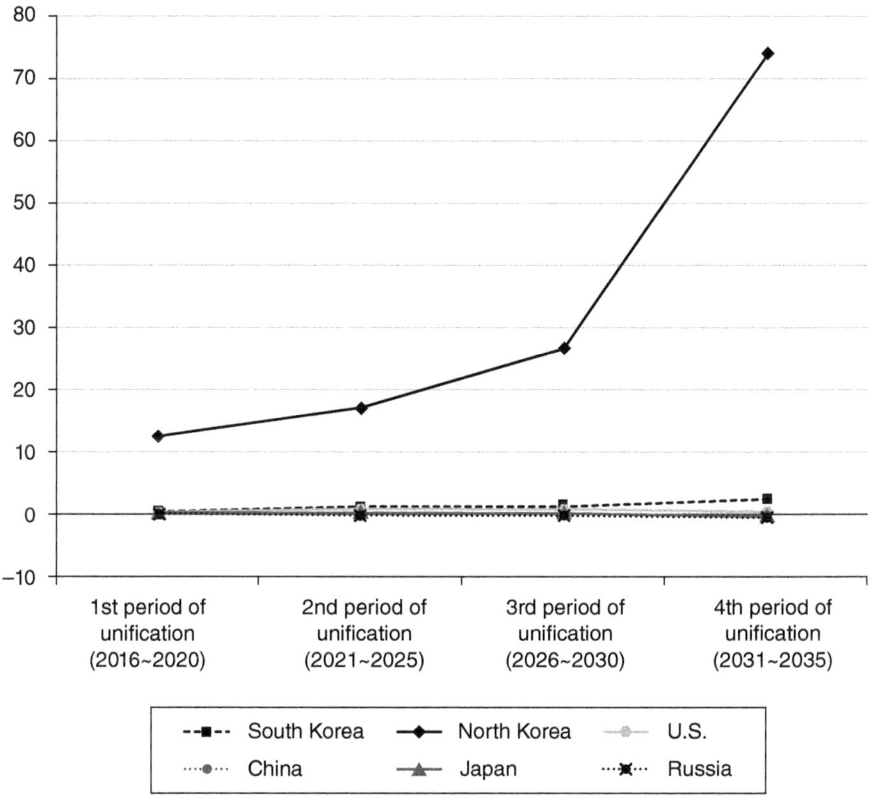

Figure 4.4 Changes in real GDP: unification scenario II-5

Source: Sung 2014

4.3 Results of KIEP (2011) and Sung (2014) compared

Both studies reflect the respective atmosphere of the times when the strategy of unification was discussed. KIEP (2011) was prepared when the Lee Myung-bak administration proposed the jar of unification for funding. Since it was focused on how many resources or funds should be prepared for unification at the time, that study aimed to set a goal for the development of the North Korean economy and to find a way to achieve it after unification. On the other hand, when Sung (2014) performed his research, President Park Geun-hye had recently proposed the idea of a unification bonanza emphasizing the beneficiary effects of unification for both Koreas. That proposal, then, aimed to gain a national consensus on unification for which Sung (2014) tried to generate the theoretical ground.

Therefore, it is difficult to compare the results of these studies. KIEP (2011) focused on the integrated economic community of the two Koreas and relied on the assumption that South Korea and related countries would support North Korea unilaterally and that the productivity of North Korean industry would increase by utilizing those aids. So it was inevitable that South Korea and related countries ended up with economic loss. Above all, KIEP (2011) tried to explain what is needed to achieve the goal of North Korea's GDP per capita reaching 65 percent of South Korea's. By doing that, KIEP (2011) came up with a somewhat unrealistic economic growth rate of 25 percent per year for North Korea.

As opposed to KIEP (2011), Sung (2014) not only draws conclusions by applying possible changes caused by economic integration between the two Koreas to the model as objective estimates, but also acknowledges the effects of economic integration between the two Koreas that is beyond inter-Korean relations in scope. In this regard, Sung (2014) is more specific and suggests more realistic scenarios than KIEP (2011).

5 Conclusion

This chapter compared the results of two studies, KIEP (2011) and Sung (2014), both of which analyzed the benefits, costs, and economic effects of a possible inter-Korean economic integration. Both studies estimated the economic effects of South Korea's aid to North Korea and free trade between the two Koreas. KIEP (2011) estimated that the annual economic growth rate, trade liberalization, aid to North Korea, and increased productivity in North Korea are necessary for North Korea to realize 65 percent of South Korea's per capita GDP. However, Sung (2014) not only estimated the economic effects of unification but also proposed the policy measures by which to achieve them. Despite these differences, this chapter draws the following implications from these previous two studies that are meaningful to understand the economic effects of an integration between the two Koreas.

First, KIEP (2011) laid out the goal of North Korea's economic growth and projected that South Korea would pay a considerable monetary amount in order to grow the North Korean economy in a short period of time. As such, it can be inferred that any North Korean economic development that relies on South Korea may not be supported in South Korea, and that concerns over this burden may lead to negative perceptions of unification. As a result, this report urged experts to present alternatives that can be beneficial to both North and South Korea.

Second, in this regard, Sung (2014) presented more realistic unification scenarios with the more realistic expected economic growth rate of North Korea. The most significant contribution of Sung (2014) was to suggest the possibility of inter-Korean economic integration as a global issue beyond the Korean Peninsula. However, it left the details to promote these unification scenarios to future studies.

At present, the previous studies summarized here are still applicable to current day Korea. The issues of South and North Korea can be resolved when the countries participating in the six-party talks cooperate. It is not just South Korea, North

Korea, and the United States that are directly involved; China, Russia, and even Japan stand to gain or lose from any future path of North Korean development, and so they should also want to have roles in the issue.

Therefore, the success of the process of economic integration and unification between the two Koreas cannot be guaranteed unless it provides all of these interested countries with benefits. Sung (2014) suggested savings on military costs due to the relaxation of tensions on the Korean Peninsula as a practical benefit that such countries can share. It claimed that if only a small portion of the reduced military expenditure is invested in North Korea's development, a dramatic development of the North Korean economy could be achieved. Although not suggested by Sung (2014), it is expected that such a dramatic development of North Korea would bring enormous investment returns to the countries of the six-party talks that invested in North Korea.

This chapter still leaves room for future research. KIEP (2011) and Sung (2014) focused on free trade, economic support from South Korea and major countries, and increased productivity in North Korea from the standpoint of economic integration. In the future, studies like this could be expanded to show the economic effects in each step of the unification process, such as free trade zones, custom unions, and common markets.

References

Ianchovichina, Elena. 1998. "International Capital Linkages: Theory and Application in a Dynamic Computable General Equilibrium Model." PhD diss., Department of Agricultural Economics, Purdue University.

Korea Institute for International Economic Policy (KIEP). 2011. "Design for Economic Community of South and North Korea." *Project Report for Ministry of Unification.*

Sung, Hankyoung. 2014. "The Effects of Economic Integration Between South and North Korea." *KIEP Research Paper No. Policy Analysis*: 14–30. http://dx.doi.org/10.2139/ssrn.2622905.

5 Industrial structure and development strategy in North Korea

Donghun Kim

1 Introduction

This chapter investigates how the economic development strategies and the industrial structure in North Korea have changed since the Japanese occupation in 1945, and suggests suitable directions of industrial structural planning to effect future economic development.

From the standpoint of North Korea, there are two possible routes for economic development in the future. First, it can maintain the inward-looking economic policy that has been practiced since the liberation – also known as an independent national economic construction, which promotes economic development by utilizing its own domestic technologies and resources. Second, it could implement an outward-looking economic policy that emphasizes export promotion by means of an economic development strategy. More specifically, North Korea can follow the track of South Korea, which utilizes industrialization and manufacturing exports as leverage for economic development. Empirically, the first of these options, the inward-looking economic policy, has not been successful. Countries that normally choose this economic policy must possess enough domestic demand to utilize economies of scale, however, in cases such as North Korea that market is too small, and so their industries have remained uncompetitive due to the lack of competition caused by domestic market protection.

There are a few advantages, in some aspects, for latecomer countries that pursue an outward-looking economic policy. Above all, the countries are able to apply technologies developed by more advanced countries to the processes of their economic development. They can also efficiently utilize the world market to export their products. Moreover, they can attract investment from foreign capital inflow in case their domestic investment resources for economic development are deficient. At this moment, maintaining its inward-looking economic policy might not be advisable for North Korea, because it is impossible to boost domestic demand with its aging population of twenty-five million. In order to ignite economic growth, North Korea has to attain necessary technical skills and market access for products utilizing financial resources for investment. The only option by which this could be achieved would be the outward-looking economic policy that enables resource acquisition.

When discussing a planned economy system like North Korea, its selected industrial structure cannot be separated from its economic development strategies and, therefore, it is necessary to look into the relationship between the two. As for North Korea's future development strategies – policies including open door industrialization, resource development-oriented growth, high-tech intensive industry development, and leapfrogging development – they have been proposed in previous literature, and in what follows I have critically analyzed the aforementioned policies. Rather than analyzing the previous studies in a single analytic framework, I have dissected the studies into one economic development strategy that concerns traditional economic development components including capital, market, and comparative advantage and another economic development strategy pertaining to catch-up or leapfrogging in order to explore North Korea's economic development strategies. This classification is, however, merely a convenience for this discussion, and contents of the aforementioned two bodies of literature quite often overlap. However, to conclude, in terms of the direction of North Korea's future economic development, as the literature suggests many different perspectives on it, I propose an idea about which industry North Korea should cultivate.

The contents of this chapter are as follows. First in the following section, I overview North Korea's economic development strategies and transition of industrial structure from the end of the Japanese Occupation to the Kim Jong-un regime, chiefly based on the existing literature. In the third section, I discuss strategies for achieving future economic development through the fostering of suitable industries, critically analyze previous literature suggesting "open economy industrialization strategy" and economic catch-up theory, and propose my policy directions based on these analyses. In the fourth, and final, section, I summarize the major points of the discussion along with my arguments and proceed to the conclusion.

2 Economic development strategy and industrial structure in North Korea

2.1 An overview of economic development strategies in North Korea: from the liberation until present day

North Korea had pursued a heavy industry-oriented economic policy until it changed its policy to one emphasizing light industry and trade in the early 1990s. The reason North Korea took a heavy industry-oriented stance was based on the view that a nation's heavy industry capacity determines to a great extent the growth of its national production capacity and provides a manufacturing base with which it can produce intermediate goods (Kim and Lee 2008).

The heavy industry-oriented policy contributed to a rapid industrialization and a likewise speedy economic growth in the early stages of economic development. However, heavy industry could not properly supply intermediary goods for agriculture, light industry, or the service sector; therefore, this policy eventually resulted in a deepening imbalance between the heavy industry sector and other industrial sectors including agriculture, light industry, and services. Along with fostering heavy industry, North Korea has based its industrial structure on the policy of establishing a self-reliant national economy. The construction of a self-reliant national economy was adopted as a national development strategy so as to justify its regime and in order to show its superiority over South Korea's economy. The basic principle of a self-reliant national economy dictates that North Korea produces all products by using its own technology and labor force with resources domestically produced in North Korea. North Korea has implemented a self-reliant national economy and also a heavy industry-oriented policy as inviolable strategies in North Korea's economic planning for a long period of time; it follows, therefore, that these policies have played a role in restraining the creativity and flexibility of North Korea's economic policy making.

The parallel policies of economic development and military buildup have made North Korea's industrial structure lopsided toward certain industrial sectors. Owing to North Korea's wish to express the superiority of its regime though military power, it has cultivated its munitions industry in parallel with heavy industry. Through the parallel policy of economic development and military buildup, North Korea's industrial structure – managed by a military-industrial complex – has transformed into a dualistic structure with both a private economy and a military economy (Kwon 2008). The expansion of military industry inevitably caused economic inefficiency in investments- and consequently eroded North Korea's economic growth potential. Also, the emphasis on heavy industry and self-reliance weakens the ability for the other industrial sectors to complement one another.

North Korea's industrial structure showed a new, different, aspect beginning in the late 1990s, which reflected the changing geopolitical settings and international trade relations in the world market. At first, the collapse of communism in Eastern Europe with the subsequent international integration of markets made communist countries apply universal disciplines in international trade. Additionally, the increase in economic transactions between the two Koreas contributed to this change. For North Korea, this all led to a shift in the industrial policy to one of light industry and trade first, rather than the former heavy industry first. Since the turn of the millennium, it has swung its pendulum of economic planning to focus on agriculture and fishery, light industry, trade, and services. In particular, the emphasis on light industry was related to strategies involved in maintaining its regime through the stabilization of its peoples' lives.

The Kim Jong-un regime adopted a parallel policy line to support both economic construction and nuclear force construction on March 31, 2013, at the full session of the Central Committee of North Korea's ruling Workers' Party. The basic discipline of this policy line was to develop scientific technology by strengthening the nation's nuclear force, which thereafter would lead to economic development in other economic sectors (The Institute for Unification Education of the Ministry of Unification 2017).

2.2 *The transition of industrial structure in North Korea: from the liberation until present day*

Table 5.1 indicates the ratio of gross value of social product (GVSP) for each sector during the period between 1946 and 1970. In 1946, the manufacturing industry – including both heavy and light industry – accounted for 23.2 percent of the GVSP, whereas agriculture represented 59.1 percent. The two sectors inversely mirrored one another until the 1970s. That is, while the manufacturing industry had steadily risen to 65 percent of the GVSP by the 1970s, agriculture had over the same time frame fallen to 20 percent. Also of note, the share of product distribution had continuously decreased. These phenomena presumably resulted from North Korea's heavy industry-oriented economic policy.

Since the 1970s, North Korea has tried to change its economic policy in order to expand its market in international trade and seek new opportunities for foreign capital inflows and technology transfer. Also, during the period between the 1970s and the 1990s, it expanded productivity of its light industry sector and the availability of consumer goods through a new system of united enterprises and other economic measures. However, despite these efforts, its industrial structure during this period did not show significant change. Whereas agriculture and fishery increased their shares from 21.5 percent to 26.8 percent the ratio of mining and manufacturing industries remained constant at 56 percent. One thing to consider is that, with regard to heavy industry and light industry, both of which belong to the manufacturing industry, the share of heavy industry escalated from 62 percent to 73.3 percent during the period. This indicates that, notwithstanding the emphasis on light industry, North Korea's heavy industry first policy persisted (see Table 5.2).

In the 1990s, during the economic crisis, North Korea experienced a decline in its heavy chemical industry in contrast with the expansion of its service industry. As North Korea's third seven-year plan (1987–1993) ended up a failure, it

Table 5.1 Ratio of gross value of social product (GVSP) for each sector between 1946 and 1970 (%)

	1946	*1949*	*1953*	*1956*	*1960*	*1962*	*1964*	*1965*	*1970*
Manufacturing	23.2	35.6	30.7	40.1	57.1	61.0	62.3	64.2	65.0
(Heavy Industry)			(11.7)	(21.7)	(31.4)		(32.5)		
(Light Industry)			(19.0)	(18.4)	(25.7)		(29.8)		
Agriculture	59.1	40.6	41.6	26.6	23.6	21.3	19.3	18.3	20.0
Transportation & Postal Service	1.6	2.9	3.7	4.0	2.2	2.8	2.8		
Construction		7.2	14.9	12.3	8.7	9.1	9.8		
Product Distribution	12.0	9.4	6.0	10.8	6.0	3.6	3.8		
Others	4.1	4.3	3.1	6.2	2.4	2.2	2.0		

Source: Adapted from Korea Institute for National Unification 1988, Hwang 1993, Kim and Lee 2008

Table 5.2 Industrial structure in North Korea (1970–1990) (%)

	1970	*1975*	*1980*	*1987*	*1990*
Agriculture & Fishery	21.5	21.8		20.0	26.8
Mining & Manufacturing	57.3	63.0		60.0	56.0
Heavy Industry	62.0	63.7	63.9	74.1	73.3
Light Industry	38.0	36.3	36.1	25.9	26.7
Other Services	21.2	15.2		20.0	17.2

Source: The Research Institute for National Unification 1995, Kim and Lee 2008

designated the period from 1994 to 1996 as a buffer in order to concentrate on prioritizing the following three principles: agriculture first, light industry first, and trade first. As the agricultural infrastructure had collapsed due to natural disasters, crop yields dropped rapidly and food shortages became a critical issue for the nation in the 1990s (Seo 1994). The agriculture first principle was implemented to overcome the aforementioned issues. The light industry first principle was a policy to resolve the problem of deficiency in daily necessities so as to help the people live better, and the trade first principle focused on the expansion of exports with an emphasis on changing the structure and modes of how North Korea conducted international trade. The shift in policy direction to international trade was affected by the collapse of socialist markets after the fall of the Berlin Wall, and it reflected North Korea's intention to increase trade with capitalist countries (Cho 1995).

In terms of North Korea's industrial structure, in the 1990s, heavy (including chemical) industry accounted for only 25.6 percent and shrank further to just 11.2 percent by 2010. This fall was mainly caused by a shortage in the supply of energy and raw materials (Hong et al. 2017). Conversely, the service sector expanded its share from 23.1 percent to 37.3 percent in 2000 (see Table 5.3).

Since the first decade of the 21st century, North Korea has tried to improve international relations with other countries in order to receive foreign aid and necessary support, relying on those plans to overcome its economic contraction. In terms of industrial policy, North Korea has proceeded with its traditional policies, mainly focusing on the four leading industrial sectors. These sectors include the coal, electricity, railway and transportation, and metal and machinery industries. They have been considered the core industries in stabilizing the overall economy after the economic crisis suffered in the 1990s. The economic management measures proclaimed on July 1, 2002, represent one of North Korea's efforts to recover from the economic crisis of the previous decade. These measures mainly aimed to accomplish an increase in wages and prices, a termination of the rationing system, the decentralization of planning targets, an expansion of the autonomous management of factories, and the adoption of the horizontal merchandising system in the market with the salary incentive system (Hong et al. 2017).

Table 5.3 Transition of the industrial structure in North Korea (1990–2016) (%)

		1990	*2000*	*2010*	*2012*	*2014*	*2016*
Mining and Manufacturing Industry	Total	40.8	25.4	36.3	35.9	34.4	33.2
	Mining	9.0	7.7	14.6	14.0	12.2	2.6
	Manufacturing	31.8	17.7	21.9	21.9	20.4	20.6
	(Heavy Industry)	25.6	11.2	15.3	15.2	13.4	13.7
	(Light Industry)	6.2	6.5	6.6	6.7	7.0	6.9
Construction		8.6	6.9	7.8	7.8	9.0	8.8
Services*		23.1	37.3	32.9	32.9	36.7	36.3
Agriculture & Fishery		27.4	30.4	23.4	23.4	21.6	21.7

Source: Adapted from Bank of Korea, DPRK's GDP-related statistics (online database); Hong et al. 2017
Note: *Services include electricity, gas, and water.

In terms of industrial structure, the opening years of the 21st century saw North Korea's agriculture sector witness its own decline in share of the total industrial output, from 30.4 percent to 23.4 percent, despite efforts to boost agricultural productivity by implementing projects such as the improvement of irrigation systems and land readjustment projects. On the other hand, shares of the mining and manufacturing industries increased from 7.7 percent to 14.6 percent and from 17.7 percent to 21.9 percent, respectively. Moreover, the share of heavy and chemical industry crept up from 11.2 percent to 15.3 percent.

During the Kim Jong-un era, North Korea's industrial structure shows a decline in the mining industry and heavy chemical industry, whereas the growth of services, agriculture and fishery, and light industry represent upward-sloping trends. The share of heavy chemical industry decreased from 15.3 percent in 2010 to 13.7 percent in 2016, while the share of light industry increased from 6.6 percent to 6.9 percent.

3 North Korea's future development strategy and industrial structure

3.1 North Korea's future economic development strategy

As discussed in the previous sections, North Korea has maintained an inward-looking industrial strategy that produces and supplies domestic consumer goods by utilizing its home-manufactured raw materials and capital goods based on its independent technologies. This strategy, as already explained, cannot succeed unless a country meets at least a moderate level of domestic demand. A heavy chemical industry, which is one of the core industries in North Korea – including metalworking, mechanical engineering, and chemical engineering – is highly inefficient in terms of technologies and facilities. It follows that this industry has lost its international competitiveness and has not functioned properly to provide facilities and raw materials for light industry and agricultural productions. Thus, in order to achieve economic recovery and development in the future, which economic development strategy should North Korea implement and how should it design any new industrial structure?

3.1.1 Conditions for economic development: capital, markets, and comparative advantage

In this section, I analyze whether the economic development strategies of North Korea, discussed herein, would be practical from the perspectives of capital, markets, and elements of comparative advantage (technology and natural resources). Additionally, I evaluate an ideal industrial structure concerning the formation of a role-sharing structure for industrial cooperation between South Korea and North Korea with the core of said industry structure in South Korea.

The primary constraints that North Korea has confronted in reality are a lack of capital and the lack of an export market needed to boost economic development. An "open door" industrialization policy is defined as an industrialization strategy that focuses on the manufacturing industry and relies on external capital and the market outside the nation's borders (Lee, Kim, and Jeong 2013). North Korea has only a small domestic market and so its industry cannot grow through economies of scale. However, if it should expand its export market to overcome its restricted economies of scale it could amplify its domestic production capacity. This strategy would utilize North Korea's abundance of well-educated labor in order to cultivate exports industries and expand its core industries by producing light industry goods, including both textiles and clothing, as well as the labor-intensive products of the electrical, chemical, and mechanical engineering industries.

Also, North Korea could realize a resource development-oriented growth policy – a strategy that exploits and exports the plentiful natural resources found in North Korea such as coal, iron ore, and magnesite and uses them as capital in the initial stages of economic development (Lee, Kim, and Jeong 2013). Lee, Kim, and Jeong (2013) estimates that the volume of the natural resources that can be used in such a growth policy is likely not as large as expected, and that the value of natural resources in North Korea would be in fact far less than estimated by some studies, particularly if it entails substantial investment in infrastructure to boost its production. Even with the likely foreign capital inflow to supply investment costs for the expansion of infrastructure (such as transportation or electricity) in order to exploit natural resources, a resource development-oriented growth policy is unrealistic. However, some portion of resources gained by exploiting natural resources can create the seed money needed for the initial stage of economic growth. It follows that utilizing natural resources as a complement to an open door industrial strategy focusing on manufacturing industry could indeed be a valid strategy.

The following strategy is referred to as a high-tech intensive industry policy. The development strategy that emphasizes technology or high-tech intensive industries has been an up-and-coming alternative aimed at the criticism that economic development focusing on a labor-intensive industry would likely remain in a low-level equilibrium of underdevelopment (Lee, Kim, and Jeong 2013). It can be understood as a "leapfrogging development" as North Korea has declared. It is also known that Kim Jong-un recently gave directions about pursuing a powerful, technical knowledge-based economy focusing on high-tech industries (Son 2017). According to Kim Jong-un's statements at the Seventh Party Congress in May 2016

> High-technology industry is the so-called pillar of a knowledge based economy. High-technology research including information technology, nanotechnology and biotechnology should be extensively initiated to focus more on high-tech industry and enhance its pivotal role in the economic development of the country.
>
> (Son 2017)

3.1.2 The pace of economic development: catch-up and leapfrogging development

In the previous section, issues about the elements of economic development, including capital inflow, capture of market share, and the selection of comparative advantage industry, have been primarily discussed. In this section, I mainly look into existing literature to find whether the economic development of North Korea can be rapidly achieved like those of other countries. "Catch-up" is defined as a latecomer attempting to obtain the skills or per capita income of the first-mover, the first moving occupant, here meaning more developed nations, at the industrial or national level, while a latecomer achieving the first-mover's level in a relatively short amount of time is known as leapfrogging (Lee and Choi 2014). In January 2001, North Korea declared a plan named "a great leap forward" in the state-run newspaper, *Rodong Sinmun*, to propose the need to achieve economic growth within the shortest period of time. North Korea's great leap forward would be conceptually identical to leapfrogging development. However, North Korea's great leap forward remains confined to the promotion of information technology (IT) services sectors and does yet appear to have had a significant impact on North Korea's economy as a whole.

In terms of policy options that can be considered in North Korea's system transition scenario, first, it is necessary to impose regular transitional structure policy measures (Kim and Roland 2012). These regular transitional structures include the means of production such as agricultural privatization, promotion of small enterprises, promotion of labor-intensive export industries, and attraction of foreign direct investment (FDI), etc. However, in order for North Korea to achieve rapid economic growth and development in a very short amount of time, rather than pursuing normal economic growth during the transition period, it is necessary to introduce additional policies for explosive growth alongside regular transitional structure policy measures (Lee and Choi 2014).

The three policy options suggested for North Korea in literature include a labor-intensive and export-oriented model similar to that of Fujian Province in

China, the Indian IT services-led business model, and the African way of selecting next-generation industries (Lee, Kim, and Lee 2009; Lee and Choi 2014; Lee and Mathews 2012). First, the model of Fujian Province in China is based on the case when Fujian Province achieved economic growth in a short period of time by accepting capital from overseas Chinese. In the case of North Korea, this policy option has a high likelihood of success on the condition that it cooperates with South Korea. The second policy option is a strategy that utilizes the IT services sector. India's transition of the industrial structure did not go through the usual pattern of achieving economic growth, as the country did not first achieve growth in the manufacturing sector before focusing on the development of the services sector. Instead, India demonstrated service-oriented growth in which the proportion of service sector market share increased without accomplishing growth in the manufacturing sector (Lee and Choi 2014). Though the IT service sector requires comparatively less capital in the early stage of development, the level of knowledge required is high. This means that for developing countries with an outstanding level of education, the IT service industry has a comparative advantage for developing countries, and India made full use of the opportunity. North Korea has also recognized this and in the early 2000s concentrated on fostering IT services as a key industry for "the great leap forward."[1]

The third policy option is a strategy for fast economic growth wherein a nation makes an entry in the next-generation industries such as renewable energy and takes advantage of its resulting early leadership position. Developed countries are already attempting to implement strategies based on renewable energy, however, as the technology itself is in the embryonic stage there is still a window of opportunity for North Korea in this area (Lee and Choi 2014). Whereas there is no great advantage for South Korea in adopting new energy infrastructure, such as smart grids, since existing infrastructure for hydraulic power and thermal energy resources that have already been established in North Korea are either very outdated or inadequate, gains from investment in existing infrastructure through new renewable resources would be relatively greater. North Korea can also utilize funds obtained by exporting its abundant mineral resources to build infrastructures for new energy resources. This method has been carried out by some countries in South America and Africa, and Mozambique also adopted a strategy investing in solar energy with the revenues accumulated by exporting coal to other countries (Lee and Mathews 2012).

3.2 North Korea's future industrial structure

North Korea's future industrial structure would be inevitably driven by complicated scenarios in terms of which industries North Korea will foster in the future. It is also not clear whether the North Korean regime will maintain the status quo or choose a rapid system transition scenario, or what kind of policy North Korea will pursue in either case. However, the inward-looking development policy that North Korea has thus far pursued has empirically failed to lead to economic development. Policy directions for fostering industry growth, such as an open-door industrialization policy or leapfrogging development, suggested by the existing literature discussed in the preceding section, are not always identical. However, it appears that they have a unified view of the ideal focus for economic growth through labor-intensive light industry by attracting foreign capital, cultivation of IT service industries, and exports expansion.

3.2.1 Light industry

Light industry in North Korea currently has the duty of providing necessities to the residents. However, it seems that North Korea's light industry has been declining ever since the financial crisis in the 1990s, and it has been operating below capacity in recent years. As a result, it is known that for considerable amounts of necessities, North Korea depends on imports, especially from China. Currently, North Korea is prioritizing investments in four leading industrial sectors, as there is a lack of investment sources. It follows that there is a lack of investment sources for light industry, and investments for the purpose of the construction of new facilities for light industries or renovation of existing facilities are very limited.

In the case of small and underdeveloped countries where domestic markets are small and lack capital, they are obliged to depend heavily on foreign markets and capital. Light industry, including the garment industry, has an advantage of being able to grow production in a short amount of time because the size of the market for such products is large and the industry is capable of attracting foreign capital (Hong et al. 2017). As for North Korea, it is necessary to nurture light industry by utilizing its labor force, which is one of its more competitive factors of production. In particular, North Korea has favorable conditions for fostering light industry because it is adjacent to South Korea and China, both of which can provide markets and funds in the early stages of economic development.

The garment industry would be significant in North Korea's economic growth as the industry can establish a production base in a short period of time through foreign investment, etc. Since the Asian financial crisis in the 1990s, unemployment has been high for unskilled and semi-skilled workers, and therefore utilizing this segment of the labor force in an efficient way might catalyze rapid growth (Hong et al. 2017).

As for Vietnam, the fastest growing export industry was the garment industry. Its garment exports are led by foreign investment companies. The main advantage of the Vietnamese garment industry was its relatively low-cost labor force, and in recent years, the industry has continued to grow through productivity improvements as they have faced a rise in labor costs. In Cambodia's case, the garment industry succeeded and experienced a boom through FDI. There, this industry accounts for as much as 30 percent of FDI and primarily targets its production to export markets. However, for North Korea, it is critical to enhance market accessibility to developed countries and to create a favorable environment for attracting foreign investment. The best way to do so would be by making progress in resolving nuclear issues and improving foreign and inter-Korean relations. As existing facilities are falling behind and foreign investment is essential for expanding production capacities, the possibility of foreign investment from South Korea and China, which are geographically close to North Korea, should be considered as one of the greatest potential monetary sources for light industries in North Korea.

3.2.2 IT industry

Historically, North Korea's IT technology development began twenty years before South Korea's (Kim and Lee 2008). Started as a means of building a self-reliant national economy, the IT industry has been promoted in order to expand automation in heavy industry. The IT industry field of software has developed into an independent industry since the 1990s and it helps with foreign exchange earnings, which have become one of the main sources of revenue. Despite its long history of technological development, North Korean IT industry has been unable to utilize overseas technologies and information, operating as an independent actor, because of North Korea's self-reliant ideology (*Juche*) and self-reliant national economy. In particular, North Korea has traditionally invested a great deal of effort in hardware development to foster its heavy chemical industry, but the production capacity of the hardware sector has nearly collapsed due to the fall of socialism, the disruption of industry infrastructure during the North Korean famine in the 1990s, and North Korea's closed economic strategies and financial difficulties, etc. However, as North Korea possesses an outstanding labor force, its potential in the software industry is perceived to be high.

Countries such as China, Vietnam, and Cambodia have utilized FDI to expand their IT manufacturing industries' capacities. China is a case where a nation has attracted foreign capital to lay its groundwork for the IT industry, attained independent technology and strengthened product competitiveness. Also, since Vietnam launched an economic renewal campaign, the "Doi Moi" policy in 1986, it has implemented economic reform. The Vietnamese administration recognized the importance of the IT industry and established a plan for developing IT industries ever since the early 1980s. Also, for Cambodia, its market expansion through foreign capital is a key element of its IT development policy, and its rapid economic growth has seemingly benefited in turn from the IT industry. The IT industry has mainly grown through the mobile communication and software industry, though it is still at the incipient stage.

IT industry can grow rapidly with the proper conditions for development, and it can also create a high forward and backward linkage effect. This is also the reason why a huge number of less-developed countries utilize IT industry as an engine for economic growth. In the case of North Korea, the North Korean administration has made an effort to train high-quality workers as its labor force is already highly skilled and low-cost. Therefore, the industry can expect rapid growth once its effort has paid off. Unlike the cases of the aforementioned three countries, the IT manufacturing industry in North Korea did not see growth because North Korea could not facilitate an inflow of foreign capital through opening its market. Though North Korea's IT industry began earlier than that of South Korea, North Korea's IT industry did not make any significant progress due to its constrained market environment. The growth and development of the IT industry will be facilitated once North Korea, which is deficient in technology and capital, acquires the required capital and technical skills in conjunction with its highly skilled labor force by opening its market to build infrastructure. Moreover, the IT industry's forward and backward linkage effect with other industries can have a great impact on the whole economy.

As for North Korea, the most practical way of attracting foreign capital to invest in the IT industry is through inflows of investment capital from South Korea. As South Korea already has international competitiveness in the IT industry, North Korea's competitiveness can be enhanced through capital from South Korea by creating a value chain in the IT industry.

4 Summary and conclusion

In this chapter, I recapitulated economic development strategies and reviewed the transition of the industrial structures of North Korea after the liberation from Japanese occupation. Looking to the future, I also investigated economic development strategies and the formation of ideal industry structures for the economic development of North Korea. In pursuit of a self-reliant national economy in the post-occupation period, North Korea had implemented a heavy industry-oriented economic policy related to the munitions industry. However, the development of heavy industry could not benefit the development of the whole economy due to a small domestic market size. Additionally, heavy industry failed in creating a forward and backward linkage effect and North Korea's inefficient facilities have only been further run down by time. Its linkage between the industries was weak, and the overlapping investment between industries has made the entire economy highly inefficient. North Korea's inward-looking economic policy could not capture enough market share and thus its entire economy has remained inefficient without being able to utilize economies of scales. Even though North Korea has emphasized light industry, agriculture, fisheries, and the service industry, it has not been able to surmount the issues left over from its past heavy industry-oriented economic development policy.

For economic recovery and economic development, the economic policy directions that North Korea should choose are clear. No matter how fast it is, unless North Korea should switch its policy to an open door industrialization policy, leapfrogging development is absolutely impossible. If North Korea were pursue the leapfrogging strategy, it would have to initiate a policy of attracting foreign capital and expanding its exports market beyond a simple open economy policy. As North Korea has a highly skilled labor force, it should work to foster light industries including the garment industry and IT industry (focusing on the field of software) by utilizing the labor force in order to have a comparative advantage in the world market. However, to cultivate these industries, it should facilitate the inflow of foreign capital through the use of SEZs. The expansion of the incentive system depends on the successful transition of North Korea as well as the extent of its market-opening policy. North Korea is adjacent to South Korea and China, and it is located in a geographically advantageous area for capital inflow and the capture of market share. After improving inter-Korean relations and the removal of economic sanctions by, for instance, making progress in resolving nuclear issues, it is highly likely that North Korea can rapidly foster its comparative advantages through establishing inter-Korean cooperation. Also, if North Korea expects to realize this rapid economic growth in the future, its system transition (to an open market) will be necessary and additional policies to promote its economic growth must be ensured.

Note

1 Rodong Sinmun in 2012 explained that India emphasized the development of information technology industry but that considering its weak manufacturing industry, India's administration trained its work force in computer programming and development of internet-based experts in the IT sector (Yonhap News, June 16, 2002; Lee and Choi 2014).

References

Cho, Kang Il. 1995. *The Trade First Principle is a Revolutionary Strategy to Lead to a Tremendous Success in the Development of Socialist Economy*. Pyongyang: Science and Encyclopedia Publisher.

Hong, Soon Jick, Seog Ki Lee, Bong Hyun Cho, Youn Seek Lee, and Il-Young Jeong. 2017. "Ways to Reform Industrial Structure of North and South Korea and Nurture Growth Industries in North Korea after Unification." *Korea Institute for International Economic Policy: Mid & Long-Term Strategies toward an Advanced Trading Economy* 17 (2). www.kiep.go.kr/eng/sub/view.do?bbsId=policyAnalyses&searchCate1=ORGNZT_0130010070000&nttId=200793.

Hwang, Eui Gak. 1993. *The Economy of North Korea*. Seoul: Nanam.

Kim, Byung Yeon, and Gérard Roland. 2012. "Scenarios for a Transition to a Prosperous Market Economy in North Korea." *International Economic Journal* 26 (3): 511–539. Doi: 10.1080/10168737.2012.707878.

Kim, Tae Woon, and Kang Bok Lee. 2008. "Changes and Future Prospects in the Industrial Structure of North Korea." *The Journal of Asian Studies*: 107–134. www.dbpia.co.kr/journal/articleDetail?nodeId=NODE06681944.

Kwon, Young Kyong. 2008. "North Korea's Economic Status with its Reform and Open Door Policy." In *The Understanding of North Korea*, 127–172. The Institute for Unification Education of the Ministry of Unification. www.unikorea.go.kr/books/understand/understand/ebook/under_NK_2008/assets/contents/download.pdf.

Lee, Keun, and John Mathews. 2012. "South Korea and Taiwan." In *The Innovative Firms in the Emerging Market Economies*, 223–248. Oxford: Oxford University Press.

Lee, Keun, and Ji Young Choi. 2014. "The Possibility of Achieving Economic Catch-up in North Korea: Policy Options Under Transition Scenarios." *BOK Economic Research* (15). https://ideas.repec.org/p/bok/wpaper/1415.html.

Lee, Keun, Byung Yeon Kim, and In Sook Lee. 2009. "The Possibility of Economic Reform in North Korea." *Journal of Contemporary Asia* 39 (2): 279–294. Doi: https://doi.org/10.1080/00472330902723865.

Lee, Seok Ki, Seok Jin Kim, and Geun Ju Jeong. 2013. "The Potential of Industrial Development in North Korea and Inter-Korean Cooperation: Focusing on the Special Economic Zones, Light Industry and IT Industry." *The Research Report of Korea Institute for Industrial Economics and Trade* (672).

Research Institute for National Unification. 1995. *A Handbook of Economic Indicators of South and North Korea*. Seoul: Research Institute for National Unification.

Seo, Seung Hwan. 1994. *The Light Industry First Policy Is a Significant Strategic Task for the Development of the Socialist Economy in the Current Stage*. Pyongyang: Science and Encyclopedia Publisher.

Son, Young-Seok. 2017. "Establishment of the Economic Structure Based on the High-Technology Is a Significant Requirement to Be an Economic Power." *Journal of Kim Il Sung University* 63 (4).

The Institute for Unification Education of the Ministry of Unification. 2017. "Understanding of North Korea." *Understanding Unification Issues*. www.unikorea.go.kr/cms/getFile.do?file=201908271522403821 2.pdf&orgname=Understanding%20North%20Korea_2017.pdf&mgmtId=MGMT_0000001473&siteId=SITE_00003&filePath=eng_unikorea/common/file/&count=Y.

6 Financing the reform and opening of North Korea

What is the precondition?

Tae Soo Kang and Dahyun Kang

1 Introduction

On June 12, 2018, US President Donald Trump and Chairman Kim Jong-un of North Korea reached a comprehensive agreement (the first ever US-North Korea summit talk in history). At the South-North Summit Meetings in April 2018, Chairman Kim expressed his interest in the "Vietnamese reform and opening model," which shows that the normalization of relations with the US is a prerequisite to attract international money.

The scale of the North Korean economy is similar to that of Mongolia and Laos. According to the Bank of Korea's statistics, the North Korean economy is just 2.2 percent the size of South Korean economy. In 2017, the population was 25.01 million, with a per capita GDP of 1.45 million won, and the total amount of trade equaled 5.5 billion dollars (1.8 billion dollars in exports, and 3.7 billion dollars in imports). In contrast, during the same year, Vietnam's per capita income was approximately $2,400, with its population approaching 100 million, and the nominal GDP exceeding $220 billion, 15 percent of South Korea's economy.

In December 1986, Vietnam started a "reform and opening" process with the *Doi Moi* Declaration, leading Vietnam's economy to expand to thirteen times the size of North Korea's. For North Korea to reach Vietnam's current economic capacity would require at least twenty years, at a rate of 10 percent annual growth.

It is impossible for South Korea alone to afford the funds for North Korea's reform and opening. The key point is to attract international investors through international financial institutions and private investors. To incentivize such investors, North Korea needs to build trust, which first requires a major financial system reform.

This chapter proceeds as follows. First, we will examine the road map established in the international community for the countries transitioning toward a market economy. Then the chapter analyzes the Vietnam case that North Korea singled out as its role model. Next, we will explore the reform task of the financial system in North Korea, which is a prerequisite for attracting international private investment. Lastly, this chapter will present North Korea's accessibility to an international payment and settlement network.

2 Transition to market economy and financing: the case of Vietnam

In the international society, a road map has been set up for countries moving to a market economy system, which is described in Box 6.1:

Box 6.1 Process for transitioning to market economy

①Lifting of UN sanctions→ ②Imroved relations with the US→ ③Membership in international financial institutions (IMF, World Bank, ADB, etc.)→ ④Trade normalization → ⑤Membership in the WTO→ ⑥Acquisition of market economy status

Source: Author created

2.1 The process of reform, opening, and financing in Vietnam

2.1.1 Lifting of US sanctions against Vietnam

In December 1986, Vietnam declared the *Doi Moi* (reform and opening movement), however, there was little support by way of investment from the international community. It wasn't until diplomatic relations between the US and Vietnam were normalized through the withdrawal of Vietnamese troops from Cambodia that international investors started taking Vietnam's reforms seriously. It took eleven years to reach the normalized diplomatic relations between the two countries after the *Doi Moi* reform and opening declaration. From the moment of the *Doi Moi* declaration, it took eleven years for diplomatic relations between the US and Vietnam to stabilize, and twenty years to reach a trade agreement. By 2001, the international community had made a full-fledged investment in Vietnam because the investment conditions were regarded as greatly improved after the ratification of the US-Vietnam trade agreement (Kwon and Kim 2019).

When US sanctions were lifted against Vietnam, support from the international public sector – concessional aid, loans of the international financial institutions, and official development assistance (ODA) – was allowed. It took a long time for Vietnam to attract private investment. In the meantime, this public support from the international organizations played an important role in filling the gaps that private investments could not bridge. For example, IMF standby loans of 194 million USD were funded immediately when the Clinton administration approved the resumption of loans to Vietnam in July 1993. Later the Donner Conference was held in December, which allowed the increase of the international community's ODA and FDI to Vietnam. In November 1994, branches of Citibank and Bank of America (BOA) in Hanoi were authorized (see Figure 6.1).

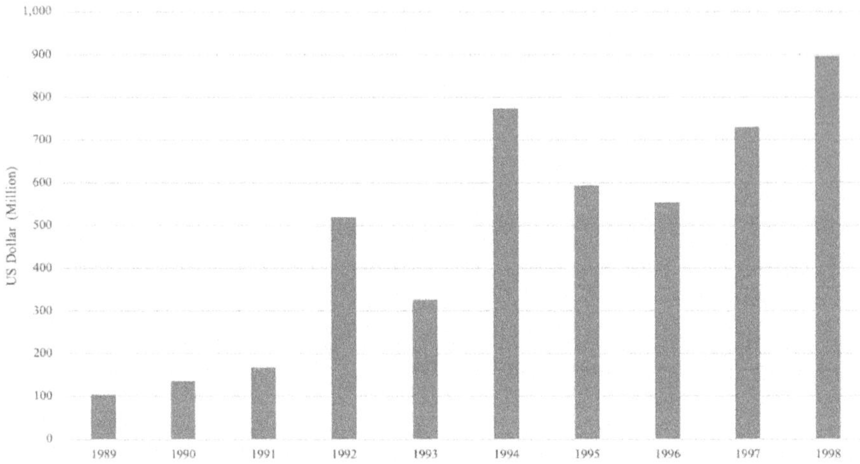

Figure 6.1 Official direct investment (ODA) during 1989–1998 in Vietnam

Source: Adapted from OECD 2019

2.1.2 Normalization of diplomatic relations (July 1995), ratification of the US-Vietnam trade agreement (2001), and accession to the WTO (November 2006, 150th member country)

When the trade agreement between the US and Vietnam were ratified in July 1993, Vietnam's exports and FDI were increased with a small margin. The amount and scale of exports and FDI were largely increased only after Vietnam joined the WTO in November 2006 (see Figures 6.2 and 6.3). WTO membership is required to conclude negotiations with "each and every" member country. Developed countries, such as the United States, require new member states to establish a system that incorporates laws and basic infrastructures meeting international standards. Therefore, North Korea's accession to the WTO signifies that North Korea has successfully joined the international community and abides by the international order of the market economy.

2.2 Implications for North Korea in financing

Recently, it was assumed that North Korea has long been suffering from a decrease in economic activity and a serious shortage in foreign reserves due to international sanctions (UNSCR [UN Security Council Resolution] 2397, December 23, 2017). As shown in the case of Vietnam's reform and opening, the normalization of relations with the US is a prerequisite for attracting foreign capital. Thus, the normalization of diplomatic relations between the US and North Korea will be the starting point of attracting international capital.

Figure 6.2 Trade inflows of Vietnam

Source: Adapted from IMF 2019

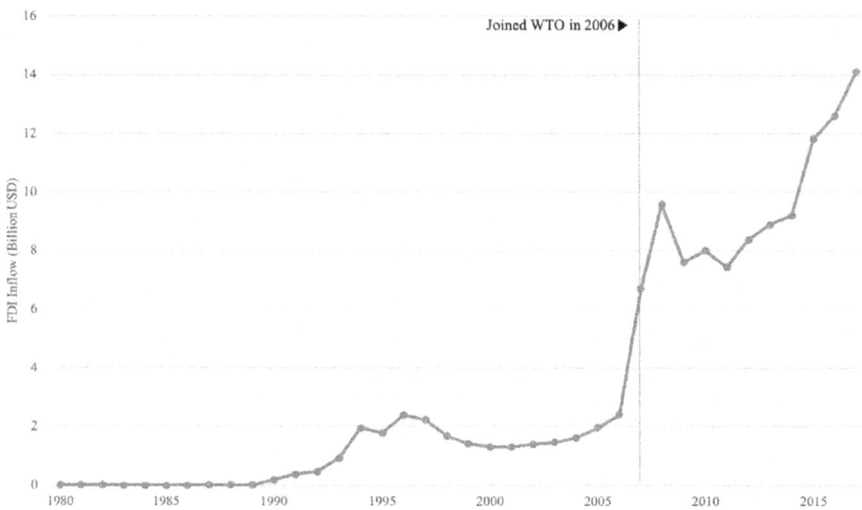

Figure 6.3 FDI inflows of Vietnam

Source: Adapted from World Bank 2019

2.2.1 The impact of international sanctions against North Korea

Since the launch of the ICBM-class missile on November 29, 2017, North Korea has faced strong international sanctions (UNSCR 2397, 2017.12.23.).

Due to these sanctions, exportation to North Korea of many essential goods (agricultural products, machinery, electronic equipment, wood, ships, etc.) has been prohibited (UNSC Resolution 2397 on sanctions against North Korea). As a result, North Korea has experienced a significant reduction in industrial production as well as in economic activities.

In particular, North Korea's imports and exports were largely decreased after the sanctions were imposed. The total trade activity between North Korea and China dropped by 51.3 percent from 2017 to 2018 (from $4.98 billion to $2.4 billion). North Korea's exports to China totaled $2.09 billion; down by 87.3 percent ($1.65 billion) from 2017. Exports of anthracite coal, iron ore, and clothing are banned, and therefore it is assumed that the related industries were directly affected by the embargo. Imports from China amounted to $2.2 billion; down by 33.4 percent from $3.3 billion in 2017. In particular, the import sanction on electronic devices, facilities, and transportation vehicles against North Korea has made it difficult for North Korea to produce industrial products. Additionally, international humanitarian aid plummeted by 60 percent to $10.1 million in the first half of 2018.

Securing foreign reserve in order to maintain the bare minimum level of imports necessary for sustaining its economy is an urgent matter for North Korea. Their strategy for trade is that the exports (minerals such as anthracite, textiles, clothing,

Table 6.1 Sanctions on North Korea

UN Security Council Resolution on North Korea	*Related Events*	*Main Contents of Sanction*
UNSCR 2375 (September 11, 2017)	Sixth nuclear test (September 3, 2017)	• Prohibition of exports to North Korea: setting up a cap on refined oil and crude oil • Prohibition of imports to North Korea: textiles, apparel, finished goods • Prohibition of new employment for North Korean workers dispatched overseas • Ban on economic cooperation: prohibition of establishment and operation of joint venture with North Korea
UNSCR 2397 (December 23, 2017)	ICBM level missile launch (November 29, 2017)	• Restrictions on exports to North Korea: reduced cap on refined oil and crude oil • Overseas workers should be recalled to North Korea within twenty-four months • Maritime Interdiction: strengthening crackdown on ships entering and leaving North Korea • Prohibition of transactions for all fishing rights trading

Source: Author created

aquatic products, food, agricultural products) are used to procure foreign reserve needed for importing goods, such as crude oil, refined oil, electronic equipment, machinery, and transportation vehicles. Also, activities such as outsourcing workers, operating restaurants overseas, selling fishing rights in North Korean waters, and selling tourism products, are all used to expand foreign reserves.

The main goal of the sanctions is to block North Korea's foreign currency procurement. For instance, UNSCR 2397 (December 2017) includes repatriation of "all" North Korean expatriate workers within twenty-four months (until December 2019) and prohibition of trading for "all" territorial fishing rights.

2.3 *Normalization of US-North Korean relations and the accession to international financial institutions*

A huge amount of financial resources is required for rebuilding the North Korean economy, and the export profit is mobilized as a crucial resource. Thus, reaching a trade agreement with the US and Japan is a prerequisite for a groundbreaking increase in exports from North Korea. The first step that North Korea needs to take is to normalize relations with the US. In the case of Vietnam, the international community's support of and investment in Vietnam doubled after diplomatic relations with the US were normalized in 1995.

North Korea's accession to the international financial institution will only be possible when relations with the US and Japan are normalized, however, the

US strongly refuses entry to the international financial institution by any "terrorist nation." Therefore, if North Korea is not released from the list of terrorism-supporting countries, it will be impossible for North Korea to join the international financial institutions, as the US and Japan hold the largest equity shares in those institutions.

In the process of North Korea's reform and opening, the first step is to become a member country of the international financial institutions. Vietnam and other transition countries used to rely on ODA from the international financial institutions such as the IMF, the World Bank, and ADB, before receiving private investment from international communities. For instance, the eligibility requirement for joining the IMF is to maintain a stable exchange rate system, and membership for the World Bank is only given to countries having IMF membership. If North Korea receives funding from international financial institutions, North Korea is obliged to submit national statistics to the IMF. It is expected that North Korea will be reluctant to disclose statistics to the international community. Another concern is that North Korea's ability to generate statistics may fall behind the international standard. There has been a case in which the IMF set a "grace period" for any country whose statistical data compiling capabilities are weak. In such a case, the IMF provides technical support to cultivate the necessary skills for submitting statistics. In the past, the IMF provided training on statistical skills to the practitioners of Eastern European countries.

In principle, the World Bank does not provide funds to non-member countries. However, if the Standing Committee approves, it may be possible to support non-member countries through "special trust funds."[1] If international sanctions on North Korea are lifted and the relationship between the US and North Korea improves, it could be possible to provide funding to North Korea in the form of a special trust fund (tentatively called the "North Korea Trust Fund").

The last step of North Korea's transition to the international market economy would be to join the WTO. In the early stage of the normalization of diplomatic relations, international financial institutions are the channels for receiving external

Box 6.2 Available resources prior to joining the international organization

Multi-Donor Trust Fund

- When international sanctions are eased or lifted, multilateral trust funds can be used to support North Korea's economic development even before joining the international financial organization
    - Examples of using the multilateral trust fund before joining the international financial institutions: Palestine Trust Fund, Bosnia-Herzegovina Trust Fund, etc. (see Table 6.2)

Table 6.2 The World Bank's multilateral trust fund prior to the accession to the international financial institution

Type	*Contents*
Palestine trust fund	$ 4,103.5 million in development restoration support (1993–2000)
East Timor trust fund	Support for $ 800 million (1999–2003) Over twenty-six international organizations including the World Bank, ADB and EU
Bosnia trust fund	Established trust funds of $150 million in 1996 to support development recovery
Kosovo special trust fund	Created in 1999 with retained earnings of $25 million

Source: Kim 2008

funding for development. In the long term, North Korea can attract private-sector-driven FDI, which has no burden of repayment. This is the model for transitional countries.

3 A system for attracting private investment from the international community

Overall reform of the North Korean financial system is an important prerequisite for the inflow of international private capital to North Korea.

3.1 The task of reforming the financial sector

For North Korea's economic development, it is important to attract private investment from the international community. As a result, North Korea has made an effort to establish a "specialized financial institution" to attract foreign investment,[2] to expand the "economic development districts[3]," and to introduce a "foreign investor protection system."[4] It is assumed that the legal infrastructure for protecting foreign investment is already established in North Korea, however, foreign investors' trust in the institutional operations of North Korea is still low. A typical example is the failure of remittance by the Egyptian company Orascom[5] in 2008.

Thus, it is a pressing task for North Korea to initiate financial reform and gain the trust of foreign investors in the North Korean economy. In other words, receiving attention from foreign investors depends on the success of the financial reforms.

3.1.1 Establishment of a market-oriented, two-tiered banking system and readjustment of non-performing loans

North Korea laid the foundation for financial reform by enacting the Central Bank Act and the Commercial Banking Act in 2004 and 2006, respectively. The Central

Bank Act explicitly grants the status of "Bank of Banks" to the Central Bank of Korea. This can be seen as North Korea's declaration of "introduction of dual banking system."

In order to make a deposit at commercial banks, the preconditions are the guarantee of withdrawal at the depositor's request at any point and the appropriate level of real interest rate payment. In most socialist countries, the interest rate of bank deposits is very low, and it is also difficult to withdraw a deposit. As a result, households in these countries show a strong preference toward cash holdings. In 1985, bank deposits in Soviet households, for instance, totaled 1.87 billion RUB, with cash holdings of 1.4 billion RUB (Kim 1999).

Records indicate that North Korea has low deposit rates and restrictions on withdrawals. Depositors in North Korea feel anxiety about exposing their identity, and people often feel a sense of deprivation due to the concerns related to periodic currency reforms. Until recently, it was only possible to withdraw personal deposits by paying a 20–30-percent commission. This is why bank deposits were often avoided, while foreign currency holdings and utilizing private funds became widespread among North Koreans.

In 2015, the Commercial Banking Act was amended to add provisions for bank deposit confidentiality and repayment of deposit principal, however, the North Koreans' trust in their banking system is still so low that no additional commercial banks have been established. Thus, "informal private finance" replaced the role of commercial banks, and therefore, loan-sharking businesses have become popular.

People in transitional countries consider "fund" as a "financial activity" given by the national budget, which has no obligation of repayment. It takes time to change the concept of "fund" into "finance" (bank loans), which requires repayment of the principal. This was the same reason Vietnam had such a high volume of bad loans, even well after adopting the dual banking system.

In the case of North Korea, there is a high probability of increasing non-performing loans, as a loan risk assessment system is absent. When a country

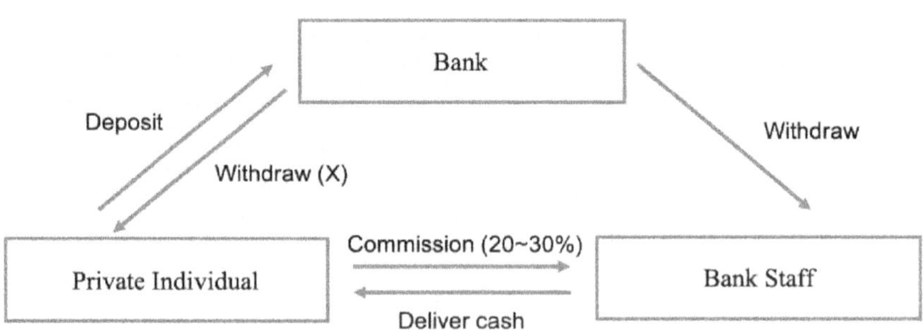

Figure 6.4 North Korea's deposit and withdrawal system

Source: Adapted from Ministry of Unification 2019

moves toward a market economy, an efficient allocation of resources in the financial sector is a key factor in determining whether the bad debts will be resolved or not. Therefore, it is a prerequisite to accurately measure the size of non-performing debts in order to maintain the health of commercial banks. Also, it is necessary to put all insolvent loans into an asset management company.

Tackling bad debts in a prompt manner will be imperative. As long as bad debts remain on banks' balance sheets, uncertainties will persist that will hinder normal business activities. Thus, wiping out non-performing assets is the very first step in increasing the business force. In the case of Vietnam, the country received assistance from international financial institutions to scale down large bad debts.

3.1.2 Reform of the exchange rate system

The gap between the official exchange rate and the market exchange rate (see Figure 6.5) should be minimized in order to absorb foreign currencies into the official market system. In 1985, the exchange rate of the Vietnamese market was eight times higher than the official exchange rate. But the gap was narrowed down to 1.7 times in 1988. For North Korea, this gap is eighty times higher (official exchange rate: 107.3 won against the US dollar, and 8,000 won at the market exchange rate). This leads North Korean citizens to avoid local currencies, thereby defaulting to "dollarization," in which local people favor foreign currencies like US dollars and Chinese yuan.

Dollarization is already deeply rooted and widespread in North Korea. In a situation like hyperinflation, holding a dollar brings an advantage in protecting asset value. On top of that, it has another advantage in that the dollar is excluded from any currency reform initiated by the North Korean government.

3.1.3 Problems related to inflation

Almost all transition countries, without exception, have experienced hyperinflation during the reform and opening process. The main reason for hyperinflation comes from an excessive currency caused by the policies of retail price subsidies and the duplication of money circulation. In socialist countries, the retail price subsidies are provided to businesses in order to control consumer prices at lower levels. Price liberalization means abolishing the subsidy system, which sparks hyperinflation. In 1993, Georgia recorded an inflation rate of 15,442 percent. Armenia and Ukraine had similar experiences, reaching hyperinflation rates in excess of 2,000 percent.

In 2002, the North Korean government abolished the retail price subsidy system when it introduced the "7.1 Measure to Improve Economic Management." Thus, the pressure on inflation is unlikely to be high when the price liberalization is initiated. In fact, no severe inflation has been observed in North Korea since 2013.

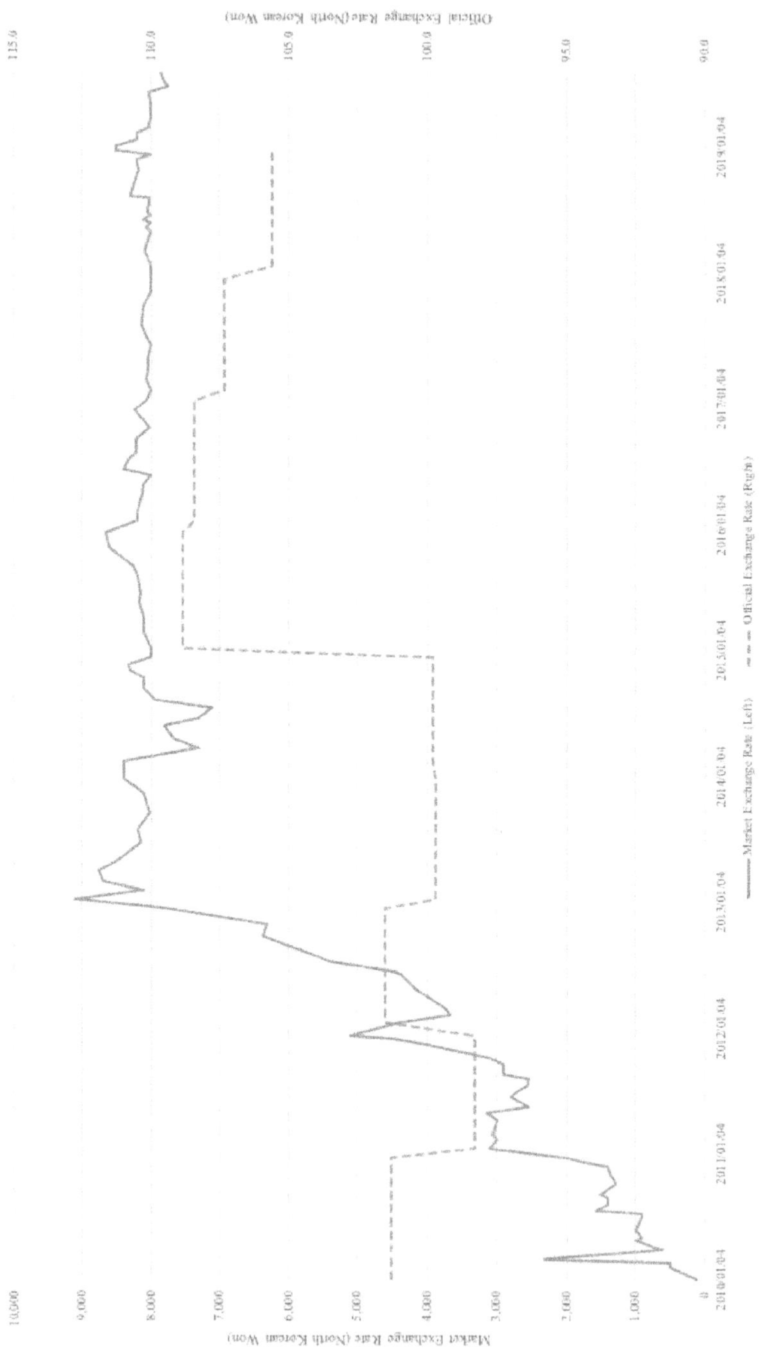

Figure 6.5 North Korea's official exchange rate vs. market exchange rate

Source: Adapted from Daily NK 2019 and Bank of Korea 2019

North Korea's monetary circulation is divided into the following two types: cashless circulation and cash circulation (Duplication of Currency Distribution). Cashless circulation (distribution) refers to an inter-company transaction via the accounts at the Central Bank of Korea. Cash circulation (distribution) refers to transactions between individuals, or between individuals and businesses, which is mainly used for the income and expenditure of workers.

3.1.3.1 BIMODAL CASH DISTRIBUTION AND INFLATION

In the structure of cash distribution, cash is paid to local people through institutions and enterprises in the form of wages from the account of the Central Bank of Korea (Joseon). When people purchase goods with their wage income, cash returns to the Central Bank of Korea through the institutions and enterprises.

Since North Korean citizens avoid making bank deposits due to the difficulty of withdrawals, the problem has become exacerbated. The cash transaction system is practically paralyzed, because the amount of leakage (capital or income that exits an economy or system, rather than remaining within it) is becoming greater than that of the cash returned to the central bank. Due to leakage, the amount of cash held by local people in 2002 was nearly double that of North Korea's national budget.

The pressure that cash leakage puts on a currency often leads to inflation. Thus, the North Korean government needs to stabilize prices by periodically recollecting excess cash through currency reform. The North Korean government carried out currency reforms twice in 2001 and 2009 but failed to prevent inflation because the reforms caused people to distrust the North Korean currency. Today, the average citizen prefers foreign currencies, such as the US dollar or the Chinese yuan, to their own national currency, out of fear of unexpected monetary reform and high inflation.

Most transition countries respond to a situation of hyperinflation by using a "currency board" scheme (a kind of fixed exchange rate regime). Under this scheme, the exchange rate is fixed between reserve currency and the currency issued by the "currency board" (Buch 1993). Estonia, Lithuania, and Bulgaria had used this system in the past. For Estonia, it used the German mark (DM) as its reserve currency.

As North Korea looks for a solution to high inflation, the fixed exchange rate system is expected to be desirable in the early stages of transition toward a market economy. It will be necessary to deliver a message to the people that the government is doing everything they can to stabilize the price by fixing the exchange rate. The fixed exchange rate system has an advantage in that the fixed exchange rate acts as a nominal anchor, greatly reducing economic uncertainty. It has been demonstrated through previous cases that countries that adopt the fixed exchange rate system show a higher economic growth rate than those with non-fixed system (Fischer, Sahay, and Garamont 1996; Lougani and Sheets 1997).

Today, the volatility of the inflation and exchange rates in North Korea have been relatively stabilized as dollarization has increased. Even after the UN's sanctions on North Korea, prices in the *Jangmadang* (unofficial private market) remain stable, and exchange rate volatility is low (see Figure 6.6). In the national economy, the North Korean won does not play a major role in terms of functional currency. It appears as though the spread of the US dollar and Chinese yuan indicates that the fixed exchange rate system, or "currency board" system, is already in effect in North Korea.

It is clear that international sanctions against North Korea have dragged industrial activities down. However, despite the sanctions, prices and exchange rates haven't been affected much. This suggests that a more detailed analysis is needed on how the international sanctions have affected the North Korean economy. To do so, it is necessary to take into account North Korea's own payment method for imports. North Korea does not import goods and pay commodity prices at the same time. The actual payment to exporters is made only after the goods are imported to the local markets. As a result, it is prevalent in North Korea to see an inconsistency in time of between importing goods and making payment. Because of this practice, when North Korea imports goods from China, it does not show a decrease in North Korea's foreign reserves, whereas import statistics reflect an increase. This is because the payment can only be made once the imported goods are sold. International sanctions focus on blocking North Korea's procurement of foreign currency. If North Korea takes a 'muddling through' strategy, however, the effect of sanctions may be diminished. Also, stress test analysis is needed to check the resilience of the North Korean economy against external sanctions. For instance, it is necessary to precisely analyze how long North Korea's foreign reserve can bear the current international sanctions.

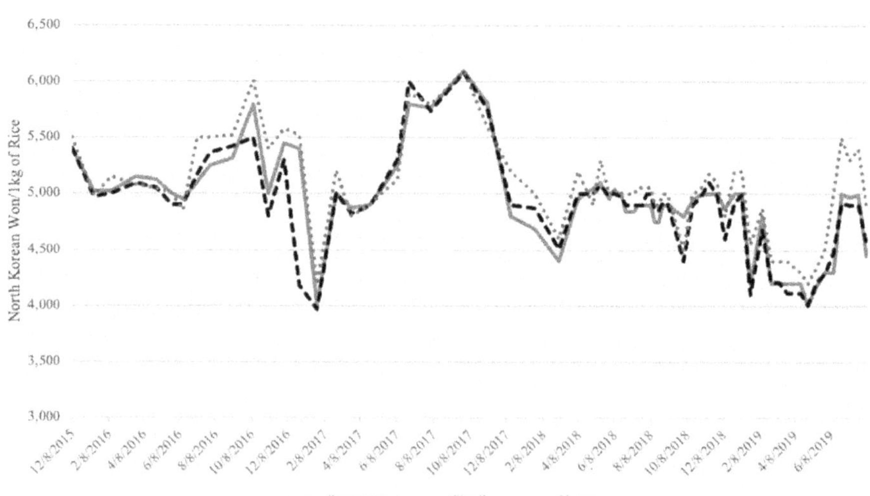

Figure 6.6 Trend of rice price after sanctions

Source: Adapted from Daily NK 2019

3.1.4 Accessibility to international payment and settlement networks

3.1.4.1 SETTLEMENT BETWEEN COUNTRIES

In 1987, North Korea defaulted on debt repayment, and since then it cannot use a letter of credit in transactions with foreign countries. For this reason, North Korea currently relies on a remittance method.

Since 1992, North Korea and China have used a bank located in Macau as a transfer channel for making payments and settlements between the two countries. The North Korean bank (Chosun Trade Bank) and the Chinese bank (China Construction Bank) transfer funds through accounts set up in the bank in Macau. Unfortunately, this process tends to be difficult and time consuming (Figure 6.7).

As a result, the central banks of these two countries signed a settlement agreement in 2004 to use the yuan remittance payment method through the account set up in the Chinese Construction Bank.

3.1.4.2 INTER-KOREAN SETTLEMENT

In cases where transactions take place between South and North Korea, it is impossible to use a letter of credit method. The only way that the two can transact

Table 6.3 Payment and settlement between countries

Type	*Contents*
Letter of credit method	Issuance of draft based on the letter of credit of the importer's bank → Request for the purchase of the draft to exporter bank with shipping documents → Receipt of export payment
Remittance method	Receipt of goods by the importer → Remittance to the exporter

Source: Author created

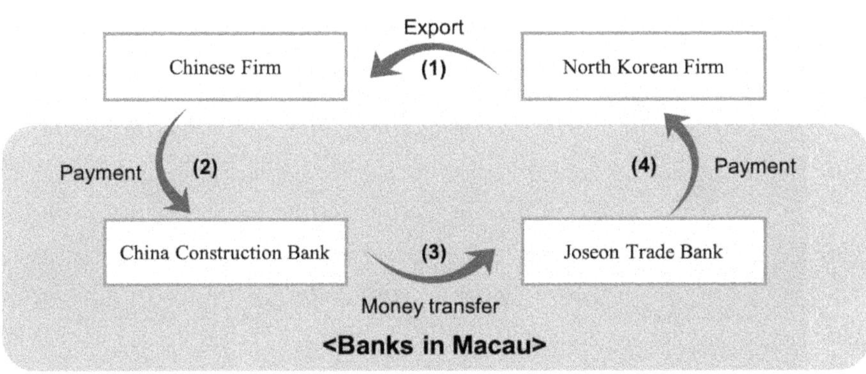

Figure 6.7 Money transfer via the bank located in Macau

Source: Author created

is by using the remittance (cash) payment method, setting up North Korea's bank account in a third country (Figure 6.8).

The problem with the remittance (cash) payment method is that it isn't time- or cost efficient. For this reason, South and North Korea signed an agreement on clearing settlement at the ministerial-level talk in December 2000, which was projected to go into effect by 2003.

Typically, transactions conclude by settling payment at the point of service, however, clearing settlement is different from the typical payment method. It records the amount of inflows and outflows on the clearance accounts established in both sides of a bank for a certain period of time (normally one year) and then payment for the remaining balance is collected after a set period of time. In the agreement between South Korea and North Korea, South Korea designated the "Export-Import Bank" and North Korea designated the "Trade Bank" as clearing settlement banks. The clearing settlement limit was set at 30 million USD, with an interest rate of 1 percent. Since the inter-Korean relations have deteriorated, however, the clearing settlement has only remained as a symbolic agreement between two countries. The clearing settlement system was utilized by East and West Germany starting in 1949, leading to their eventual successful unification. Considering the fact that North Korea is incapable of settling transactions in the US dollar due to a foreign currency shortage, the clearing settlement system could be useful in a way to enhance the stability of the payment and settlement intermediation.

As it has remained merely an agreement, there has been no actual settlement between the two Koreas. At this point, it is assumed that North Korea will have difficulty in accessing the international settlement network for a considerable time. To resolve this situation, there should be at least a provisional solution. An international payment method used in between the Iranian central bank and the (South) Korean commercial banks (e.g. Woori Bank and Industrial Bank of Korea (IBK)) could be an alternative, for example, though consent from the US government would be a prerequisite. When Korean companies trade with Iranian

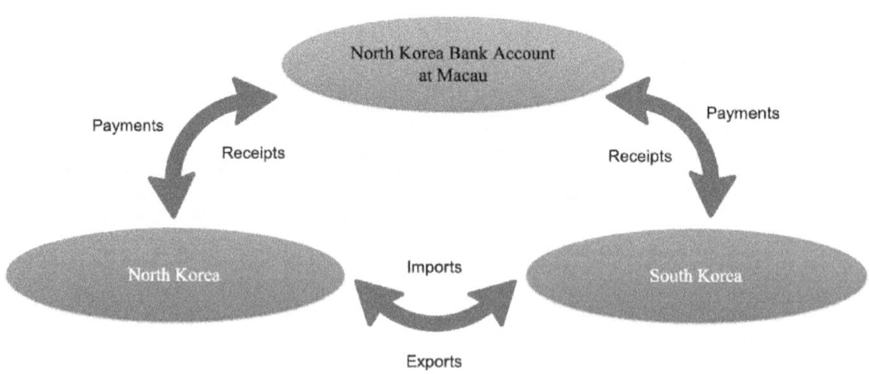

Figure 6.8 Example: payment scheme using North Korean bank account at third country

Source: Author created

companies, the Korean exporters and importers settle their transactions through accounts that the Iranian central bank established at either Woori Bank, or the Industrial Bank. Since 2010, when the agreement for this process was reached, the two countries have made their payments in Korean won. For instance, when the Iranian Oil Company exports crude oil to a Korean company, the payment for export is deposited in a Korean won (KRW) account of the Central Bank of Iran, set up at Woori Bank or the Industrial Bank. And when the Korean company exports products to the Iranian company, it also receives payments through this account (Figure 6.9).

The settlement system shown in Figure 6.9 was implemented in 2010 after consultations between South Korea and US governments took place. Through this system, Korea and Iran were able to trade crude oil and commodities with no actual foreign exchange transactions. Since May 2, 2019, however, the United States suspended this system, as the US continued to impose sanctions on Korea's import of Iranian oil. As a result, the KRW account of the Central Bank of Iran, which used to be a trade channel between Korea and Iran, has lost its function. Due to the frozen KRW settlement account, it has become difficult for Korea to export goods to Iran.

In the past, South Korean firms have used US dollars to pay North Korean agencies, for example, during the Kaesong Industrial Complex project. South Korean banks established branch offices in the Kaesong Industrial Complex and the Mt. Kumgang Tourism Zone in order to perform duties related to currency exchange and remittance business for both tenants and tourists.

More than 130 South Korean companies used to do business in the Kaesong Industrial Complex in the past. Today more than 90 percent of those companies wish to continue working in the Kaesong Industrial Complex, and the number of

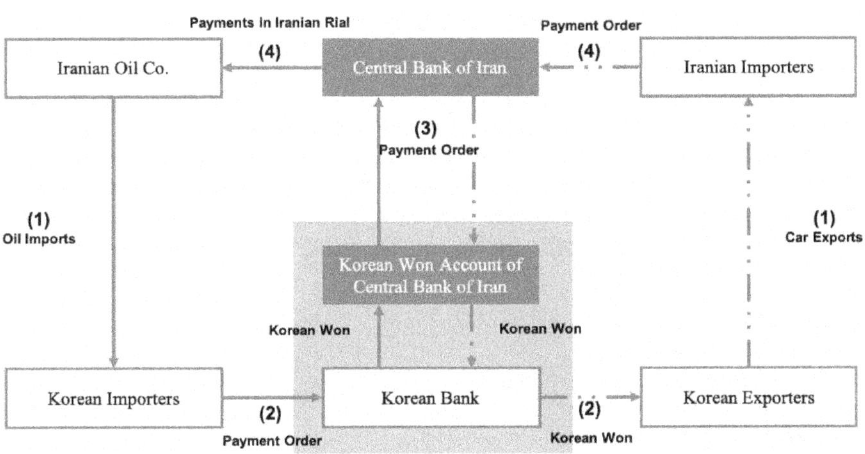

Figure 6.9 Settlement scheme between Korea and Iran

Source: Author created

jobs created by the Kaesong Industrial Complex has been estimated to be as high as 100,000 on the South Korean side alone.

For the North Korean workers' wages, South Korean companies exchanged the wages in US dollars at a Woori Bank branch in the Kaesong Industrial Complex and paid directly to North Korea's Special Provincial Development Administration. The Special Provincial Development Administration took 70 percent of the deposited amount from South Korean companies. The remaining 30 percent was delivered to the North Korean workers in the form of "necessity products" or North Korean won through the commercial joint venture company.

4 Conclusion

At the inter-Korean summit in April 2018, North Korea expressed its interest in the Vietnamese reform and opening model. This shows that North Korea's reform and opening will likely be implemented in a similar way. As it is discussed in this chapter, normalizing relations with the United States is essential for North Korea to pave the way for its transition to the market economy. It is also a critical point in attracting international funds. Judging by the success Vietnam has had with this program, the open expression of interest in utilizing the model holds important implications for North Korea.

Once the diplomatic relations between the US and North Korea are normalized, there will be two stages in the inflow of international funds to North Korea. The first step will be the inflow of aid from public sector development (ODA) through international organizations such as the IMF and the World Bank. After that, the international private sector investment (FDI) is expected to follow.

North Korea's success of reform and opening depends on attracting international private sector investment. This chapter presented four prerequisites for attracting money from the international community: the establishment of a market-oriented banking system, the reform of the exchange rate system, the stabilization of inflation, and access to the global payment network.

It is still a difficult task to figure out North Korea's economic situation from the outside. Moreover, it is unknown how the international community's sanctions on North Korea, including UNSCR 2397, are currently affecting the North Korean economy. Thus, the success of the four reform tasks presented in this chapter highly depends on the reliability of sources reporting North Korean statistics.

Notes

1 The trust fund is a fund created by the contributions of donors and NGOs, including international financial institutions. International organizations are entrusted with and manage the trust funds.

2 In 2011, North Korea announced the "Ten-Year Strategic Plan for the National Economic Development" and proposed the establishment of a "National Development Bank." However, it is difficult to establish the bank due to sanctions from the international community.

3 They established the legal foundation for this by enacting the "Special Economic Development Zone Act" in May 2013. Currently, five large economic zones and twenty-one economic development zones are designated as major cities in the border region of North Korea.
4 Restrictions on nationalization of foreign firms, a guaranteed return on investment proceeds to foreign investors, prohibition of discrimination.
5 Orascom, an Egyptian company, cooperated with the North Korean Communications Agency to establish the Koryo link (75 percent owned by Orascom). There are about five million mobile phone subscribers in North Korea. Orascom failed to transmit the money from the investment proceeds to Egypt. The North Korean authorities demanded the exchange of Orascom's profits to the market exchange rate (8,000 won=1 dollar) instead of the official exchange rate (108 won=1 dollar). If you exchange money at the market exchange rate, the value will drop to only 1/80. Orascom ceased new investment in North Korea in 2013.

References

The Bank of Korea. 2019. "Economic Statistics System." Accessed August 21. https://ecos.bok.or.kr/EIndex_en.jsp.

Buch, Claudia. 1993. "Die Waehrungsreform in Estland." *Weltwirt* 4: 441–465.

Daily NK. 2019. Accessed August 21. www.dailynk.com.

Fischer, Stanley, Ratna Sahay, and Carlos Garamont. 1996. "Stabilization and Growth in Transition Economies: The Early Experience." *IMF Working Paper* 96 (31). www.imf.org/en/Publications/WP/Issues/2016/12/30/Stabilization-and-Growth-in-Transition-Economies-The-Early-Experience-1929.

International Monetary Fund. 2019. "DOT." Accessed August 21. www.imf.org/en/Data.

Kim, Byung Yeon. 1999. "The Income, Savings, and Monetary Overhang of Soviet Households." *Journal of Comparative Economics* 27 (3): 644–448. Doi: https://doi.org/10.1006/jcec.1999.1614.

Kim, Yeong Geun. 2008. "The Role and Aid-Scale of International Official Development Assistance (ODA) in the Development of North Korea." *International Area Studies Review* 17 (4): 1–31. http://hdl.handle.net/10371/96204.

Kwon, Yool, and Mirim Kim. 2019. "Policy Implications of the Vietnam Reform Model on the South-North Economic Cooperation." *KIEP World Economy Today* 18 (24).

Lougani, Parakash, and Nathan Sheets. 1997. "Central Bank Independence, Inflation, and Growth in Transition Economies." *Journal of Money, Credit and Banking* 29 (3): 381–399.

Ministry of Unification. 2019. "North Korea Information Portal." Accessed August 21. https://nkinfo.unikorea.go.kr/nkp/main/portalMain.do.

Organization for Economic Cooperation and Development (OECD). 2019. "Aid Disbursements to Countries and Regions." Accessed August 21. https://stats.oecd.org.

World Bank. 2019. "World Bank Open Data." Accessed August 21. https://data.worldbank.org.

7 Effect of WTO accession on North Korea and its implication for economic development

Hongshik Lee and Sung Taek Cho

1 Introduction

Former communist countries took various measures to improve production efficiency and strengthen competitiveness through legal and institutional reform during the transition to a free market system.

In so doing they established a new economic growth engine by breaking out of economic isolation and solving internal reforms through the introduction of a free trade system. They recognized that normalizing relations with the Western world and the subsequent expansion of trade would be a prerequisite for economic growth in the process of reform.

At that time, the US was putting political pressure on communist countries in refusing credit grants from requesting financial institutions. Former communist countries needed to eliminate these trade barriers for minimizing discriminatory measures in trade in the process of transition. Improvement of political relations and a stable incorporation into the global economy based on international trade standards could be possible through WTO accession. As a result, representative communist countries such as China, Vietnam, and Russia are seeking to join the WTO as well as undergo internal reforms.

After joining the WTO, international trade in most transition countries has increased dramatically. China's total trade amounted to only $75 billion in 1987 when it applied for membership in GATT, but trade has increased rapidly since 2001, when WTO membership was confirmed, surpassing $4 trillion in 2016. Russia's total trade was only $70 billion in 1993, but likewise rose to $ 850 billion by the time when it was approved for entry into the WTO in 2012 (KIEP 2018a). Vietnam's trade volume was only $14 billion in 1995, but was soared to $430 billion in 2017. In particular, Vietnam was granted the status of normal trade relations (NTR) through the US-Vietnam Trade Agreement in 2001, and trade with the United States also played a large part in increasing trade volume (KIET 2007).

In terms of investment, these countries have seen a surge in capital inflows from the global market since joining the WTO.

Foreign capital inflows to these countries became a driver of economic growth, and in the process, it brought with it the creation of jobs and technology transfer. As mentioned earlier, the former communist countries have continued their economic growth to date by expanding trade and investment after joining the WTO. Such cases of achieving a stable incorporation into the free trade system while maintaining fundamental systems like China and Vietnam are suggested as good models to apply to North Korea.

There may be some holding the opinion that discussions on joining the WTO are not realistic or timely, as North Korea's accession to the WTO requires a number of prior tasks be completed first such as normalizing relations with the United States, ending support rendered to terrorist supporting countries, and lifting economic sanctions. In order to lift economic sanctions, the denuclearization of North Korea must be prioritized. This is expected to take a long time depending on the interests of North Korea and the United States. Moreover, the geopolitical peculiarities of the Korean Peninsula, where the interests of each country are sharply intertwined, make it difficult to lift economic sanctions.

Even when this is completed, accession to the WTO requires a long process of bilateral and multilateral agreements from application to full membership, and in some cases, it may take more than ten years to become a full member. In addition, considering the long-term vision of forming a joint economic zone on the Korean Peninsula, much preparation for North Korea's market opening is required. Therefore, starting the debate on North Korea's accession to the WTO at this point in time seems preferable given South Korea's preparations aimed to prepare for North Korea's openness and inter-Korean economic integration in the long run.

Thus, this chapter will assess the impact of WTO accession on North Korea through the study of foreign cases and will likewise examine the WTO accession process and the various issues that may arise in this regard, before concluding by drawing policy implications.

In this chapter, we will look at the impact of WTO accession on North Korea through past examples of transition economies that did so, and consider the tasks that must be done before joining the WTO. In addition, we will discuss North Korea's plans to join the WTO, taking into account North Korea's particularity.

This chapter is organized as follows. Section 2 explains the meaning of North Korea's accession to the WTO and the accession procedure. In Section 3, we examine the impact of WTO accession on North Korea through the example cases of prior transition economies. Section 4 explains the prerequisites for joining the WTO, and Section 5 concludes the study and offers policy implications.

2 The meaning of North Korea's WTO accession and its process

North Korea's accession to the WTO implies that it is incorporated into a free trade system. Compliance with WTO rules and obligations will be a new experience for North Korea. During the Cold War, although North Korea conducted some trade with China, the USSR, and Eastern Europe, it basically pursued an industrialization strategy based on *Juche*, North Korea's official policy of self-reliance.

This is an extreme strategy to reduce the role of international trade and seeks policies of import substitution. Since Kim Jong-un came to power, this strategy to achieve localization and import substitution throughout national production has been further emphasized (KIET 2007). It would be unfamiliar for North Korea to abandon existing policies and establish trade policies under the new system. However, considering that accession to the WTO is the final step to becoming a normal state, WTO accession is necessary and will require a lot of preparation and measures.

Only once economic sanctions against North Korea are lifted, will the process of joining the WTO be possible. In the process, North Korea would face many difficulties in decision-making. They would also have internal friction in following membership conditions and engaging in bi/multilateral negotiations. However, on the premise of solving these problems in order to join, if North Korea were indeed to be accepted into the WTO, it would mean that North Korea will have already complied with, and have experience in, following, or otherwise participating in the principles set by international agreements. The experience in negotiation and cooperation, along with the building of trust in the international community should work to ease North Korea's transition into the WTO

The first is the principle of most favored nations (MFN) and national treatment (NT) according to the principle of non-discrimination. MFN is a basic WTO principle that prevents countries from discriminating against trading partners. This means that if North Korea has given trade privileges to certain countries, those privileges should be revoked, and those trade partners should be treated the same as other WTO members.

Of course, there are exceptions depending on the contents of the FTA or the specificity of each country.[1] However, MFN is an essential principle that WTO member countries must follow. NT is a principle that imported goods and domestic products should be treated equally. In other words, as long as foreign goods are imported into North Korea, North Korea should treat them equally as though they were its own products.

This principle aims to prevent the introduction of various domestic regulations aimed to discriminate against foreign imported products, and the scope of its application is quite wide, so disputes with trading partners may arise in relation to its application. North Korea must comply with both the principle of equal opportunity in competition between exporting countries and the principle of fair competition between domestic and imported products (GwangEun 2005).

The second is the principle of negotiation, which is that market opening should be conducted only through negotiation, not unilateral demand. The purpose of the WTO was to ease trade barriers between countries and promote free trade through market opening, which requires internal reforms such as new trading laws and institutions.

Although the principle of negotiation has advantages such as easing confrontation between countries and reducing the burden of restructuring due to a gradual market opening, North Korea, which has little experience in trade negotiations with countries in the market economy, has the potential to cause significant internal conflicts in bilateral and multilateral negotiations.

The third is the principle of transparency and predictability, which means that North Korea's trade laws and systems should be disclosed and reviewed to be transparent and predictable externally so as not to be used as a trade barrier. The WTO is obliged to promulgate all trade-related policies to all member countries and to conduct formal reviews in accordance with trade review procedures. Under these principles, all Member States have their trade policies circulated to Member States and are subject to regular review.

The predictability principle is a kind of promise that each country will comply with the concession schedules submitted to the WTO, which will enable all member states to clearly see each other's mitigation of trade barriers. This means that North Korea needs policy reform similar to the international level to comply with the WTO's basic principles.

If North Korea promises to comply with the WTO's rules and wants to join, the process can be summarized as follows. To join the WTO, North Korea begins negotiations by submitting an application form and MFTR (Memorandum on Foreign Trade Regime) to the WTO director general.

At this time, the MFTR will take a kind of trade policy report explaining North Korea's trade system. Subsequently, the Working Party, composed of WTO member countries, will discuss North Korea's terms of accession through multilateral negotiations based on the previously submitted application and MFTR.

In the case of North Korea, it will take a lot of time to prepare a transparent economic and trade policy report corresponding to the general WTO member states. When the series of negotiations is completed, the concession plan is submitted to the WTO secretariat based on the result of the negotiation. After the working party report and concession proposal are submitted to the ministerial meeting, if more than two-thirds of the member states agree, the signing of North Korea's accession agreement proceeds along with the Congressional Protocol Ratification. Finally, the acceptance of North Korea is submitted to the WTO Secretariat.

North Korea will become an official member of the WTO thirty days after the receipt of all relevant documents, including the acceptance and Protocol on the Accession of North Korea. Since WTO membership is conducted through multilateral and bilateral negotiations with the affiliated working party group, there is no formal form of membership. The reason for the difference in the concessions between countries is because the economic conditions of the signatories are reflected.

Due to these characteristics, it is common for the application period to become a full member country to last more than ten years. Table 7.1 shows that China, which is considered to have been active in joining the WTO, took fifteen years from application to approval and only thirteen years for multilateral negotiations. It can be seen that Russia also has had many difficulties in the finalizing the agreement, and as a result took a total of 19 years to become an official member.

In North Korea, multilateral and bilateral negotiations that require internal openness and reform in the process of joining the WTO will be a significant burden. In the case of GATT's original member countries, it was possible to

Table 7.1 WTO accession period

	China	*Russia*	*Vietnam*	*Laos*
Application for membership	July 10, 1986	June 4, 1993	April 1, 1995	July 16, 1997
Working Party committee	18th (1996–2000)	31st (1994–2008)	14th (1998–2006)	10th (2004–2012)
Multilateral negotiations	13 years	14 years	6 years	11 years
Bilateral negotiations	5 years (37 countries)	19 years (58 countries)	5 years (26 countries)	7 years (9 countries)
Approval	December 11, 2001	August 22, 2012	January 11, 2007	February 2, 2013

Source: Adapted from KIEP 2018a

Table 7.2 WTO accession process

Steps	*Procedural Works*
Step 1	○ Submission of the request ○ Circulation of the request ○ Transmission to the General Council/Ministerial Conference ○ Working Party Establishment
Step 2	○ Accession negotiations – Multilateral negotiations/Bilateral negotiations
Step 3	○ Adoption of the Report of the Working Party ○ Transmission to the General Council/Ministerial Conference ○ the General Council/Ministerial Conference approval ○ Acceptance of the protocol of accession

Source: Adapted from Korea Ministry of Foreign Affairs

obtain qualifications without examination. However, it can be said that the entry barrier has increased because the applying member state has to go through a certain examination. For North Korea, it will be necessary to increase its understanding of bilateral and multilateral negotiations that discuss the procedures for accession and the level of concession. This procedure can be summarized in Table 7.2.

The WTO grants exceptionally long grace periods for transitions to developing countries and least developed countries in the process of joining. If North Korea is recognized as a developing or least developed country, a period of grace may be allowed for certain periods of time for obligations imposed on WTO members. It may also be subject to the general system of preferences (GSP) provided by developed countries to aid developing countries.[2] In addition, depending on the economic system, the benefit of exceptions to the Principles of the Most Favored Nations may also be granted.

3 The effect of WTO accession on North Korea

If North Korea is guaranteed the MFN status from the major trading partners such as the United States, the EU, and Japan through WTO membership, it is expected to increase in trade and investment through regulatory reform, market opening, and industrial structure reorganization that meet international standards.

Transition economies such as China, Vietnam, and Laos experienced trade and investment growth as they joined the international market after joining the WTO, which was the driving force for economic growth. In addition, institutional reforms appropriate to the international standard will be accompanied by the principle of transparency among member countries on trade policy. The impact of WTO accession on North Korea would be as follows.

3.1 Impact on trade

The MFN is based on the principle of non-discriminatory treatment when trading between WTO member countries. Under this principle, if North Korea applied a preferential price that was only to be applied between communist countries in the past then, after joining the WTO, that price should be abandoned, or should be applied to all WTO member countries.[3]

The principle of MFN, which means that goods and services in the country should be treated as equivalent to imported goods and services, exists to reduce trade barriers along with the National Treatment Principles.

Since the member countries comply with the WTO trade rules under the principles of MFN and NT, there is an opportunity for market entry to each other, which can lead to increased trade. In particular, if North Korea's economic sanctions are lifted and it joins the global economic system, it can be expected to experience increased trade through advanced relations with the United States.

If the United States treats North Korea as a normal trade relationship (NTR) and gives North Korean products the benefits of the GSP applied to developing countries instead of the high rate column two-tariff rate, it can likewise be expected to increase trade with the United States. The same prediction can be made when the GSP is applied to the EU relations.[4]

This prediction can also be confirmed in the following research results of Anh Thi Le (2017) who analyzed the change in trade volume based on the gravity model before and after Vietnam joined the WTO. As a result of the analysis, after Vietnam joined the WTO, total trade volume increased significantly, and exports have increased by 215 percent over the past eight years since 2007.

Wakasugi and Zhang (2016) analyzed the impact of WTO accession on corporate exports using Firm-level data for electrical machinery and communication equipment sectors. As a result of the analysis, the WTO accession promoted corporate productivity and the increased productivity lead to enhance its export.

The same result was also obtained in the study of the whole of the WTO member states, not just in specific countries. Subramanian and Wei (2007) concluded that using the gravity model, WTO/GATT membership increased global trade by 120 percent. Along with the results of these studies, the key statistical indicators make it clearer to understand the changes in trade volume after joining the WTO.

Figure 7.1 shows the change in trade volume before and after WTO member states (0 (t = 0) indicates the year of WTO membership). The figure shows that after joining the WTO, the trade volume increased sharply and remained at a higher level for a considerable period than before.

China, Cambodia, and Vietnam, which joined the WTO while still having socialist economic systems like present day North Korea, also show that trade volume has increased since joining the WTO. Figure 7.2 shows the trade volume of three countries. 0(t=0) is the WTO accession year 0 is the time of joining the WTO, indicating 2001 in China, and 2004 and 2007 in Cambodia and Vietnam, respectively.

It can be seen that the trade volume has increased since joining the WTO in all three countries, and it has been steadily higher than before joining for all until the 10th period after WTO accession. Thus, if North Korea becomes a WTO member by complying with international trade rules and ensuring transparency in its own policies, trade volume is expected to increase as well.

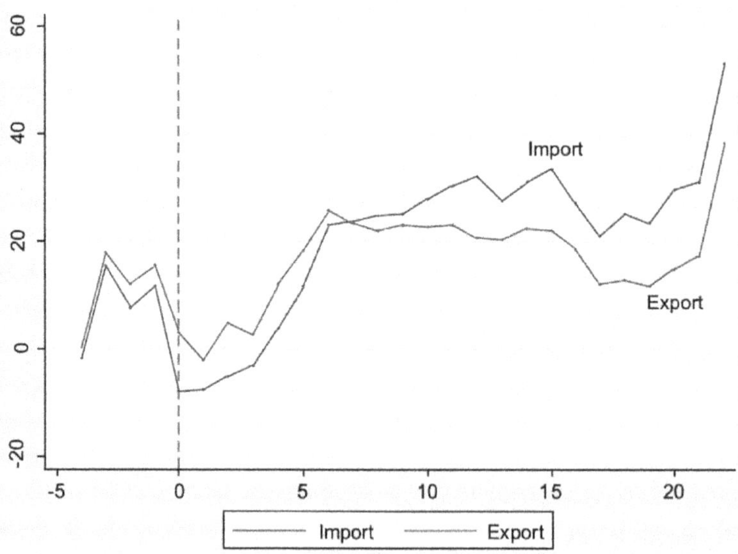

Figure 7.1 Trade in WTO member countries

Source: Adapted from WTO

Note: 1) This data is the error term that country and time specific effect are removed; 2) 0 is WTO accession year and the number of countries is 157

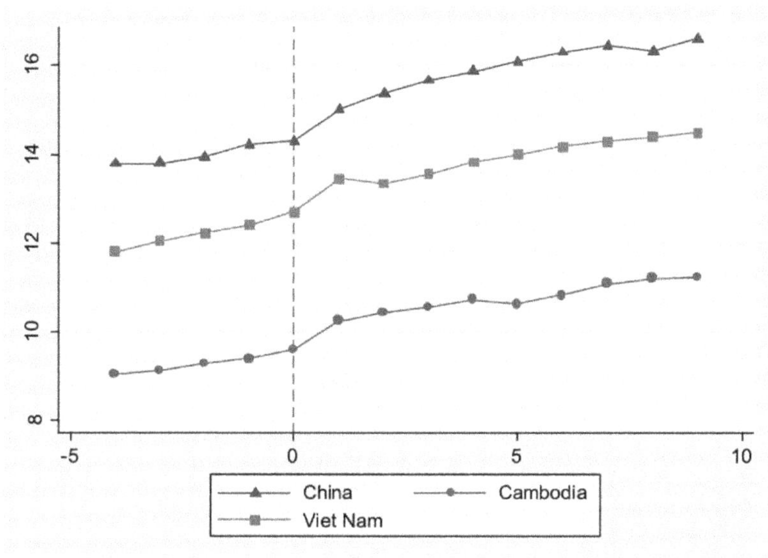

Figure 7.2 Change in trade after WTO accession (China, Cambodia, Vietnam)

Source: Adapted from WTO

Note: Trade volume is a logarithmic value

3.2 Impact on FDI

Joining the WTO not only expands trade, but also lowers investment barriers between member countries. In the least developed countries, e.g. North Korea, foreign investment inflow is an essential factor for economic growth, so the biggest benefit of joining the WTO for North Korea will be the expansion of investment through incorporation into the world market. In the economic growth of developing countries, it is desirable to attract foreign investment rather than aid in the long term, so it is necessary to pay attention to the investment aspect of the WTO membership effect.[5]

Hong (2008) analyzed China's FDI by province for eleven years after joining the WTO. As a result of the analysis, the amount of foreign investment inflow increased significantly after joining the WTO, and it was found that the WTO accession was an important factor for foreign multinational companies to select investment regions.

Norbäck, Urban, and Westerberg (2007) analyzed the effect of WTO accession on FDI, and concluded that joining the WTO increased exports of foreign subsidiaries. Statistical data can confirm this fact. Figure 7.3 shows the changes in FDI among member countries after joining the WTO. In the figure, 0 (t = 0) means the year of entry into the WTO. Immediately after joining, the size of FDI increased

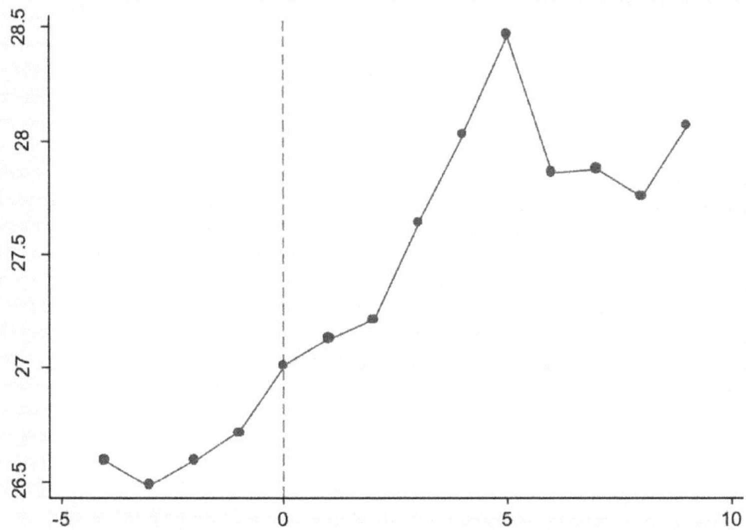

Figure 7.3 FDI in WTO member countries

Source: Adapted from WTO

Note: 1) This data is the error term that country specific and time effect are excluded; 2) 0 is WTO accession year and the number of countries is 141

rapidly, and since then, even with repeated fluctuations, the level of FDI remained at a much higher level than before the accession.

Looking at the cases of China, Cambodia, and Vietnam, which are the representative transition economies of Asian countries, they show that the trend is the same. Figure 7.4 shows the amount of FDI in China, Cambodia, and Vietnam since joining the WTO. It can be seen that the FDI has increased since the accession. More detailed analysis is required, but based on related research and actual data, it can be expected that WTO membership will have a direct relationship with investment expansion.

3.3 North Korea's system reform

The WTO is a liberal trading system that seeks to improve the welfare of each country by reducing interference and restrictions on trade (Qin 2007). The WTO is expanding its focus not only on goods and services, but also on investment and intellectual property, and it requires member countries to comply with the WTO's commitments and obligations. Commitments to increase market access are different in each Member State and regular renegotiation is required.

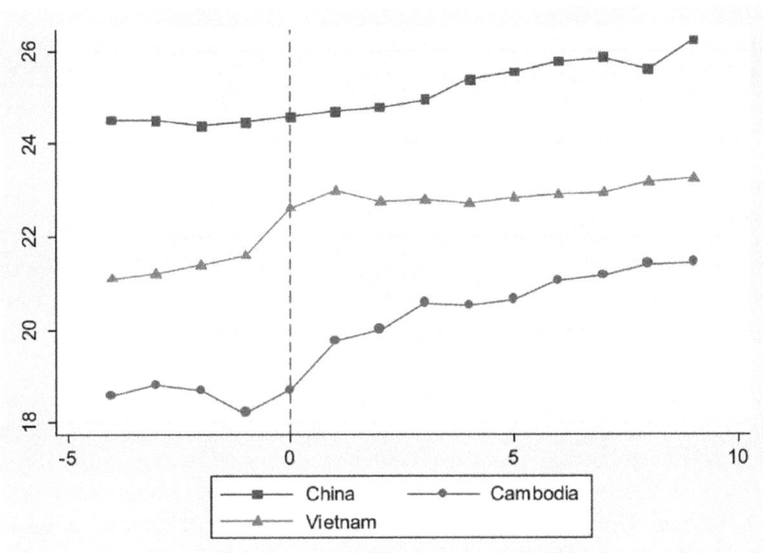

Figure 7.4 Change of FDI post-WTO accession (China, Cambodia, Vietnam)

Source: Adapted from WTO

Note: FDI is a logarithmic value

However, the obligations required by the WTO cannot be easily changed and include not only the trade system, but also the policies and institutions of member countries on the scope of its regulation.

Therefore, when North Korea joins the WTO, it is necessary to develop a system suitable for the international level and establish a legislation corresponding to the WTO agreement. Through this, North Korea needs a high level of internal reform and external openness. If North Korea joins the WTO and reforms the system, it can be expected to see increased efficiency in its economic sector (KIEP 2018a).

China, which has opened the market to a higher level than the WTO requires (WTO-Plus), has also experienced significant changes in laws and institutions. For example, except for cigarettes, medicines, and public companies, a system was established wherein the prices of most goods and services are determined in the market, and foreign companies' participation in imports and exports was recognized. In addition, the Foreign Trade Act was revised by reducing the existing governmental role of directly controlling overall trade.[6]

North Korea adhered to the principle of a national monopoly in trade, but now seems to be improving in a more market-oriented direction where many trade companies are in charge of trade.[7] Contrary to this, North Korea is also pursuing policies to enforce the use of domestic products (2015.1), so policies and institutions that are commonly used in the international trade environment are needed.

In order to join the WTO, both multilateral and bilateral negotiations have to be carried out, so North Korea can induce consideration of its internal policies on international trade norms and create an appropriate institutional environment.

4 North Korea's essential prerequisite for WTO accession and policy implications

The meaning and procedure of North Korea's accession to the WTO and its effects have so far been discussed. In order to join the WTO, North Korea must first be recognized by the international community as a normal state and improve foreign relations.

Specifically, North Korea's incorporation into the world economy must be preceded by the lifting of economic sanctions and the removal of itself from the list of terrorist supporting countries. Under sanctions, it is impossible for North Korea to be a WTO member and carry forward economic cooperation between the two Koreas. Only through the actual completion of denuclearization of the Korean Peninsula and the lifting of economic sanctions, would it be possible to be incorporated into the international market as a normal state and to take various measures to promote growth.

Since no conclusion has been drawn on the lifting of economic sanctions at the second US-North Korea summit, it is not advisable to make hasty predictions about North Korea's future. However, as becoming a member of the WTO requires bilateral and multilateral negotiations, it often takes more than ten years, and various discussions are needed to establish North Korea's strategy for the accession. Therefore, at this point, it is necessary to pay attention to the improvement of foreign relations with North Korea, the lifting of economic sanctions, and the internal reform of the system to implement international trade norms. As mentioned earlier, considering the peculiarity of North Korea's regime, much preparation is required to join the WTO. The details of what will be required shall be discussed in what follows.

First, it is necessary to promote inter-Korean economic cooperation in order to learn consistent international trade norms. The objective of the WTO is to ensure free international trade activities by reducing the trade barriers imposed by the governments of each member country and by enacting and implementing unified norms that stipulate them (Lee 2003). Member States must comply with the WTO's international trade rules and implement the concessions submitted by each country.

In addition, any problems arising in the implementation process should be resolved only by the WTO's judicial mechanism, not by unilateral action of the Member States.

The consistent promises between these countries are what North Korea lacks in experience. Considering that it takes a long time to join the WTO, it is necessary to increase inter-Korean exchange and cooperation and raise the level of economic cooperation, thereby cultivating practical skills for international trade and helping North Korea in learning about consistent policy formulation.

In fact, North Korea enacted the "Geumgangsan Tourism District Act" in 2002, the entire revision of the "Raseon Economic and Trade Zone Act" in 2013, and the "Foreign Investment Enterprise Work Act" in 2015 in the course of promoting economic cooperation projects with South Korea and China. North Korea, then, has some experience in establishing a system different from that of the past through the improvement of these laws and systems.

Just as the external factors of economic cooperation has led to changes in laws and institutions, North Korea has a need to deepen economic cooperation with South Korea to bring about gradual changes (KIEP 2018a).

In the case of China, the gradual learning in terms of the understanding of international trade norms, market openness, and the importance of all preliminary preparations can be seen. In 1985, China decided to apply for membership, and it wasn't until 1993 that the negotiations began. China took a total of 16 years to become a full member. This is known to be due to internal disputes with the Chinese authorities' understanding of norms and the concession plans of the goods and services market, in addition to bilateral and multilateral negotiations to join the WTO.[8]

Trade between the two Koreas has been made tariff-free, and has unique characteristics that are different from general international trade, such as policy support directly from the Korean government to North Korean-invested companies (KNDA 2018). With such favorable trade conditions, there would normally be a possibility of violating regulations in the WTO agreement, but it is accepted by the international community considering North Korea's political specificity and trade volume. Based on this special relationship, it is necessary to provide opportunities for North Korean authorities to understand and learn about international trade norms.

Second, we need to devise a strategy to recognize the two Koreas' trade as the exception of the MFN under the WTO system. To this end, it is necessary to recognize the uniqueness of inter-Korean economic cooperation in the international community and to review the provisions of the WTO law.

Some of the possible ways in which South-North Korean economic cooperation can be recognized as an exception to the WTO system may be through the use of the WTO waiver,[9] the WTO Accession Clause (Article XII),[10] and the Enabling Clause.[11] The WTO's waiver provision is a legal mechanism that exempts an institutional obligation in the event that the obligation cannot be fulfilled for any particular reason (Dukgeun and Park 2014). It could be argued that, alongside the unique relationship already accepted to exist between the two Koreas, that South Korea is also helping a developing country to grow – a possible avenue to garner exemptions from obligations within the rules of the WTO accession clause.

When considering the accession clause, South Korea's WTO protocol needs to be revised and North Korea must specify its special relationship with South Korea when it joins the WTO. In the case of using the enabling clause, there is the problem that South Korea must prove that trade between the two Koreas must be done to support the economic development of North Korea.

In reality, it is more likely that the inter-Korean relationship can be recognized as an internal transaction through the waiver clause. Looking at past trade between East and West Germany, one sees that they were not exempted from the aforementioned waiver clause, however, that trade relationship was an example of the GATT/WTO's recognition of political specificity, and there are great implications in that precedent for inter-Korean relations. However, in order to utilize the various legal mechanisms of the WTO, including the waiver, the specificity of inter-Korean relations must be recognized in advance by the international community, which takes a long time and requires inter-Korean patience.

Third is that the policy-making process needs to be reshuffled in a direction that is gradually transparent and predictable. The WTO attaches great importance to the transparency and predictability of trade policy. By securing the transparency of the policies of a member state, it is possible to determine whether trading partners are using trade barriers and to clearly predict the degree of market opening based on the concessions.

The transparency of trade policy ensures that member countries can judge whether trading partners have trade barriers and can clearly predict the degree of market openness based on concessions. To this end, the WTO requires that trade policies be reviewed every two to six years, depending on national characteristics. Meanwhile, because the concession schedule, which can be called a promise between member countries, has a legal effect that forms part of the WTO agreement, it can further increase predictability.

In the case of North Korea, there is no experience under control through external management and supervision in its policies and measures, and it may have a desire to reject such a foreign concept. Therefore, it is necessary for North Korean authorities to improve their awareness of trade norms and to review trade systems that meet international standards.

Fourth, the price and financial system needs to be reviewed. Since the WTO aims to expand free trade around the world, North Korea needs to check its price structure to prepare for the WTO system. Since the prices of planned economy countries are not determined by the market, it is possible that the prices of the raw materials, energy sector, and the prices of industrial goods and consumer goods are determined by policy. It is necessary to review this price structure, and North Korea will have to enact and revise customs procedures, trade in services, laws and systems related to intellectual property rights, exchange rates and financial systems to meet international standards.

So far, we have discussed what North Korea needs to prepare for joining the WTO. Of course, there are other issues to consider when joining the WTO, but this chapter only discusses the items to be prepared for. North Korea's actual preparations depend on North Korea's will and international political situation. Since North Korea's incorporation into the international community is to be prepared gradually, it will be meaningful to discuss it closely in a broad sense.

5 Conclusion

This article comprehensively looked at the meaning and procedures of North Korea's accession to the WTO. It also examined the probable effect of WTO accession on the North Korean economy following its entry into the WTO.

Currently, North Korea is under several trade restrictions by the international community as well as facing economic sanctions. If North Korea agrees to the international community's peaceful resolution to its nuclear program, North Korea would be recognized as normal state, and thereby they would be allowed to try to incorporate into the world economy.

WTO membership can be seen as the final step in becoming a normal country. What needs to be considered here is that North Korea's transition is not achieved through WTO membership, but that the final stage of North Korea's transition is to join the WTO. Therefore, a lot of preparation and effort must be made to join the WTO. In the past, North Korean allies, such as China and Vietnam, saw accession times of more than 10 years from application to completion. This fact implies that there are internal and external difficulties in the transition process.

It is expected that North Korea will face the same difficulties that faced its former allies. This study examined several issues that could be discussed in this regard and can be summarized as follows. Since North Korea's stable transfer to the free trade system will be completed by joining the WTO, it needs to be promoted from a long-term perspective. By joining the WTO, North Korea will see increased revenue in trade and investment, which will be a driving force for economic growth, but in the process of preparing the reform, it will need to be ready to prepare laws and institutions suitable for international standards. The reform of North Korea's system will be costly, so preparatory work must be done.

To this end, North Korea needs to learn the standard rule of international trade through inter-Korean economic cooperation, and further accumulate trade experience through practice in regional trade agreements. In addition, it is necessary to make the international community more aware on the peculiarities of inter-Korean economic cooperation from now on in order to be recognized later on as a legitimate exception of MFN.

It will also be necessary to gradually reorganize North Korea's policy-making process to be transparent and predictable, and the discussion on reform of the price and financial system that has been carried out in the planned economic system should begin as soon as possible.

These discussions are aimed at minimizing the cost of North Korea's eventual involvement in the international community. This study focuses on discussing the problems and issues related to joining the WTO and providing information for discovering new issues.

There is of course a limitation that any rigorous analysis based on quantitative analysis of data concerning North Korea, due to the secretive nature of that state, is lacking, and is consequently in need of more data for detailed considerations regarding North Korea's trade and industrial system.

Thus, future, technical follow-up studies including quantitative analyses are needed along with studies concerning legal issues based on WTO rules. Additional detailed analyses of North Korea's industrial policy and trade system, as well as specific strategies for incorporation into the global economic system through the WTO accession, should also be sought.

Notes

1 GATT Article XXIV for trade between India and Pakis, WTO Article XII for inter-Germany trade.
2 The WTO does not provide criteria for status in developing countries. Therefore, the country wishing to join the WTO can declare whether it is a developing or developed country at its option. However, since the status of the least developed country is designated by the WTO according to the UN's socio-economic index, it can be said more clearly that a standard is proposed rather than the status of the developing country.
3 The WTO recognizes exceptions to rational discrimination, such as the status of member countries and FTAs.
4 According to the European Commission (2002), the EU states that it is possible to impose general preferential tariffs on North Korea if practical steps are taken to liberalize trade and investors. Therefore, such negotiations are possible through bilateral negotiations in North Korea's accession to the WTO.
5 Since FDI is accompanied by technology transfer and job creation, it is essential to secure essential elements for long-term economic growth rather than aid.
6 According to KIEP (2018b), Laos modernized its law system through WTO accession, and Russia also promoted institutional reform in the economic field with its entry into the WTO.
7 Article 36 of the "Socialist Constitution" of North Korea, revised in 1992, stated the principle of national monopoly on trade. However, in 2012, in the revised constitution, the power of the state was somewhat reduced as many trading companies were in charge of trade.
8 *Ibid.*, 4.
9 GATT 1947: Article XXV Joint Action by the Contracting Parties.
10 Marrakesh Agreement establishing the World Trade Organization Article XII Accession
11 GATT, Decision of 28 November 1979 (L/4903) (Differential and More Favourable Treatment, Reciprocity and Fuller Participation of Developing Countries).

References

Ahn, Duk Geun, and Jeong Joon James Park. 2014. "A Study on Internal Trade Between South/North Korea in the WTO System and Gaesung Industrial Complex." *Journal of International Area Studies* 3 (4): 139–170.

Korea Institute for International Economic Policy (KIEP). 2018a. "Transition Economies' Experience of WTO Accession and Its Implication for DPRK." *KIEP Report* 18 (2).

Korea Institute for International Economic Policy (KIEP). 2018b. "Study on North Korea's Trade System: Implications for the CEPA Between South and North Korea." *KIEP Policy Analysis* 18 (14).

European Commission. 2002. "The EC—Democratic People's Republic of Korea." *European Commission Country Strategy Paper* 2001–2004.

Hong, Jun Jie. 2008. "WTO Accession and Foreign Direct Investment in China." *Journal of Chinese Economic and Foreign Trade Studies* 1 (2): 136–147.

Korea Institute for Industrial Economics and Trade (KIET). 2007. "North Korea's Plan to Normalize Foreign Trade with a focus on Vietnam." *Issue Paper* 222.

Korea National Diplomatic Academy (KNDA). 2018. "Trade and Diplomacy Strategy for Institutional Stabilization of Inter-Korean Economic Cooperation." *IFANS* 18.

Le Anh Thi. 2017. "Effects of WTO Accession on Vietnam's Trade: The Gravity Model Approach." Master's thesis, University of Oslo.

Lee, Gwang Eun. 2005. "The Basic Principles of WTO." *Journal of International Area Studies* 1 (1): 171–200.

Lee, Hyo Young. 2003. "China's Accession to the WTO: Implications and Prospects for the Future Reform of Her Economic System." *Business Management Review* 36 (1): 231–248.

Norbäck, Pehr-Johan, Dieter Urban, and Stefan Westerberg. 2007. "Gravity Estimation for Multinational Enterprises: An Application to the GATT/WTO Puzzle." *Working Paper*.

Qin, Julia Ya. 2007. "The Impact of WTO Accession on China's Legal System: Trade, Investment and Beyond." *Wayne State University Law School Legal Research Paper Series* 7 (15): 1–30.

Subramanian, Arvind, and Shang-Jin Wei. 2007. "The WTO Promotes Trade, Strongly but Unevenly." *Journal of International Economics* 72: 151–175.

Wakasugi, Ryuhei, and Hong Yong Zhang. 2016. "Impacts of the WTO Accession on Chinese Exports." *Journal of Chinese Economic and Business Studies* 14 (4): 347–364.

Part II

Sectoral approach and strategy

8 Analysis of North Korea's agricultural revolution after economic crisis

Young-hoon Kim and Hyo Chan Oh

1 Introduction

As the global socialist economy was being dismantled in the late 1980s, North Korea's economy entered into a serious recession. Agricultural production decreased significantly, and food supplies gradually declined. In the mid-1990s, after Kim Il-sung's death, North Korea's cereal production hit a record low due to natural disasters. Since then, food shortages have become a chronic phenomenon and the country has had to get assistance continuously from the international community.

When Kim Jong-il came into power, the revival and development of the agricultural sector became a paramount objective for North Korea's economy. New agricultural policies were introduced and several attempts for the reformation of the agricultural sector had been proposed to promote these policies. Nevertheless, agricultural production levels were disappointing; agricultural productivity did not improve significantly, and even after Kim Jong-il's death, food shortages continued to prevail well into Kim Jong-un's era. This suggests that reforms were sluggish in the agricultural production sector. If agricultural reform, which aimed at strengthening the incentives to induce motivations for production, had been successful, North Korea's agricultural production would not have been stalled for so long.

This chapter aims to summarize and thoroughly analyze the major reformation measures that influenced North Korea's agricultural sector. The analysis will be performed in the following three stages: first, the major contents of the reformation measures will be compiled and summarized by referring to relative documents and statutes; second, the expected impact of the reform measures will be logically projected with consideration of North Korea's economic and agricultural situation; third, the effectiveness of each of the reformation measures will be analyzed to the greatest possible extent. The end goal of this study is to determine by careful analysis, whether the expectations of agricultural production and subsequent policy changes were realized.

2 Agricultural reformation in Kim Jong-il's era

2.1 The legacy of Kim Il-sung and the basis for new agricultural conditions

After Kim Il-sung's death in 1994, the legacy inherited by Kim Jong-il, the Chairman of the National Defense Commission, was a prolonged economic recession and a severe food shortage. North Korea not only failed to produce sufficient food supplies, a paramount goal for their economic policy from the early stage of their socialist revolution but also experienced a long-term economic downturn that culminated with a decrease in agricultural production at the end of Kim Il-sung's reign. In 1995, disastrous flooding caused huge amounts of damage, which plummeted food production to 3.45 million tons. This was a period when the impacts of long-term economic recession compounded, with a resulting agricultural production drop to a level where it was unable to recover to even that of 1980s.

North Korea's agricultural policy after the death of Kim Il-sung focused on overcoming this chronic agricultural recession and the insurmountable food shortage at hand. Since the mid-1990s, North Korea began to promote new agricultural policies, such as the enhancement of food production, the revival and development of the livestock industry, and the restoration and repair of the basis for agricultural production. Unlike in the previous approaches, these agricultural policies set realistic targets and included practical initiatives.

To ensure that the new agricultural policies proceeded smoothly, favorable conditions for the agricultural sector, external and internal, had to be created. The most important factors among them were institutional improvement (reformation measures), and capital procurement (the opening measures to attract foreign capital). North Korea conducted various approaches to achieve these conditions. When North Korea's agricultural industry is assessed overtime, its agriculture promotion policy may be understood as outlined in Figure 8.1.

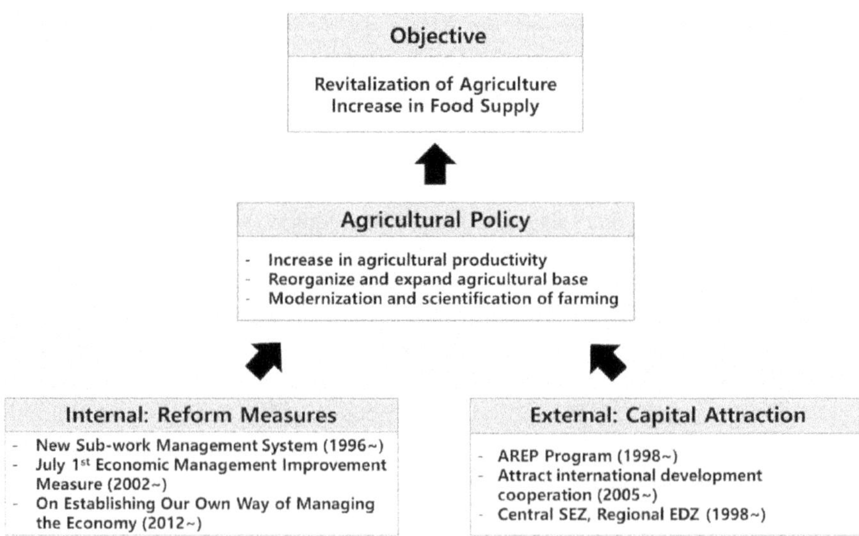

Figure 8.1 Major agricultural objectives and strategies in the Kim Jong-il era

Source: Kim Y. H. 2012

2.2 Agriculture reformation measures of the 1990s

2.2.1 Improving the distribution of the new sub-work team management (NSTM) system

In 1996, when the food shortage reached its most critical point, North Korea introduced the new sub-work team management (NSTM) system for cooperative farms. Significant features of the NSTM system may be summarized as three points. First, the size of a "sub-work" team has been reduced to increase the bond between the team members. A team under the former system comprised of ten to twenty-five members, would be reduced under the new system to a size of five to ten members. Second, the production target of each sub-work team was diminished to increase each team members' opportunity for receiving additional allocations. Third, authority to dispose of any excess production was given to the sub-work team, perhaps the most reformative feature of the policy (see Table 8.1).

With the presence of a farmer's market, farmers' incomes can increase significantly if the government does not purchase the excess production but gives it out as actual goods to the farmers, allowing them to dispose of these materials freely. This is explained in Table 8.2. In the late 1990s, the official price of rice hit a record low at 0.08 KRW/kg. At the same time, the market price of rice at a farmer's market was 47 KRW/kg – 587 times higher than the official price. Price disparity of corn crops was also huge; during the same period, the official price of corn crops was 0.03 KRW/kg, however, the farmer's market price of the corn crops was 27 KRW/kg, 900 times higher than the official price (see Table 8.2). Due to this large price discrepancy between the state market prices and the open market prices, it can be assumed that the conditions for higher income are met when the cooperative farms receive excessive production of crops in kind.

Table 8.1 Comparison of the changes of sub-work team management system (1966/1996)

	Sub-work Team Management System (1966–1995)	*New Sub-work Team Management System (1996)*
Composition	• 10–25 members • Place members in consideration of their abilities, needs, and age	• 5–10 members • Composed of family and relatives
Production Objective	• Planned amount suggested for the sub-work teams according to the production objectives of the country in corresponding year	• Set as the average harvested amount of the average of the previous three years and the average of the previous ten years.
Disposal of Agricultural Products	• Government purchase of over production	• Free disposal of over production

Source: Kim and Ji 2006

Table 8.2 Comparison between rice and corn prices in North Korea (KRW/kg)

	Settlement Distribution Price of the Cooperative Farms	*Official Price*	*Retail Price in the Farmers' Market*		
			1998	*1999*	*2000*
Rice	0.50	0.08	77	64	47
Corn	0.45	0.03	40	33	27

Source: Adapted from Ministry of Unification 2000; Kim and Ji 2006

2.2.2 Assessment of the NSTM system

Therefore, has the establishment of the new sub-work team management system contributed in increasing agricultural production and improving farmers' income? Contrary to expectations, the new sub-work team system failed to induce the expected motivational goals in North Korea's agricultural sector in the late 1990s. Since 1997, there has been no report of this new system being implemented on the national level. Furthermore, agricultural production did not recover for three to four years after the introduction of the NSTM system.

If the sub-work team of cooperative farm produces more than the originally planned target, team members receive additional shares that correspond to that of the excess production; sub-work team members receive higher income by selling the additional shares of excess production at a nearby farmer's market; sub-work teams finally expand their investment independently and increase future agricultural production. Then, if this all works as planned, it may be concluded that a motivational effect of the NSTM system should have been realized. However, the increase in agricultural production after the introduction of NSTM system was not evident. On the contrary, North Korea's agricultural production was affected much more immensely by the introduction of agricultural materials. This means that the impact of the introduction of the NSTM system was minimal in North Korea's agriculture.

2.2.3 Economic reform measures in the 2000s: 7.1 economic management improvement measures

2.2.3.1 REALIZATION AND DECENTRALIZATION OF PRICES, WAGES, AND EXCHANGE RATES

In July 2002, North Korea enforced "Economic Management Improvement Measures" for the realization of the prices of its major goods and services. North Korea described the measures as a way to strengthen its socialist economic system, however, considering the series of economic measures included line items such as the creation of the Sinuiju Special Administrative Region, the establishment of the trust banks,[1] it is reasonable to interpret the "7.1 Measure" as more than just a newly proposed economic improvement measure.

Table 8.3 Major price and wage increases described in 7.1 Measure

Division	*Product/Class*	*Unit*	*Price/Wage*		
			Before Adjustment (A)	*After Adjustment (B)*	*Rate of Increase (B/A)*
Price	Rice	1kg	0.08 KRW	44 KRW	550 times
	Corn	1kg	0.07	33	471
	Diesel	1kl	1	38	38
	Electricity	1kWh	0.035	2.1	60
	Tram fare	1 time	0.1	1	10
	Subway fare	1 Section	0.1	1	10
	Sleeping car fare	Pyeongsong-Namyang	50	3,000	60
	Amusement park entrance fee	Songdo Beach	3	50	17
	House rent	Pyeongyang standard	0.03% of income	2 KRW per month per $1m^2$	(15–20)
Wage	Production worker	KRW/month	110	2,000	18
	Mine worker	KRW/month	–	6,000	–

Source: Kim and Ji 2006

The most evident innovation in the "7.1 Measure" was the realization of unified prices, wages, and exchange rates. Previously, the government of North Korea sold rice for 0.08 KRW per kilogram, but the rice price was set to 43–45 KRW after the measure, which is close to that of the farmer's market. The price of corn rose sharply from 0.07 KRW to 33 KRW. Subway fares, bus fares, and the prices of household goods also increased significantly. Housing rents for a single house that were previously 5 to 10 KRW per month increased to 2 KRW per month for each $1m^2$ area of the house.

At the same time, wages increased greatly. The monthly salaries of soldiers and public officials increased fourteen to seventeen times, while laborers' salaries increased ten to twenty times. Production workers' salaries were raised from 110 KRW to 2,000 KRW, while those of mine workers were raised to 6,000 KRW. Along with inflation, new 1,000 won bills were issued. Exchange rates were adjusted to a similar level to that of Rajin-Sonbong region, increasing from 2.15 KRW per dollar before the measure to 150 KRW after the measure. In addition, the 'money sheet exchanged with foreign currency (convertible notes)' was abolished.

After the 7.1 Measure, the official prices of all products were raised to the level of market prices. This is directly related to the reduction of the rationing system. When 7.1 Measure was announced, some argued that the rationing of daily necessities had been abolished. However, it is believed that the rationing system was not fully terminated at that time since ration tickets were still issued.[2]

The realization of the newly set prices and wages was the most evident reformation in the 7.1 Measure, but studies show that it has brought about various other transformations (Kwon 2010). It is believed that the government controlled only the strategic indicators and also the companies that were led by the so-called "planning by the companies," which expanded the decentralization to their management as well. This measure also introduced performance-based differential rate of payments. When most of the goods were distributed through the state-owned distribution network, the 7.1 Measure, allowed the establishment of permanent markets and market distribution. The expansion of market distribution had side effects such as dualization of price structures between the official and market prices, which led companies to concentrate on land acquisition based on price differences.[3]

2.2.3.2 EVALUATION OF THE 7.1 ECONOMIC MANAGEMENT IMPROVEMENT MEASURE

The essence of the 7.1 Measure is price reform and the expansion of decentralization policies. The expected impact of these measures on North Korea's agricultural sector was increasing agricultural production. The expectation was, then, that the effect of these price adjustments and increases would affect the sub-work teams and farmers of each farm through a decentralized system (motivational system through differential rates of payments) and finally increase agricultural production.

To determine the feasibility of increasing agricultural production by implementing the 7.1 Measure, two-way analysis seems necessary. First, the relative scope of the purchasing price received by the farms should be analyzed. If the prices for agricultural goods – set by the government – increase faster than labor wage rates or other commodities' prices, then agricultural production is likely to increase.

Second, whether real motivational effects can be realized through a performance-based differential rate of payment policy should be analyzed. When differential distributions can be realized according to the performance of each farm worker, agricultural production is likely to increase.

Using rice as an example, the rate of increase for government purchasing price following the 7.1 Measure was higher than that of both wages and daily necessities. However, when it was compared to the rate of increase in the price of the raw materials (electricity, energy)[4] purchased by the farms, it was found to be at a similar level (see Table 8.4). If the increasing rate of the product price does not exceed the rate of price increase for the factors of production necessary to create said product, additional investments for the factors of production will not increase, and overall production is not likely to be enhanced unless there is a change in other factors, such as a technological innovation. The net effect of the price increase on agricultural production, therefore, was neutral.

However, if the relative value of grains distributed by the farm members increases, a partial motivational effect can be expected when the distribution exceeds the requirement for one's self-consumption. This is related to whether systematic improvements have been successfully realized. As it can be seen in the case of the NSTM system in 1996, it was incorrect to expect any more than a partial success because the motivation inducement system was not successfully established.

Opinions vary in interpreting the intentions behind North Korea's intentions for their economic measures in 2002, but there is agreement in that there were no significant differences in the prospects for its outcome. Price increases and the temporary strengthening of motivation may contribute to the enhancement of productivity in short-term, however, the mid-to long-term prospects were dismal unless external capital was supplied. Furthermore, the reformation measure itself contained several problems, which can be summarized as follows:

First, although the wages increased only 10 to 20 times, the most important food price increased by about 500 times. The purchasing power then, was still low. This is a clear sign that the state has given up its policy stance of taking responsibility for the basic living requirements of its people.

Second, some pointed out that the effectiveness of readjusting the exchange rate to a realistic level was invalid. Since 1999, North Korea ceased the use of 'money sheet exchanged with foreign currency (convertible notes)', while foreigners have used foreign currency directly at foreign shops and hotels. Therefore, any measure to readjust the exchange rate to a more realistic level was merely a formal acknowledgement of this phenomenon. Also, the North Korean Won was expected to depreciate significantly as the shortage of all supplies was not resolved. Under such circumstances, the possibility of the influx of foreign currency reserves held by the residents compared to the market seems very low.[5]

Third, since the prospects of an improvement of the supply sector were dim, the effect of the Measure was in question. For instance, the supply of rice must be ample enough to stabilize the price of rice at 44 KRW per kilogram. This is because when the supply of rice remains short of the required amount, new black market-based prices arise.

Table 8.4 Comparison of 7.1 Measure's rate of price increase

Division	*Unit*	*Before Adjustment (A)*	*After Adjustment (B)*	*Rate of Increase (B/A)*
Purchasing price of rice	KRW/kg	0.8	40	50 times
Wage (Production Worker)	KRW/month	110	2,000	18 times
Daily necessities & fares		–	–	10–40 times
Price of raw materials				
– Diesel	KRW/kl	1	38	38 times
– Electricity	KRW/kWh	0.035	2.1	60 times

Source: Chosun Sinbo 2002, Kim and Ji 2006

Fourth, the 7.1 Measure was a strategy to hold fast to the principles of socialism and to obtain political practicality. In this view, the economic measure was considered a dualistic strategy to both absorb the large informal open market sector into the official command market sector while simultaneously transferring the government's role of procuring and supplying goods to businesses and farms.

3 Reformation and opening in the Kim Jong-un era

3.1 Reformation in the agricultural production sector

After the inauguration of the Kim Jong-un regime, there were notable reformation measures in North Korea's economic and agricultural sectors in 2012. This is known as the June 28th Policy, which can be summarized as seen in Box 8.1.

The contents of the Measure appear to be reformative, however, not to the degree that this could be judged as a genuine reform for the following reasons. First, the government's supplying of agricultural materials and the government's purchasing of agricultural products were both already de facto socialist agricultural management policies pursued by North Korea. Thus, "guarantee of the initial cost of production by the state" constitutes a reaffirmation of the function that the socialist government already must perform. Second, the effectiveness of the declaration was also very low. In the middle of deepening inflation, providing agricultural materials as currency rather than providing actual food or necessary materials, may be seen as an avoidance of the responsibility to procure and supply these goods by the state. Third, contents about liberalizing the disposal of excess from one's allocated share after production quotas are met is only a measure that reaffirms what was already happening in the market.

Box 8.1 Major aspects of North Korea's reformation in the agricultural production sector, 2012

1. The state guarantees initial cost for the production by cooperative farms and factories
2. The state and the cooperative farms (factories) distribute agricultural products at certain rate
3. Set prices equal the market prices
4. Privately owned shares may be disposed of freely
5. Diminish the size of sub-work teams in cooperative farms to 4–6 members

Source: Author created

The reduction in the size of sub-work teams was the most reformative aspect of this measure. This is meaningful in terms of changing the management structure of the agricultural sector from collective management to individual management. While motions for the reduction of the size of sub-work teams was included in previous measures (1996 and 2002), implementation in all cooperative farms in North Korea or whether these teams administered their activities independently had not been previously confirmed. The reform measures of 2012 neither contained practical reformation contents, nor helped North Korea's agricultural productivity significantly increase.

In 2014, North Korea took reformative measures that went a step further in their agricultural production sector (Kim Jong-un's 5.30 Laborious Work)[6]. The key points of this measure are summarized in Box 8.2 (Hyundai Research Institute 2014).

The major contents of the measures represented in the reform measures in North Korea's agricultural production sector in 2014 in Box 8.2 may be regarded as reformative enough. It is particularly reformative that the Measure supported the allocation of 3,300m^2 of farmland for each member citizen of the agricultural labor force for cultivation. This is comparable to the "Production Responsibility System" reforms that have rapidly propelled the Chinese agricultural sector since their introduction in 1978. The reformation of China's Production Responsibility System, which began in 1978 known as "Bao chan dao hu (包産到戶)," allocated responsible farmlands to the farms provided additional incentives to the farmers for products exceeding the government's purchasing target. This incentive allocation system developed into the form of 'Bao gan dao hu (包幹到戶)', which gave farmers all the products that exceeded the government's purchasing target allowing their free disposal by each farm house. China's 'Bao gan dao hu' production responsibility system has increased their agricultural production greatly. The fact that the agricultural production of China has increased by 48.2 percent in the 1980–1985, after the introduction of production responsibility system, proves it (see Table 8.5).

Box 8.2 Major aspects of the reform measures in North Korea's agricultural production sector in 2014

1 Introduce self-managing system at cooperative farms and factories in DPR Korea, abolish sub-work teams in cooperative farms, and adopt family-unit based farming

2 Allocate 1,000 pyeong (3,300m^2) of farmland per person (of the farm labor force) for agricultural purposes and divide agricultural products produced from the land into 40 percent and 60 percent shares to be distributed to the state and individuals respectively

Source: Adapted from Hyundai Research Institute 2014

Table 8.5 Changes in China's agricultural production in reform period (%)

Year	*Crop production*	*Forestry*	*Livestock industry*	*Sideline production*	*Total*
1975–1980	13.0	36.1	31.9	26.2	16.9
1980–1985	36.2	54.9	65.5	170.8	48.2
1985–1990	17.3	1.8	38.5	71.5	26.1

Source: Lee 1997

North Korea's agricultural reformation measure in 2014 was similar to China's 'Bao gan dao hu' production responsibility system in that they both gave new forms of incentives to individual farmers. If the reforms had been implemented in all cooperative farms in North Korea, it is highly probable that their agricultural production would have increased greatly. However, food production in North Korea has fallen from 2014 to 2018, which indicates that the effect of the reformative measures in the agricultural production sector have been, if anything, minimal.

3.2 Efforts to attract agricultural investments through the open door

North Korea has also taken steps to further expand its openness in managing its economy under the Kim Jong-un administration. It has supplemented investment related laws in order to promote foreign investment and expanded the designation of special economic zones. It has also reorganized the existing central economic zones and made greater efforts to attract foreign investment by designating new regional economic development districts (Institute for Unification Education 2007).

In 2012, North Korea amended the "Foreign Investment Companies Registration Act" and "Foreign Investment Companies and Foreigners Tax Act."[7] There are two notable features about this change: one is that the government exempts the corporate income tax in the first year's profit if a foreign investment bank has operated a business for a period of more than ten years; another is the exemption of the business tax for the interest earned by providing loans in favor of North Korean banks and companies.[8]

Efforts to attract foreign capital through the designation of new special economic zones are illustrated in the "Law on Economic Development Zone," announced on May 29, 2013. The law enforced the designation of the special economic zones (SEZs) by classifying them into central and regional economic development zones (EDZs) and demanded provincial people's committees (based on the provinces and cities under the direct control of the central government) to apply for the installation of regional economic development districts to the central Special Economic Zone Guidance Agencies. Under this law, North Korea designated thirteen economic development districts for each province by November 11, 2013, and added five more districts in 2014 (see Tables 8.6 and 8.7).

Table 8.6 Central and overseas SEZ, EDZ (after 1990)

Region		*Major Contents*
Overseas	Rajin·Sonbong	– 1991, Establish Free Economic and Trade Zone (FETZ) – 2011, Designate "Rason Economic and Trade Zone" – 2008–present, DPRK/RUS promote "Rajin-Khasan Project"
	Sinuiju	– 2002 Sept., Designate "Sinuiju Special Administrative Region" – 2012, Designate "Hwanggumpyong·Wihwado Economic Zone" – 2014, Designate "Sinuiju International Economic Zone"
	Others	– 2014, Designate "Wonsan·Mt. Kumgang International Tourist Zone" – 2014, Designate "Gangryeong International Green Demonstration Zone" (Hwangnam), "Unjong High-Tech Development Zon" (Pyongyang), Jindo Export Processing Zone (Pyongnam) – 2015, Designate Mubong Special Zone for International Tourism (Ryanggang)
Republic of Korea	Kaesong	– 2002, Designate "Kaesong Industrial Complex" – 2004–2015, In operation and Inter-Korean trade of goods – 2014, temporal shutdown, closed in 2016
	Mt. Kumgang	– 2002, Designate "Mt. Kumgang Tourist Region" – 2008, Closed

Source: Adapted from Ministry of Unification; North Korea Information Portal

Table 8.7 Regional overseas economic development zones

Division	*Designated in 2013*	*Designated in 2014*	*Designated after 2014*
Economic Development Zone	Hamgyongbuk-do: Chongjin Chagang-do: Manpo Ryanggang-do: Hyesan Pyonganbuk-do: Amrok River		Hamkyongbuk-do: Kyongwon Pyongyang: Gangnam
Industrial Development Zone	Chagang-do: Wiwon Hamgyongnam-do: Heungnam Gangwon-do: Hyondong	Pyongannam-do: Chongnam	
Agricultural Development Zone	Hamgyongnam-do: Bukchong Hamgyongbuk-do: Orang	Pyongannam-do: Sukchon	
Tourism Development Zone	Hwanghaebuk-do: Sinpyong Hamgyongbuk-do: Onsong Island	Pyonganbuk-do: Chongsu	
Export Processing Zone	Hwanghaebuk-do: Songrim Pyongannam-do: Waudo		

Source: Adapted from Ministry of Unification; North Korea Information Portal

Despite North Korea's efforts to attract foreign capitals, foreign investments have not been not arranged in a favorable manner. The investments for the central SEZs and major cities were mainly comprised of small investments for consignment processing. The large-scale investments that North Korea expected were limited to infrastructure-oriented investments by investing countries that intend to secure their shipping channels in the Pacific. North Korea failed, then, to invigorate domestic industrial activities. Foreign investment in regional Economic Development Zones was at its best, minimal. Further compounding these situations, international sanctions on North Korea have only strengthened since 2016, further dampening foreign investment.

3.3 Evaluation of agricultural reform and opening policy in the Kim Jong-un era

In the 2010s, there was an element that constituted reason for a positive outlook and thought that perhaps North Korea's agricultural production may improve significantly. It was in the shape of a reform measure that was adopted as part of the "Economic Management System in Our Style" in 2012. The purpose of this measure was to dramatically increase agricultural production by granting greater incentives to famers than before. However, this reform measure did not lead to significant increases in agricultural production. Production of food crops increased only 3 percent over the two years from 2012 to 2014, and the production even decreased in 2015, compared to the previous year (see Table 8.8)[9]

The analysis indicates that the first reason for insignificant increases in North Korea's agricultural production despite the 2010 agricultural reform measure was that there were "external constraints" in the operation of the reform measures. This means that there are limitations to improving productivity when there is insufficient capital for reform. Second, there are "internal constraints" of food supply in North Korea. This constraint refers to the difficulty to initiate thorough agricultural reform under chronic food shortages. If incentive-based agricultural reform is applied at the production site and the productivity is enhanced in the agricultural sector, and if some or all of the shares of this increase in production

Table 8.8 North Korea's agricultural production, requirement, and shortage

	2012	*2013*	*2014*	*2015*	*2016*	*2017*
Production	5,025	5,113	5,126	5,329	4,985	4,763
Requirement	5,558	5,588	5,617	5,646	5,673	5,701
Shortage	533	475	491	317	688	983

Source: Food and Agriculture Organization of the United Nations 2020. "FAO Statistics" and DPRK FAO/WFP Joint Rapid Food Security Assessment

Note: 1) Productivity is sum of rice, corn, barleys, pulses, potatoes (FAO-2 items), and other cereals (FAO-5 items); 2) requirement is based on 1 person/year, which is calculated as 175.4kg (based on the required amount suggested by FAO/WFP, 2019)

is then continuously distributed as an incentive for the agricultural producers, the increase in production could be settled as permanent phenomenon.

However, the chronic food shortage has made it difficult for North Korean agriculture to get into such a virtuous cycle. Strengthening the distribution of incentives for the farmers could temporarily reduce the government's purchasing volume amid the inability to supply even the minimum amount of food. The decrease in government purchase power inevitably results in a reduction in rations and means that the residents who were relying on rations will face greater difficulties. If the measure is not backed up by a sustainable increase in food supply, agricultural reforms are likely to result in failure. In order to initiate the reforms, incentives for agricultural producers and food supply to urban residents should increase at the same time, and the government must be able to secure enough agricultural products from home and abroad to be able to meet supply demand for the time being.

North Korea also took steps to open its economy. With the hope of expanding foreign trade and increasing foreign investment, an open-door policy was expected to have a positive ripple effect on the agricultural sector. However, active foreign investment was not made in the special economic development zones. The closed nature of North Korean society and lack of improvement in basic infrastructures failed to provide foreigners with an attractive environment for investment. In addition, North Korea's trade and foreign investment conditions have exacerbated since 2016.[10] The Inter-Korean economic cooperation project in Kaesong Industrial Complex was suspended, and international economic sanctions on North Korea have increased, putting North Korea's economic opening and investment attraction policies on the verge of collapse.

4 Conclusion

Since 1966, North Korea had implemented a sub-work team management system in their cooperative farms for effective agricultural production and the distribution of agricultural products. As food shortages grew in the 1990s, North Korea introduced the 'new sub-work team management system' as a new form of distribution system for cooperative farms. However, there are no reports that the system was universally implemented on North Korean farms. Given that North Korea's agricultural production has remained stagnant without increasing, this experiment of distribution system reform in North Korea's agriculture failed to produce successful results.

In July 2002, among a wide range of economic reform measures, the Economic Management Improvement Measure (7.1 Measure) was enacted. Among the contents of the 7.1 Measure those directly related to the agricultural sector included the directive to increase the purchasing price of food (price reform), the expansion of the right to self-disposal of agricultural products among farms (decentralization) and the opening of markets for production components. This was expected to motivate production and significantly improve the production of the agricultural sector. However, any effect on the increase in production was not evident. In the case of rice, the effect of price hikes on the increased production was neutral as there was virtually no difference between the rate of price increase for rice and the rate of the price increase for agricultural materials under the 7.1 Measure.

What is notable as the greatest change in the North Korean agriculture since the inauguration of Kim Jong-un regime is the agricultural reform that began in 2012. These reform measures[11] can be characterized as a "Garden Production Responsibility System" in cooperative farms, which assigns the responsibility for farmlands not only to the sub-work teams in the cooperative farms but also to the individual farmhouses and makes them take charge of their own agricultural production. North Korea announced that this reform has greatly increased the production of food products. Given the stark reality of stagnant and declining food production observed in North Korea since 2012, however, it can be inferred that the reform has not, in actuality, been successfully established.

Meanwhile, North Korea has tried to attract capital from the international community through the establishment of special economic zones and the designation of development zones. The baseline strategy of the special zones was to promote economic development by efficiently operating a decentralized planned economic system in the mainland, while utilizing special economic zones as a channel for capital and foreign currency inflows to boost exports. However, North Korea has been sluggish on its economic opening due to the lack of human and material resources, and the international community has been slow to invest in North Korea. This situation is partly due to poor investment conditions, partly owing to the absence of a domestic market and partly because of the external economic risks possessed by any investment in North Korea. Due to such restrictions, foreign investment in North Korea's economic opening has failed to materialize.

Despite various reform measures and open-door efforts, North Korea's agriculture was not able to escape the "trap of lack of capital and sluggish reform." It is also difficult to see any clear difference between past agricultural policies and the new "economic development strategy," announced at the seventh party congress convened in May 2016. Moreover, the aforementioned decline in trade and in investment is becoming a more permanent reality following the international sanctions on North Korea. As a result, agricultural production has been declining recently and food supply and demand has been exacerbating.

At this point, North Korea must seek an alternative course. As part of that, it is necessary to pursue agricultural development programs for the areas near North Korea's special economic zones. There are three main reasons for this: the first is the creation of associated effects. The government should develop hinterland industries so that any capital that flowed into the specialized zones could flow into the mainland through the residents' consumption of goods. Second, the government should prepare for increasing demand for agricultural products in the specialized zones. The inflow of foreign investment into the specialized zones increases income and thus increases demand for agricultural products. In response, preparation for the agricultural products' supply bases in the hinterland specialized zones seems crucial. Third is the development of a new model for foreign agricultural cooperation. By promoting agricultural cooperation projects near the specialized zones, the government can develop commercial cooperative models that produce open agricultural markets and new supply sources for agricultural materials.

Cooperation between the two Koreas is also essential for pursuing such agricultural developments. Inter-Korean cooperation can be pursued in three directions: humanitarian-level agricultural cooperation projects (private aid groups), infrastructure and capacity development cooperation projects (public sector), and commercial trade and investment cooperation projects (private companies). This will not only create direct economic benefits but also establish a foundation for driving agricultural development. North Korea should be active in pursuing such cooperative projects.

Notes

1 In September 2002, Deputy Minister of External Economics Relations of North Korea Yong Sul Kim mentioned in the seminar on North Korea's Economy held in Tokyo that a new type of bank called Trust Bank was established in North Korea in last July (Kim and Ji 2006, 51).

2 However, it seems that there were attempts to alleviate the rationing system. To consider the abolishment of the rationing system, it is known that Cheongjin, North Hamgyong Province, was selected as a pilot area in early 2002 and an experiment to abolish the distribution of daily necessities (other than food) was conducted (Segye Ilbo)

3 Lee (2009, 12) described it as the "institutional land" that is created by an institution but under the quality control by the state.

4 Although the representative raw materials in the agricultural sector are fertilizer, seeds, agricultural chemicals, agricultural equipment, and vinyl, we used electricity and energy price as the representative prices of raw materials because there is no data on the supply and demand or prices of these materials (Kim and Ji 2006, 54).

5 Despite of the dramatic increase in official exchange rates in July 2002, North Korea has taken physical measures to ban dollar circulation since mid-November. Regardless of North Korea's claims, the practical purpose of this measure was to gather any remaining dollars (Kim and Ji 2006, 59).

6 Choson Sinbo (2016. 01. 08); *Yonhap News* (2015. 01. 09.); Kim Jon Un, "On Establishing Our Own Way of Managing the Economy in Line with the Demand for Actual Development," 2014. 05. 30; quoted in *Tongil News* (2015. 01. 06).

7 Yonhap News, 2012. 02. 10, "DPRK, Amends Foreign Investment Companies Registration Act and Tax Law"; Yonhap News, 2012. 03. 11 "DPRK Adopt Inter-Korean Economic Cooperation Insurance Model to Attract Investment", etc.

8 Yonhap News, 2012. 02. 09, "DPRK Exempts Business Tax for Foreign Investment Banks . . . Law Amendment"

9 Although it cannot be compared directly with the figures in Table 8.8, FAO/WFP (2019) reportedly estimated that the food production in North Korea dropped further to 4.17 million tons in the years 2018 and 2019.

10 The United Nations and the international community have tightened the sanctions on North Korea due to its nuclear experiment and long-range ballistic missile test in early 2016. (UN Security Council Resolution 2270).

11 These are known as the "June 28 Policy" in 2012 and the "May 30 Measure" in 2014.

References

Chosun Sinbo. 2002. Article on North Korea's Rice Purchasing Price. *Chosun Sinbo*. www.chosunshinbo.com. Accessed July 19.

Food and Agriculture Organization of the United Nations. 2020. "FAO Statistics." Accessed February 2. www.fao.org/home/search/en/?q=statistics.

Hyundai Research Institute. 2014. "The Impact of North Korea's Agricultural Reformation on Its GDP." *Current Issues and Tasks* 14 (36).

Institute for Unification Education. 2007. "Trend and Characteristics of North Korea's Consolidation of Legislation." Accessed February 2. www.uniedu.go.kr/uniedu/home/cms/page/unieng/main.do?mid=UNIENG&main=true.

Kim, Yeon Chul. 2012. "Probability of Kim Jong-um Regime's Reform and Liberalization." *KDI Review of North Korean Economy* 14 (6).

Kim, Young Hoon. 2012. "North Korea's Agriculture and Food Conditions Under Kim Jong-un's Era." *EXIM North Korea Economic Review* Summer 2012: 25–28.

Kim, Young Hoon, and Ji Bae. 2006. *A Study on Changes in North Korean Agriculture Since the Food Crisis*. Korea Rural Economic Institute.

Kwon, Young Kyoung. 2010. " '2012 System' Deployment Strategy and Changes in North Korean Economy." *KDI Review of North Korean Economy* 12 (3).

Lee, Il Young. 1997. *China's Agricultural Reform and Economic Development*. Seoul: Seoul National University Press.

Lee, Young Hoon. 2009. "Characteristics and the Implications of the Changes in North Korea's Economic Structure after the July 1st Measure." Unpublished draft.

North Korea Information Portal. 2020. "Ministry of Unification." Accessed February 2. https://nkinfo.unikorea.go.kr/nkp/main/portalMain.do.

9 Innovative urban planning and development for Pyongyang through collaboration with developed cities

Hong Soo Lee and Cheon Woon Choi

1 Introduction

In order to initiate a timely collaborative relationship between South Korea and North Korea (if and when there is any early movement toward an easement regarding existing economic sanctions from the international communities such as the United Nations), it is necessary to understand the direction of North Korea's economic openness thoroughly. In this chapter, we would like to explore some innovative methods of collaboration in the area of urban planning and development.

In this concise chapter, we therefore wish to first introduce the definition of "city to city" (C2C) for city level relationships, rather than between two countries, in order to pursue a much closer and more active collaboration between the two Koreas. Then, the land value of areas reserved or utilized by urban planning and development strategies, completed in South Korea and Singapore based on state-owned lands, would be reviewed for the C2C engagement. For North Korea, especially in Pyongyang, multilateral collaborations with the capital cities of neighboring countries could be considered, including public-private partnership (PPP) oriented urban development projects. The bilateral land swapping model, explored and successfully implemented between Singapore and Malaysia, could be used as a benchmark for the collaborative urban planning and development projects in Pyongyang with other cities as well.

When we (i.e. South Koreans) speak of discussions or negotiations with North Korea – for any business deals or public matters – we tend to mistakenly understand that we (i.e. South Korea) would have a priority over the other neighboring peoples (e.g. China, Russia), stemming from our single shared historical ethnicity. However, it would not be so simple as the history of North Korea and of East Asia could be interpreted in many different ways. First, North Korea has long been exchanging trade with its neighbors as well as some other countries in Eastern Europe and has apparently continued to do so even under the current stringent economic sanctions. When the sanctions are alleviated or lifted, there is no guarantee that South Korea will take priority as a partner for future collaborations. Looking at physical borders, a countless number of landmines are buried in the Demilitarized Zone (DMZ), located between the two Koreas, and it will take more than simply time to eliminate the physical risk buried over the past 70 years. However, when you look at the northern borders of North Korea facing China and Russia, there are already a multitude of planned or completed pieces of infrastructure in Special Economic Zones and ready for cooperation works (e.g. thorough joint venture) with its northern neighbors. For example, The Rason Special Economic Zone, earlier called Rajin-Sonbong Economic Special Zone and located in the northeastern part of North Korea facing the territory of Russia, was established in 1992 to promote economic growth through foreign investments and Chinese and Russian companies have already invested in that economic zone. As such, when the sanctions are eased or North Korea's economic development begins in earnest, South Korea may find the basis for these expectations of primacy in economic collaborations with the North to be more or less just that: merely expectations.

This chapter begins by forming an understanding and review of the current status of urban planning and development in Seoul and Singapore and will summarize the know-how of rapid and successful urban planning and development performed in those countries in order to discuss applications for Pyongyang. In introducing some useful techniques of urban planning and development, including ones related to real estate and finance, we hope that this chapter contributes to the next generation of urban policy making, and will be taken into consideration whenever collaboration between developed cities, and Pyongyang occurs in earnest, hopefully, in the near future.

2 A brief analysis of urban planning and development in Seoul, Singapore, and Pyongyang

2.1 Urbanization of the cities after the 1950s–1960s

The goal of urban policies in Seoul represents provisions for quality of life taking into consideration ecology, comfort, safety, and welfare in the metropolitan city, while the goal of Pyongyang's is summarized as convenience of its peoples' lives considering hygienic, cultural and global tourism under socialist ideological propaganda. Given the population concentration of the Seoul Metropolitan area, it has been regulated by the Seoul Metropolitan Area Readjustment Plan to balance the overcrowded status and has benefited from the decentralization plan. In order to achieve the goal of balanced urban planning and development there are three major measurements used as part of the development control for the Seoul Metropolitan Area, these are: urban growth control, avoiding overcrowding, and conservation of natural environment In addition, urban policies promote the development of self-sufficient (e.g. job-housing proximity) new cities located around the periphery of Seoul. The Seoul Metropolitan Government is also pursuing various initiatives for the balanced developments between the southern part of the city, south of the Han River (e.g. Gangnam, Seocho, Songpa), where the living quality is generally higher than other areas, and older part of the city, north of the

Han River where the living quality is generally lower. We clarify the definition of Metropolitan Area as an urban area having the relationship or characteristic of a Metropolis including its suburban area. Therefore, any urban planning and development of Pyongyang as a Metropolitan Area is representing development beyond just the capital itself as it is closely related to the entire economic growth of North Korea as well.

With this in mind, we can review then the degree of urbanization of the three cities to understand how the different urban planning and development systems have been planned and achieved. Coincidentally, the three cities all had been colonized under Japan and have an independent history starting afterwards, in the mid-20th century. They therefore represent three cities that have been rebuilding since 1950s or 1960s. Figure 9.1 shows aerial maps of the three cities for a better view of their individual urbanizations. Careful observation of these maps reveals the distinctive differences of the urbanized areas and the three remarkable points. First, as you can see from Figure 9.1, Pyongyang's urbanized area appears to be less than 20 percent of the entire city; small compared with the other two cities where almost 100 percent urbanization has been achieved. Second, given the limited access to Pyongyang from outside areas and less-urbanization, only about 12 percent of the population of North Korea living in Pyongyang, compared to South Korea, where over 20 million, over 50 percent of the population, is living in Seoul and the Seoul Metropolitan area including Gyeonggi and Incheon provinces. Singapore's city country area is slightly larger than Seoul and there are about 5.7 million people living in that city (KOSIS 2020; Park 2016; The World Bank 2020a). Third, the GDP of Pyongyang (about 2,700 USD) is much lower than the other two cities (approximately 40,000 USD for Seoul and approximately 60,000 USD for Singapore) and as such, we strongly believe that urban development is one of the potential areas for new economic growth. There is a need to further review the relationship between GDP and key urban developments (KOSIS 2020; Park 2016; The World Bank 2020b).

For example, we can review how urban development supports the economic growth of the cities based on Singapore's case as given the city country status, it is easier to look at for a for quick comparison than the more complicated dynamics of Seoul. We selected two representative urban development elements, the construction sector and the transport sector, among all the elements comprising the total GDP. As we can see from the last three years' (i.e. 2016–2019) average information, approx. 4,500 SGD and 8,000 SGD of the value of the GDP value were contributed from the construction sector (including public housing) and the transport sector (including bus, metro, cycling as well as the road for private vehicle) respectively. If we sum up the two elements, the combined contribution to the GDP is approx. 10,000 USD and it is about 3.5 times that of Pyongyang's total GDP (i.e. 2,700 USD). As such, we wish to reiterate that urban development will be one of the key areas for the next economic growth phase of Pyongyang for North Korea (Trading Economics 2020).

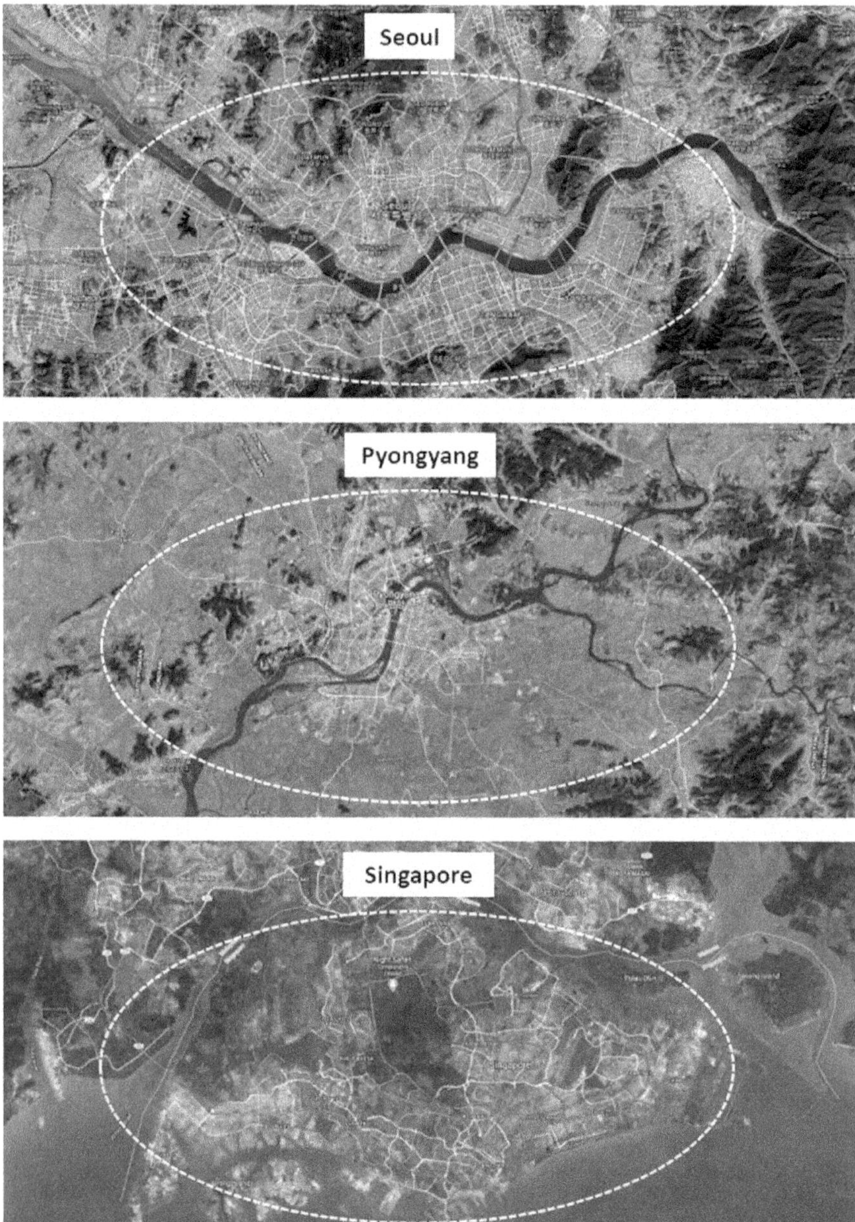

Figure 9.1 Seoul, Singapore, and Pyongyang – urbanization of cites following the 1950s–1960s

Source: Adapted from Google Maps 2020, "Location of Seoul, South Korea," "Location of Singapore," and "Location of Pyongyang, North Korea"

2.2 History of urban planning and development in the cities

The first modern urban planning system in Pyongyang was established in 1952 as the Pyongyang City Restoration Construction Plan. In 1953, the College of Construction was established to cultivate construction professionals and in 1960, the Pyongyang General City Plan was prepared and reported to have formed the framework for urban planning. The formation of such a planning system by North Korean authorities appears to be quite advanced considering that the South Korean Urban Planning Act was not enacted until 1962. The Housing Area Planning is the most systematically organized North Korean urban planning document and it is five years ahead of South Korea's urban planning. Due to the speed of the city's restoration and urban renovation under the full support of Russia (the USSR at that time), it seems that the urban planning and organization system in Pyongyang was established earlier than its counterpart in Seoul.

Urban planning and development management in South Korea – including Seoul – is carried out under the Act on National Land Planning and Utilization, a basic urban planning act, establishing urban management planning and district scale planning. In addition, the techniques for implementation such as zoning systems, urban infrastructure projects, and urban development projects are measured and proceeded by the guidelines set forth in the Act. The process of participatory planning by the residents has emerged and has expanded from the progress of democratization and localization in the Act and the participation of private capital (e.g. Public Private Partnership) is also stabilized as part of urban planning and development management under the Act. In addition, according to the Land Planning and Utilization Act, South Korea's urban planning is implemented as a regulation (e.g. land use zone and district system) and a development project (e.g. urban development project, urban infrastructure project) and as and when the individual property rights are violated from incorrect implementation processes, the Act is the medium used to resolve the resulting cases. Usually, the budget of urban planning and implementation is provided by the central and local governments and the principle of financing is borne by the implementer or beneficiary.

On the other hand, North Korea's urban planning character is still in its infancy compared with South Korea's one. While we can see the character of urban planning and development techniques are also presented along streetscapes (e.g. magnificent landscape effects, three-dimensional arrangement effects, non-reversive and unique architectural facades and baroque urban design techniques), it is difficult to find a detailed regulatory system for the specific urban planning and implementation of each project. This is likely related to the nature of the state regime where the government can influence the working and living places in the city based on state-owned land. Since the country monopolizes all means of production, the resources for urban developments are, in principle, the state's burden and the execution of such a project is thus handled by the enterprises and cooperative farms under the authority of the state.

2.3 Character of existing urban structure in the city centers

One of the important elements in determining the urban shape is the high-rise mixed-use buildings in the CBDs (i.e. Central Business Districts) of Seoul. Offices for financial and business functions are mainly located in the center of each CBD district and its land is accordingly priced higher than other areas. Urban planning also reflects this market trend, allowing high density and mixed-use at the central area and as a result, urban landscapes are largely determined by the land price distribution. However, since there is no land sale market in North Korea, there is no competition and the land use planning and decisions rely more on the planning norms of socialist states, or as set by North Korea's socialist policy of self-reliance: Juche. As such, we see there are many residential areas – even in the center of the city – with this large scaled baroque style architecture and many plazas with examples consisting of People's University Hall, Juche Idea Tower and Kim Il-sung Square. This highlighting of the magnificent and splendid aspirations of the state through visual effect rather than space used for the normal citizen is in stark contrast to the South. These differences of land use as well as the types of scenery in the two cities' central areas are stark, reminders of their different origins in either the capitalism-based market economy or the socialism-based planned economy system. For example, in residential units, while the living room is characteristically the center of each dwelling unit in Seoul, more individual rooms -oriented with public facilities for joint production and joint distribution – is a more typical characteristic of residential buildings in Pyongyang. Since the dwelling unit is considered as part of a socialist community, not just a family, the proportion of living rooms is relatively low compared to South Korea. Please see the summarized comparison between Seoul and Pyongyang in Table 9.1 for easy reference.

What follows is a quick analysis of the three cities using actual urban spaces to highlight the potential urban development at Pyongyang (see Figure 9.2). These are the cities' civic and adjacent districts for comparison, as a civic

Table 9.1 Characteristics of urban planning and housing in Seoul and Pyongyang

	Seoul	*Pyongyang*
Center City	Changed from low density residential use to high density mixed-use business purpose	Remained with a significant focus on large scaled public use (e.g. public buildings) with high-rise residential purpose
Residential area	Single-detached house to high-rise residential building Living room-oriented house plan	Housing complex together with public facilities (e.g. communal space, laundry plant, distribution center, day care center) More individual room-oriented house plan with small living room

Source: Author created

Figure 9.2 Seoul, Singapore, and Pyongyang – civic districts and adjacent areas

Source: Adapted from Google Maps 2020, "Location of Seoul, South Korea," "Location of Singapore," and "Location of Pyongyang, North Korea"

district is normally the representative space of a city. One of the common uses of this civic space is for holding national events of the city or country. For example, the Armed Forces Day in Seoul, the National Day in Singapore and the Military Parades in Pyongyang are the major events held in these cities' civic spaces, respectively, as these places are meaningful and centrally located spaces for the cities.

Then as these spaces are so important, we will look at each of the districts in the corresponding city context carefully. The first one is Gwanghwamun Square in Seoul (see Figure 9.3). The district is also heavily used by people for many other public purposes such as for concerts, gatherings, and other forms of entertainment throughout the four seasons and it is also the space for the expression of a citizen's right such as the popular candlelight protest. In addition, we can see from the existing mixed land use that different types of uses are coexisting in civic districts, such as office, commercial, hotel, residential, public space, historical space, school, etc., we could imagine this to be a character of the dynamic space of a civic district.

Similar with Seoul, when we look at the civic district in Singapore (see Figure 9.4), we easily understand that the central square, named Padang, is also well designed to be used by the people for public activities. Based on the mid-term and longer-term land use plan, a mixed-use development is required for different uses so that the districts could provide diverse attractions for citizens, tourists and for sustainable economic growth as well.

Finally, let us look at the Kim Il-sung Square area in the third and final city at the heart of this chapter, Pyongyang, (see Figure 9.5), although we are not familiar with all the details of events held here, other than political uses broadcast to the outside, we could imagine how the space is planned and used by their government. In addition, it seems that there is no comprehensive, transparent or consistent land use or master plan for the capital city and even if there are some exiting mixed-use developments such as hotels, restaurants, historical buildings and other public spaces, they are not impactful enough to take a lead or to be a focal place facilitating the economic growth of Pyongyang and North Korea.

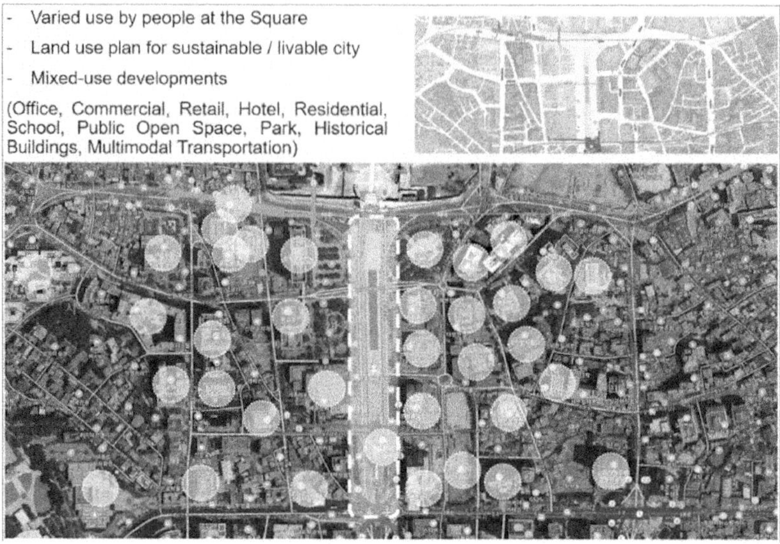

Figure 9.3 Seoul – civic district and adjacent areas

Source: Adapted from Google Maps 2020, "Location of Seoul, South Korea"; Luris 2020

Note: The highlighted circles in grey in the areal map are areas of developments and/or public activities; the color-coded map is a land use plan (e.g. red for public/blue for commercial)

Figure 9.4 Singapore – civic district and adjacent area

Source: Adapted from Google Maps 2020, "Location of Singapore"; URA Space 2020

Note: The highlighted circles in grey in the aerial map are areas of developments and/or public activities; the color-coded map is a land use plan (e.g. red for public/blue for commercial)

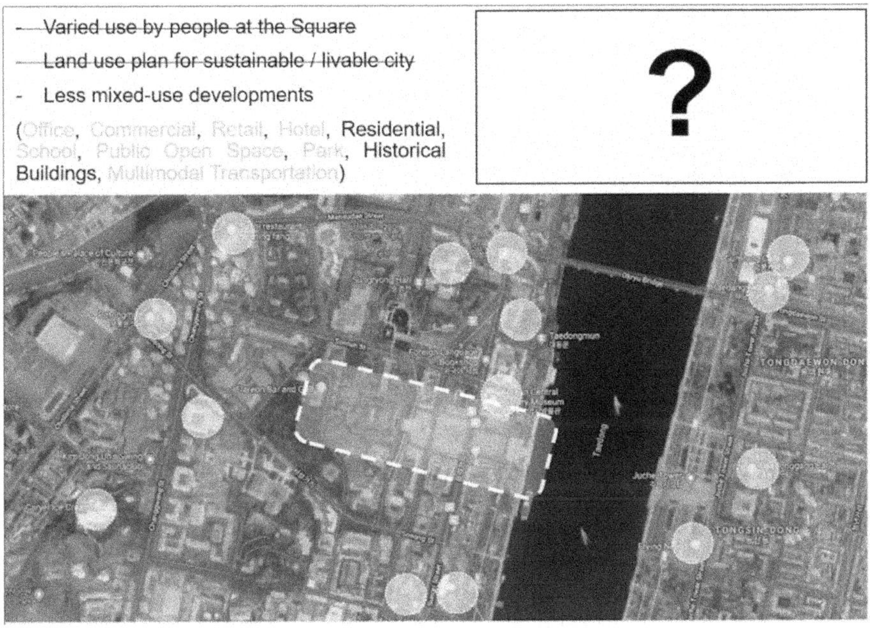

Figure 9.5 Pyongyang – civic district and adjacent areas

Source: Adapted from Google Maps (2020), "Location of Pyongyang, North Korea"

Note: 1) The highlighted circles in grey in the areas of developments and/or public activities; 2) No land use plan or mid- or longer-term master plan is published

3 C2C collaboration by Pyongyang with other cities utilizing urban planning and development experiences of Singapore and Seoul

3.1 C2C (city-to-city) approach

G2G (i.e. government to government) is a commonly used term in collaboration between governments and/or countries. However, the goal of this section is to define and explore the city level relationship as C2C in urban planning and development for more intimate collaboration between Pyongyang and other cities.

3.2 Lessons learned from Singapore and Seoul

Singapore and Seoul are perhaps the two most remarkable cities for benchmarking rapid economic growth and urbanization among all of the cities in Asia perhaps even the world. Although the two cities have many similar characteristics, one prominent shared aspect is that the cities have both achieved a swift and successful growth owing to the government led policies devised right after colonization and war had left them devastated. In addition, both cities have experienced population explosions even before proper urbanization from urban planning and development, however in both their cases, Seoul and Singapore have resolved resulting issues very well with their own solutions from government planning. As we know, North Korea leader, Kim Jong-un, took time out from planning for the historical first summit with US President Donald Trump in Singapore to take in some of Singapore's iconic urban development sites (e.g. Gardens by the Bay and Marina Bay Sands integrated resorts) and after seeing the panoramic views of successfully developed urbanization in Singapore, he may wish to benchmark the urban planning and development of Singapore for future planning in the capital of North Korea. The two nations' differences in politics, administrative systems and culture, become evident when reviewing and exploring the urban planning and development cases in Singapore which will be more meaningful in many aspects for Pyongyang as time goes on.

Singapore has an area of 725 square kilometers, slightly larger than Seoul (i.e. 605 square kilometers) through continuous reclamation projects performed over time (e.g. Marina Bay area is all area reclaimed in the 1980s) and it is less than half of Pyongyang (i.e. approximately 2,000 square kilometers). Singapore is a metropolitan city country where more than 30 percent of population is comprised by various non-Singaporean nationalities. Based on an advanced practical and efficient system in urban planning and development as well as urban-related administration, it is also widely known as one of the best cities in which to do business, in not only Asia, but also the world. Singapore could be seen as the representative urban planning story of the last 60 years, showing how transparent and consistent government-led and citizen participant driven urban growth can transform an area. Singapore's successful implementation of city strategies can also be the benchmark model for urban planning and development in North Korea, especially for Pyongyang. While not accepting of Western capitalism as it is, by maintaining an authoritarian political and administrative system that pursues Asian values, the economic system of Singapore is performing better than Western capitalism. This can be an attractive point for North Korea to choose it as a model over Seoul, as it is a model that accepts the merits of the Singapore-style open market economy while maintaining the existing political and administrative system. More specifically, introducing an agency such as the Singapore public agency, the Urban Redevelopment Authority, to readers will be beneficial in understanding this study. The URA is the main statutory board for the continuous successful implementation of urban planning and development fields in Singapore today.

The URA is an organization established in 1974 by the URA ACT (CHAPTER 340) and the statutory board under the Ministry of National Development. It is not easy to define it, as it is not exactly the same as or similar to any other domestic city-related institution, but it can be considered that the administrative hierarchy is somewhat simpler than any similar authority bodies that that exist in Korea due to the characteristics of urban countries that place importance on practicality and efficiency. The following are the six main responsibility tasks achieved through the contents of URA ACT (Singapore Statutes Online 2020).

3.2.1 Land use planning

The URA's most important task is to establish a mid- to long-term strategic land use plan for the Master Plan (i.e. Legal Plan) and the Concept Plan (i.e. Non-Legal Plan) respectively for the fifty-five planning areas in Singapore. The Master Plan is planned to be re-established every five years, however, the Master Plan is only reviewed from time to time based on the quarterly real estate market monitoring, and corrections are made only if necessary.

3.2.2 Development control

Based on the Master Plan, the URA evaluates and approves various urban development projects and the government is responsible for providing quality services taking into account public nature as well as business feasibility through cooperation with committees consisting of experts and citizens in each field.

3.2.3 Urban design

The URA is also in charge of the urban design of Singapore. Examples include Orchard Road Shopping street, Marina Bay area, and Tanjong Pagar's international financial business district. The harmonization of functional buildings, streets for transport and human activities scaled public realms including spaces such as parks for walking, and cycling are the key elements of a great city to play, work and live in.

3.2.4 Building conservation

Since its announcement in the Master Plan for Conservation in 1989, the preservation of historic buildings is one of the important tasks of the URA. Not the preservation of simple buildings, but the preservation of important buildings and districts through communication with people living inside and outside the designated building's area including guidelines and processes. Currently more than 7,000 buildings have been marked as conservation protected buildings, and in order to harmonize new and traditional ones, the work is also carried out in cooperation with the teams for urban planning, development control and urban design. We can see the variation of density resulting from the coexistence of conserved districts and business or commercial areas throughout the city.

3.2.5 Land sales

The URA is a government agency preparing and proceeding the land sale programs under the Master Plan together with many other statutory boards (e.g.

Singapore Land Authority) in order to meet the multitude of required planned private and public developments as well as maximize the land value via captured development through public tenders.

3.2.6 Carpark management

The URA is managing most of the public street parking except the housing complex maintained by the Housing Development Board (HDB) in Singapore.

3.3 Strategies of urban planning and development collaborations from experiences of Singapore and Seoul

In order to avoid hindering sustainable urban growth from sudden and reckless investment, when the economic sanctions are alleviated or lifted, cities in North Korea will find it necessary to establish a coherent and transparent urban planning and development system similar to the ones found in Singapore or Seoul. Seoul's urbanization which is now known as Dynamic Seoul was formerly the "The Miracle on the Han River" a term used to describe its rapid growth after independence from the Japanese colonial period and the Korean War. This title reflects how the modern city of Seoul is the result of the establishment of a comprehensive and integrated system for regulatory, management and policy enforcement in urban planning and development. Singapore and Seoul have been gradually implementing the required basic urban infrastructure and urban development based on medium-term and longer-term urban planning as well as on citizen's opinions. For example, intensification of existing floor area ratio (i.e. FAR) or change of land use from a planned single-use to mixed-use taking into consideration the adjacent infrastructure such as roads, public spaces, and mass transportation, has been happening on both publicly and privately owned land. All the stakeholders from the landowner, building owner, developer, transit agency, and up to and including the national and local government have benefited from this sort of urban planning and development.

Urban planning and development also includes the implementation of new development and infrastructure works for those areas not yet urbanized within the city (or adjacent to the city) under the medium-term and longer-term urban planning. The cities in North Korea like Pyongyang should consider revision of their urban policy and the restructure of urban, industrial, population centers in tandem with economic opening as anyone can easily predict that the city of Pyongyang, after the economic opening or unification with South Korea, will change drastically. It is the right time for Pyongyang to reconsider the existing urban policy step by step in order to prepare for the various possible scenarios such as population explosion and development concentration, as well as traffic congestion from both domestic and overseas influx. If not, Pyongyang may become the center of confusion seen in many cities in developing countries. That is to say, that it could find itself far from the task of achieving a sustainable urbanization as a Metropolitan city due to indiscriminate development and investment creating chaotic situations rather than becoming a future growth engine for North Korea and Asia. To prevent this, Pyongyang, like Singapore or Seoul, needs to have a city level public urban planning and development agency that will act as a source for comprehensive and consistent control for land use planning, development proposals, urban design, construction conservation, and land sale.

Finally, let us examine the collaboration resulting from the innovative land swapping project between Singapore and Malaysia. Here Singapore and Malaysia jointly developed state-owned lands. This could have potential implications for the development of state-owned lands between Pyongyang and other cities. On September 21, 2010, Prime Minister Lee Hsien Loong of Singapore and Prime Minister Najib Razak of Malaysia announced a deal on both countries' so-called Land Swap.

Singapore became a member of the Malaysian Federation, gaining independence from the United Kingdom in 1963, and two years later in 1965 Singapore became an independent state when it separated from Malaysia as well. When leaving Malaysia, the railroad and train stations located in Singapore, and from Singapore to Thailand, remained in Malaysia's possession; though the two countries continued to discuss the ownership of these places, they found a mutually beneficial agreement in 2010 and settled dramatically. In 2017, these developments were completed successfully. These interchangeable land targets, or land swaps, are the Malaysian-owned north-south train route left in Singapore and the six lands for stations for Singapore-owned lands in the Marin Bay area (i.e. new development area) and Ophir-Rochor area (i.e. old town area). Malaysia and Singapore established a joint venture company called M+S Pte Ltd by a sovereign wealth fund (i.e. 60 percent state in Khazana Malaysia and 40 percent stake in Singapore Temasek) together with the private sector for implementation of these developments (OCBC Bank 2020). Similar with the development of M+S, Pyongyang's urban development at sites on state-owned lands could be successfully achieved through an P+M or P+S (Pyongyang + Seoul) strategy based on Seoul or Singapore's global investment experience and credit (Yi 2018).

4 Conclusion

In summarizing our concise chapter, we wish to highlight two perspectives for Pyongyang to consider in its effort to become the global metropolitan center that will induce economic growth for both the city and country.

First, an establishment of public urban planning and development organization in Pyongyang similar with the URA in Singapore or the Seoul Metropolitan Government (SMG). This would allow it to set up comprehensive, transparent, and consistent urban planning as well as implementation of urban development works. For information, the URA is the organization utilized to rebuild Singapore after Independence from Malaysia in the 1960s and the organization has been acting as a key one for sustainable and livable urban development until the present day. Since 1971, they have been publishing Singapore's Concept Plan every ten years. It is a consistent and longer-term plan for the next forty to fifty years for guiding a clear direction of Singapore's economic development. The SMG has likewise been producing policies to better realize urban dynamics for a distinctive and delightful development since 1960s.

Second, Pyongyang, or other major cities, may wish to benchmark the successful bilateral urban development project between Malaysia and Singapore for Pyongyang's potential collaboration in urban planning and development with other cities. If direct collaboration with a certain city is considered too sensitive, there would be ways to engage other cities for multilateral urban projects as well.

References

Google Maps. 2020. "Location of Pyongyang, North Korea." Accessed March 2. www.google.com.ph/maps/place/Pyongyang,+North+Korea/@39.0194012,125.7556954,15z/data=!4m5!3m4!1s0x357e02dae64f4337:0xd40677e21771aa95!8m2!3d39.0392193!4d125.7625241.

Google Maps. 2020. "Location of Seoul, South Korea." Accessed February 2. www.google.com.ph/maps/place/Seoul,+South+Korea/@37.5571244,127.0784633,59741m/data=!3m1!1e3!4m5!3m4!1s0x357ca28b61c565cd:0x858aedb4e4ea83eb!8m2!3d37.566535!4d126.9779692.

Google Maps. 2020. "Location of Singapore." Accessed March 2. www.google.com.ph/maps/place/Singapore/@1.28993,103.8509803,1991m/data=!3m1!1e3!4m5!3m4!1s0x31da11238a8b9375:0x887869cf52abf5c4!8m2!3d1.352083!4d103.819836.

KOSIS. 2020. "Regional Gross Domestic Product per Capita by Administrative District (City), Gross Regional Income, Individual Income." *Statistics Korea, Regional Income*. Accessed January 2. http://kosis.kr/statHtml/statHtml.do?orgId=101&tblId=DT_1C65.

Luris. 2020. "Land Use Regulation Map Service." Accessed April 2. http://luris.molit.go.kr/web/map/LvsMapMainTotalView.jsp.

OCBC Bank. 2020. "Stay Connected with OCBC Digital Banking." Accessed February 2. www.straitstimes.com/politics/how-the-joint-venture-behind-marina-one-and-duo-came-to-be.

Park, Dae Han. 2016. "KDI 'Income per Capita in Pyongyang $2,700. . . Three Times the Size of Other Parts of North Korea." *Yonhap News*, December 22. www.yna.co.kr/view/AKR20161222070800002.

Singapore Statutes Online. 2020. "Urban Redevelopment Authority Act." *A Singapore Government Agency Website*. Accessed February 2. https://sso.agc.gov.sg/Act/URAA1989.

Trading Economics. 2020. "Singapore GDP." Accessed February 2. https://tradingeconomics.com/singapore/gdp.

URA Space. 2020. "Master Plan." Accessed March 2. www.ura.gov.sg/maps/?service=MP.

The World Bank. 2020a. "GDP per Capita (Current US$)—Singapore." *World Bank National Accounts Data, and OECD National Accounts Data Files*. Accessed March 2. https://data.worldbank.org/indicator/NY.GDP.PCAP.CD?locations=SG.

The World Bank. 2020b. "Urban Development." Accessed February 2. www.worldbank.org/en/topic/urbandevelopment.

Yi, Seow Bei. 2018. "How the Joint Venture Behind Marina One and Duo Came to Be." *The Straits Times*, January 15. www.straitstimes.com/politics/how-the-joint-venture-behind-marina-one-and-duo-came-to-be.

10 Projections on North Korea's energy use and CO_2 emissions

Tae Yong Jung and Jongwoo Moon

1 Introduction

The relationship between energy and economic development has been widely examined, because energy plays a significant role in the global economy. Economic and social activities are closely related to energy production and consumption, as energy is an essential input source for economic and social activities. Securing primary energy sources, such as coal, oil, and natural gas, has been a crucial component of a country's energy policy, and energy facilities, such as electricity grids, and oil and natural gas pipelines, are considered to be important social overhead costs (SOC). In the 21st century, in addition to securing energy sources, combating climate change has become an important energy and environmental issue globally. The international society has agreed on the voluntary reduction of fossil fuel consumption and greenhouse gas emissions. Today, all countries have established individual energy strategies that secure energy sources for economic activities and are participating in international efforts in reducing greenhouse gas emissions.

The economic development of North Korea is also closely related to its energy use. The North Korean economy has been using coal as its main energy source, and hydroelectric power has been the primary source for generating electricity. Before the economic sanctions, North Korea refined crude oil to produce oil products, or consumed imported oil products for use in the transportation and industry sectors. However, the production and consumption of oil products in North Korea has become minimal due to the current economic sanctions, which strictly prohibit the importation of crude oil or oil products. In addition, North Korea submitted its Nationally Determined Contribution to the United Nations Framework Convention on Climate Change (UNFCCC), and committed to contributing to the international efforts on reducing greenhouse gas emissions by 2030.

This chapter is structured as follows. Section 2 provides an overview of the economic, energy, and social conditions of North Korea by using data from international organizations, such as the International Energy Agency, to better understand North Korean energy consumption and greenhouse gas emissions. Section 3 uses Kaya Identity Decomposition to measure the effects of key driving factors for greenhouse gas emissions. This section examines the relationship between

North Korea's energy and economy, and provides energy and greenhouse gas emissions projections through 2030. Section 4 analyzes North Korea's Nationally Determined Contributions (NDC), and compares North Korea's contributions to the projections calculated from the previous section. Based on the analysis, Section 5 derives policy implications for establishing low-carbon development pathways in North Korea. The analysis can become a starting point for analyzing the determining factors of North Korea's greenhouse gas emissions.

2 North Korea's energy, economic, and social situations

Energy has a close relationship with economic development. Typically, a country's economic development and energy consumption have a positive relationship and move in a similar direction. North Korean economic development and energy consumption patterns have shown a similar result, but those have been changed dramatically due to internal political, economic, and social factors, as well as external factors.

2.1 Economic and social conditions

The North Korean economy has not grown significantly over the last few decades. North Korea's economy grew rapidly in the 1970s and 1980s thanks to its close relationship with the Soviet Union and other Socialist countries in Eastern Europe. North Korea's real gross domestic product (GDP) had increased from 8.29 billion 2010 USD in 1971 to 44.33 billion 2010 USD in 1989. The collapse of the communist states in the late 1980s, followed by the Soviet Union in 1991, however, significantly damaged the economic growth potential of North Korea. Those events dramatically changed the international political dynamic, as well as North Korea's domestic conditions. Afterward, the North Korean economy continued to record a negative growth rate, and serious droughts leading to the Arduous March in the mid-1990s made matters worse. The recent economic sanctions imposed by the United States, prohibiting trade and financial transactions with North Korea, as well as limiting foreign aid (Congressional Research Service 2019), have further slowed the North Korean economy, placing the estimated real GDP in 2016 at 27.1 billion 2010 USD.

The population of North Korea has increased gradually since the 1950s, however, the population growth rate has declined since the 1970s. The population of North Korea was estimated at 14.81 million people in 1971, and the population growth rate was about 1.85 percent per year in the 1970s, however, the Arduous March during the mid-1990s and the weakened economy reduced the growth rate to 1.27 percent in the 1990s, and 0.7 percent in the 2000s. The population of North Korea in 2016 was estimated at 25.37 million people (World Bank 2019). In sum, the population and real GDP of North Korea were 20.29 million people and 42.7 billion USD in 1990, respectively. In 2016 the population increased to 25.36 million people, but the real GDP decreased significantly to 27.1 billion USD (see Figure 10.1). This indicates a trend of continued economic hardship in North

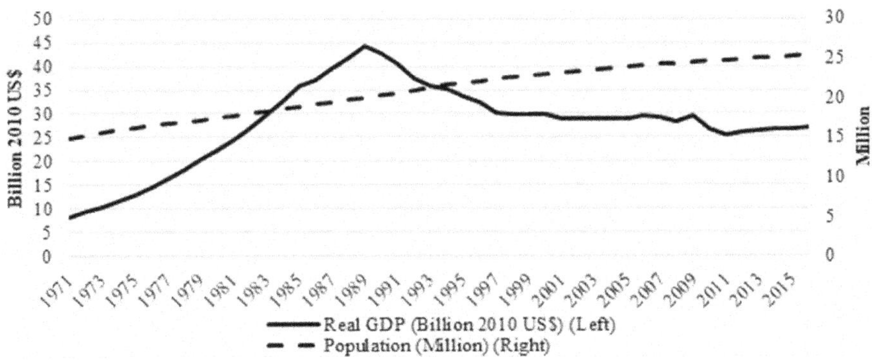

Figure 10.1 North Korea's real GDP and population

Source: Adapted from World Bank 2019 and IEA 2019

Korea, especially since strengthened economic sanctions by the UN and the United States are expected to worsen the North Korean economy in the coming years.

2.2 Energy situation

Energy is an essential input for economic activities, and a country's energy consumption increases as its economy grows. If the major energy sources are fossil fuels, such as coal and oil, an increase in energy consumption increases greenhouse gas emissions. North Korea's energy consumption and greenhouse gas emissions show a similar trend to the country's economic conditions. In general, primary energy sources, such as coal, crude oil, gas, and hydro, transform into secondary energy, such as electricity or oil products, and the total final consumption aggregates into a country's end-use energy. As shown in Figure 10.2, Total Primary Energy Supply (TPES) and Total Final Energy Consumption (TFC) showed an increasing trend in the 1970s, however, both energy supply and consumption have gradually declined since the mid-1980s. An interesting finding from North Korea's energy supply and consumption is the decreasing gap between Total Primary Energy Supply and Total Final Consumption.

The gap between TPES and TFC continued to increase until the late 1980s, however, the gap has been decreasing since the early 1990s, and has become quite minimal in recent years. According to the Energy Balance table from the International Energy Agency, the gap between TPES and TFC has a close relationship with the use of coal, oil, and oil products.

The difference in consumption of coal between TPES and TFC was 6,818 thousand TOE in 1989, but the gap decreased to 1,768 thousand TOE in 2013. This dramatic change can be explained by coal and coal products used in furnaces and coke ovens. This indicates that North Korea's bad economic condition led to a decrease of steel production, and consequentially, the use of coal products for

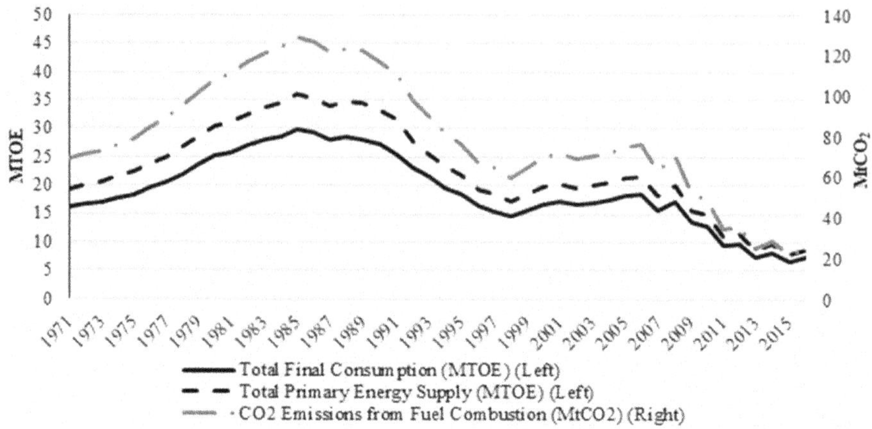

Figure 10.2 Energy and greenhouse gas emissions of North Korea

Source: Adapted from IEA 2019

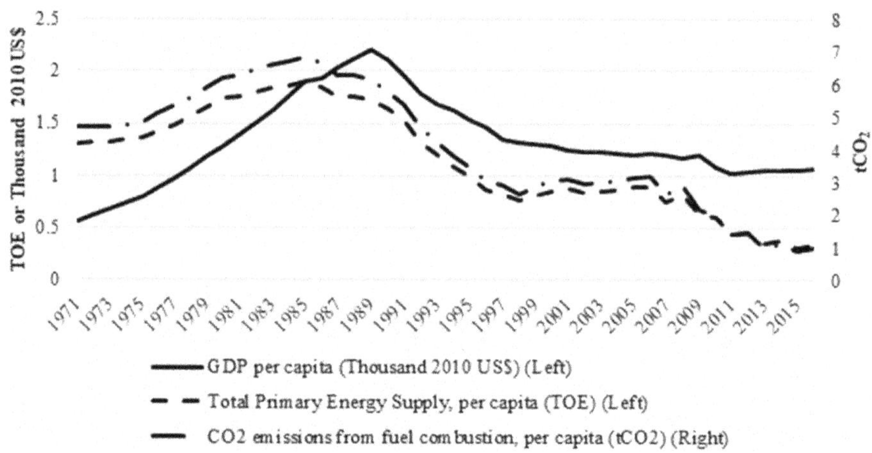

Figure 10.3 Energy and greenhouse gas emissions, per capita

Source: Adapted from IEA 2019

steel production. The use of coal and coal products in electricity generation has also declined, from 4,488 thousand TOE in 1989 to 1,699 thousand TOE in 2016. As the North Korean economy began to decline in the late 1980s, TPES continued its significant downward trend, leading to a significant decrease in the demand for coal in the process of energy transformation.

Considering that most of the fossil fuel used in North Korea is coal, and the importation of crude oil or oil products has been restricted under the current stringent economic sanctions, North Korea's greenhouse gas emissions are closely related to its coal supply and consumption. Figure 10.3 shows that North Korea's carbon emissions from fuel combustion and TPES move in a very similar direction. After reaching a peak of 129.4 $MtCO_2$ in 1985, North Korea's CO_2 emissions from fuel combustion continued to decrease gradually. The CO_2 emissions from fuel combustion have decreased by over 80 percent in the last thirty years down to 25 $MtCO_2$ in 2016. In per capita base, the economic and energy indicators reveal the harsh economic conditions of North Korea in recent decades more clearly. Though the population of North Korea increased from fifteen million people in 1971 to twenty-five million people in 2016, the real GDP increased by only eighteen billion 2010 USD. Accordingly, GDP per capita has doubled from only 560 2010 USD to 1,070 2010 USD over the last four decades.

In the same period, TPES per capita decreased by about 74 percent, from 1.31 TOE in 1971 to 0.35 TOE in 2016. Also, CO_2 emissions from fuel combustion per capita have declined since 1985 and reached only one tCO_2 per person. On a per capita basis, energy and economic indicators of a country generally tend to increase in most economies, in line with its economic development. North Korea's TPES per capita in 2016 is only 24 percent of that in 1971, however, which indicates very serious economic and energy deficiencies. During the same period, per capita CO_2 emissions had increased to a high of 6.9 tCO_2 in 1985, and from there, declined steadily to only 1.0 tCO_2 in 2016.

As shown in Figure 10.4, North Korea's electricity generation has a close relationship with the North Korean economy. Similar to the economic development, the electricity generation of North Korea had increased from 15 TWh in 1971 to 29.2 TWh in 1989. After reaching its peak in 1989, the electricity generation of North Korea decreased continuously in the 1990s. Though the electricity generation increased slightly in the early 2000s, it resumed a downward trajectory in the late 2000s. In 2016, North Korea generated about 17 TWh of electricity, which

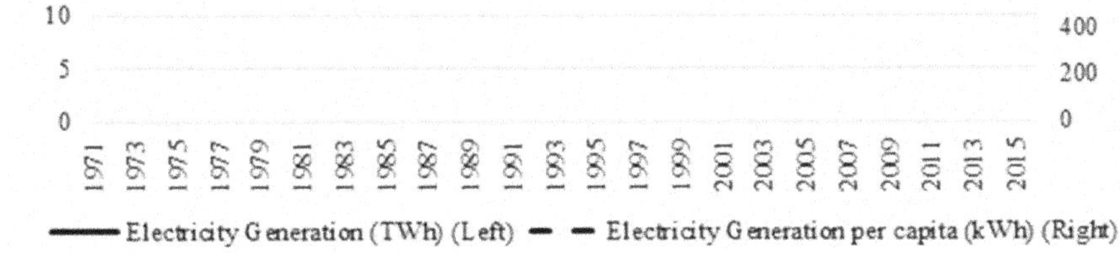

Figure 10.4 Electricity generation

Source: Adapted from IEA 2019

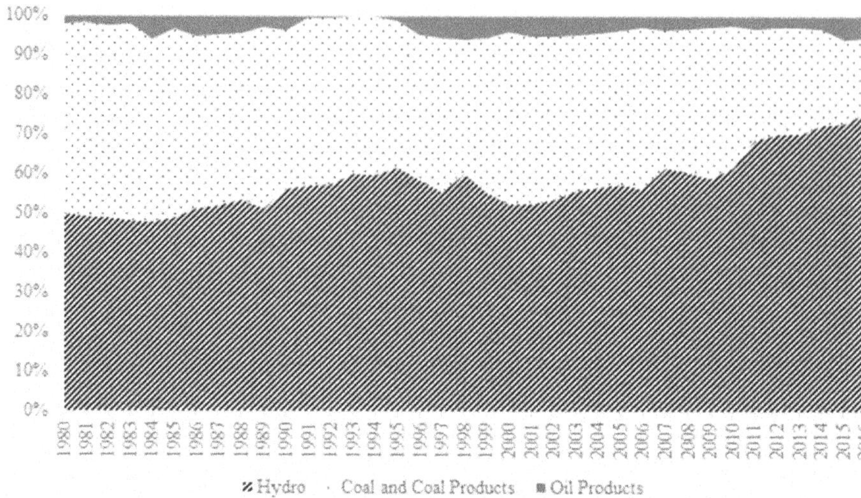

Figure 10.5 Share of electricity generation by source (%)

Source: Adapted from IEA 2019

is similar to its 1973 levels. Due to the population growth, however, electricity generation per capita decreased more dramatically than the total electricity generation. Electricity generation per capita has decreased by approximately 33 percent, from 1,003 kWh in 1971 to 667 kWh in 2016. This result reveals the serious electricity supply condition in North Korea. Improving the efficiency of existing facilities by retrofitting and installing new technology is becoming the key challenge in the electricity sector.

Hydropower has been the main energy source for electricity generation in North Korea. According to IEA statistics, hydropower accounted for about 75 percent of the electricity generation in 2016. In 1980, hydropower contributed half of the electricity generation, and coal accounted for 48 percent. The remaining 2 percent of electricity was generated from oil and oil products. The share of coal remained between 30–40 percent until 2000, but it dropped to lower than 30 percent after 2010. Except for a few years, the share of oil and oil products has contributed less than 5 percent of the total electricity generation. Figure 10.5 shows that North Korea has been largely relying on hydropower. Heavy reliance on a single energy source can cause challenges to the country's electricity generation, however, especially considering the low energy efficiency of North Korea's old hydropower plants, and the seasonality of hydropower generation. Such variables threaten the stability of electricity generation in North Korea.

3 Methodology and analysis

The purpose of this section is to examine the relationship between energy consumption and economic growth, and project the future greenhouse gas emissions of North Korea. The study uses annual energy, economic, and social data from the International Energy Agency, United Nations Data, and North Korean Statistics provided by Statistics Korea. The data shows that energy consumption and economic development trends started to decline in the mid-1980s, with contributing factors like the collapse of the Socialist Bloc in the late 1980s, and the Soviet Union in 1991, altering North Korea's economic structure. Thus, the study only covers the data periods from 1990 to 2016.

3.1 LMDI-Kaya identity decomposition

Kaya Identity Decomposition provides a way to understand and break down changes in CO_2 emissions. CO_2 emissions can be divided into categories such as population change, energy use from economic activities, efficient use of energy, and type of energy use. The method considers GDP, Energy Consumption, Population, and CO_2 emissions over time and provides a framework for evaluating factors affecting GHG emissions. The identity equation can be used to decompose four CO_2 emissions factors. (Kaya and Yokobori 1997; Peters et al. 2017).

In this chapter, the Logarithmic Mean Divisia Index (LMDI) Decomposition method is used to analyze the key factors affecting carbon emissions in North Korea.

$$CarbonEmissions \equiv \frac{CarbonEmissions}{Energy} \times \frac{Energy}{GDP} \times \frac{GDP}{Population} \times Population \tag{10.1}$$

$$(A) \equiv (B) \quad (C) \quad (D) \quad (E)$$

(GDP/Population) is per capita real GDP (pGDP); (Energy/GDP) is energy intensity of energy (EI); (Carbon Emissions/Energy) is carbon intensity of energy. The Carbon Intensity (CI) of energy is the indicator demonstrating the amount of CO_2 emissions from a unit of energy supply, because all energy sources, such as coal, oil, and gas, emit different amounts of CO_2. That is, to produce an equal amount of energy, the use of coal creates higher levels of CO_2 emissions than oil. Energy intensity shows the amount of an energy source required to produce one unit of GDP. In other words, this indicates how efficiently an economy uses an energy source during production. For example, if half of a ton of energy is used to produce one dollar of GDP, the economy has a lower energy intensity, and is considered more efficient, than an economy using one ton of energy to produce the same one dollar of GDP.

The cumulative change in carbon emissions from base year 0 to target year t can be found in Equations 10.2–10.6. The LMDI method is used to find each part of the equation. By using this equation and method, the chapter analyzes the change of North Korea's greenhouse gas emissions, and with the results of time-series analysis, the decomposition analysis provides a better understanding of North Korea's energy and greenhouse gas emissions.

$$\Delta CarbonEmissions = CE_t - CE_0 = \Delta CE_{POP} + \Delta CE_{pGDP} + \Delta CE_{EI} + \Delta CE_{CI} \quad (10.2)$$

$$\Delta CE_{POP} = L(CE_0, CE_t) \times ln\left(\frac{POP_t}{POP_0}\right) \quad (10.3)$$

$$\Delta CE_{pGDP} = L(CE_0, CE_t) \times ln\left(\frac{pGDP_t}{pGDP_0}\right) \quad (10.4)$$

$$\Delta CE_{EI} = L(CE_0, CE_t) \times ln\left(\frac{EI_t}{EI_0}\right) \quad (10.5)$$

$$\Delta CE_{CI} = L(CE_0, CE_t) \times ln\left(\frac{CI_t}{CI_0}\right) \quad (10.6)$$

where $L(CE_0, CE_t) = \frac{CE_t - CE_0}{ln\left(\frac{CE_t}{CE_0}\right)}$ is the logarithm weight average.

3.2 Analysis

In the Kaya Identity Decomposition, the analysis covers the entire sample periods from 1971–2016 to show a better picture of North Korea's greenhouse gas emissions. The study uses the same variables in Kaya Identity Decomposition. Figure 10.6 provides the result of the ten-year Kaya Identity Decomposition.[1] From Figure 10.6, the result shows that GDP per capita is the main source of the increase in greenhouse gas emissions, and the energy intensity is the main factor limiting the increase of greenhouse gas emissions. In the 1970s, North Korea's CO_2 emissions from fuel combustion increased by 38.9 $MtCO_2$. The economic growth of North Korea increased in per capita GDP, and accordingly contributed to an increase of 72.23 $MtCO_2$ in carbon emissions. A population increase in North Korea's boosted carbon emissions by 14.42 $MtCO_2$, however, energy intensity (which indicates an efficient use of energy) and carbon intensity reduced 47.64 $MtCO_2$ and 0.11 $MtCO_2$ of carbon emissions in the

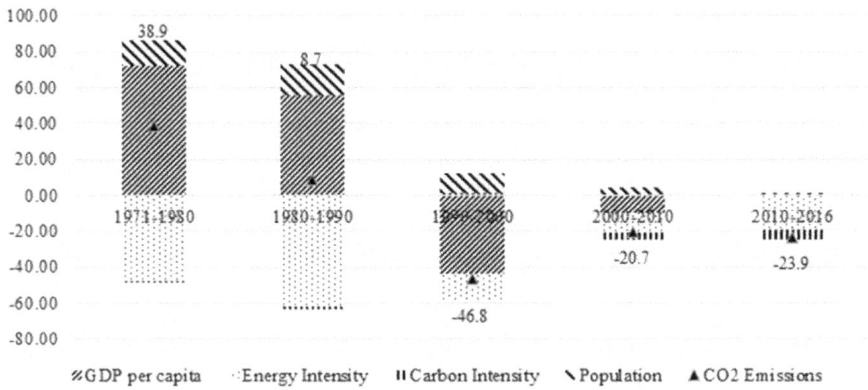

Figure 10.6 KAYA identity decomposition (10-year; $MtCO_2$)

Source: Author created

1970s, respectively. In the 1980s, the carbon emissions from fuel combustion increased by only 8.7 $MtCO_2$. Population growth and GDP per capita increased carbon emissions by 16.82 $MtCO_2$ and 55.71 $MtCO_2$, respectively. However, the improvement of energy intensity and carbon intensity reduced the emissions by 62.42 Mt CO_2 and 1.42 Mt CO_2, respectively. As a result, the amount of increase of carbon emissions from fuel combustion in the 1980s was significantly reduced compared to that of the 1970s. In the 1990s and 2000s, there was a significant decrease in CO_2 emissions from fuel combustion. While the population slightly increased emissions, the emission reductions from GDP per capita and Energy Intensity played a significant role in decreasing total carbon emissions from fuel combustion. This can be explained by the fact that the North Korean economy significantly diminished during those periods. The decreasing trend of CO_2 emissions from fuel combustion continued into the 2010s. Aside from population, all other factors have contributed to the decrease of CO_2 emissions from fuel combustion, while the low population growth rate in recent years has also slowed the increase in carbon emissions from North Korea.

Figure 10.6 illustrates the result of the KAYA Identity Decomposition and the changes in CO_2 emissions by each factor. As the North Korean economy has waned over the last decades, the amount of energy use has decreased accordingly. As a result, total CO_2 emissions have reduced since the 1990s. Especially, the decreasing trend of per capita GDP and CO_2 emissions since 1990 can be highlighted as a distinctive feature that is quite different from the cases of other countries.

4 Energy supply and CO_2 emissions projection of North Korea

Due to the limited information and various uncertainties of economic, social, and political factors, any projection of North Korea's future energy supply and consumption would not be very accurate. This chapter, however, projects North Korea's future energy supply and CO_2 emissions based on the stable correlation between North Korea's past primary energy supply and GDP, and therefore, the relationship between GDP (economic activity) and energy supply as an input of economic activity is assumed to be stable. Based on this assumption, future North Korea's GDP can be projected by multiplying North Korea's population projection and the growth rate of per capita GDP. With the emission factors of energy sources, the future emission projection can be achieved by the stable relationship between primary energy supply and carbon emissions.

4.1 Projection of North Korea's energy supply

In order to project North Korea's GDP by 2030, North Korea's per capita GDP is projected by applying the per capita GNI growth rate from Kang, Jung, and Son (2018). Kang, Jung, and Son established four different scenarios by using the economic growth rates of South Korea in the mid-1970s, China in the mid-1990s, and the Southeast Asian countries in the past when they have had similar levels of per capita GNI to North Korea today. Under the current circumstances, however, the assumption of achieving the growth rates of South Korea or China's would be unrealistic. In addition to these two scenarios, this section includes a model that assumes an annual growth rate of 6 percent after 2020. Due to the continued economic sanctions, the pace of North Korea's economic development might not reach the rates of Southeast Asian countries. This scenario thus assumes a lower growth rate than the former two scenarios, and therefore, projects North Korea's real GDP level by using three scenarios that considered the economic growth rates of the Southeast Asian countries in the past when their per capita GNIs were similar to North Korea's per capita GNI (estimated by Bank of Korea) of $1,258 in 2016.

Table 10.1 North Korea's economic development scenarios (2016–2030)

	Scenario 1	*Scenario 2*	*Scenario 3*
Average Annual Growth Rate	7 Southeast Asian Countries (7.5%)	7 Southeast Asian Countries (7.1%)	Under Economic Sanction (6.0%)

Source: Kang, Jung, and Son 2018

Note: These scenarios assume that the North Korean economy establishes the foundation of economic development in 2016–2020 and then continues to grow as the seven Southeast Asian countries (Cambodia, Indonesia, Malaysia, Myanmar, Philippines, Thailand, and Vietnam)

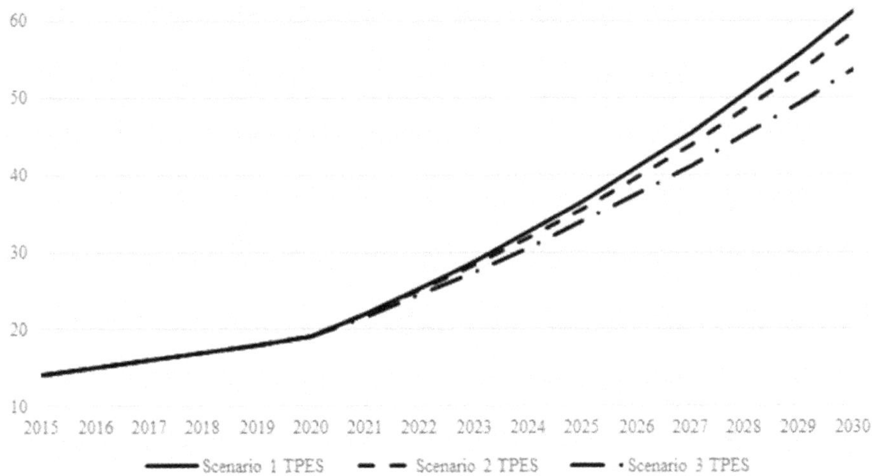

Figure 10.7 North Korea's TPES projections by GDP scenarios (MTOE)

Source: Author created

North Korea's GDP was forecasted by multiplying its UN population projection (median scenario) (United Nations 2019) and per capita GDP projection. The study assumes a stable relationship between GDP and energy use and projects the future energy use by using regression analysis. As shown by Figure 10.7, the primary energy supply is expected to reach around 50–60 million TOE in 2030.

4.2 Projection of North Korea's CO_2 emissions

Based on the projections of primary energy supply by 2030, the projections on CO_2 emissions from fossil fuel consumption can be achieved. Since the structure of North Korea's primary energy supply is largely dependent on coal, there is a very stable relationship between the use of fossil fuel and CO_2 emissions, therefore, the study assumes a stable relationship between primary energy supply and CO_2 emissions and projects North Korea's future CO_2 emissions. As shown by Figure 10.8, North Korea's CO_2 emissions are projected to reach between 196 million and 221 million tCO_2 in 2030.

4.3 North Korea's voluntary emissions reduction targets

In August 2016, North Korea ratified the Paris Agreement, which was adopted on December 12, 2015, at the Twenty-First Conference of the Parties to the United Nations Framework Convention on Climate Change. Accordingly, North Korea submitted its intended nationally determined contribution (INDC) containing its climate mitigation and adaptation plans to the UNFCCC (DPRK 2016).

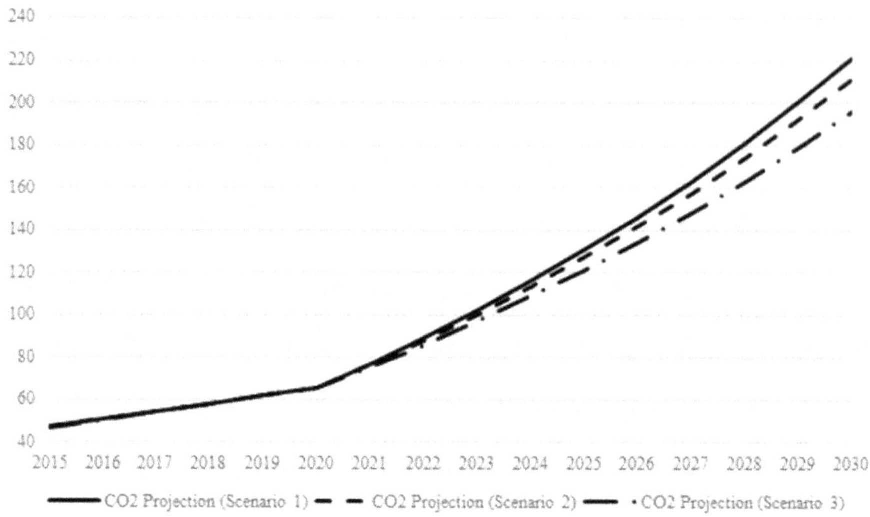

Figure 10.8 CO_2 emissions projections by GDP scenarios ($MtCO_2eq$)

Source: Author created

According to North Korea's INDC, North Korea's greenhouse gas (GHG) emissions in 2000 were 65,714 $GgCO_2eq$, which accounted for 0.16 percent of the global GHG emissions (40 Gt CO_2eq) in 2000. On a per capita basis, North Korea's GHG emissions were 2.9tCO_2eq in 2000, which made it one of the lowest GHG emitting countries in the world. Though North Korea's GHG emissions are expected to increase to 6.5 tCO_2eq, this rate will still be lower than the global average.

North Korea understands the importance of incorporating climate change into its national, social, and economic development plans and strategies as an important measure for achieving national sustainable development. As per North Korea's five-year economic strategy, national energy and climate change issues can be addressed by enhancing the efficiency of generating facilities, as well as expanding the use of renewable energy sources. Considering North Korea's development priorities and its need for climate adaptation, the international supports on developing countries, agreed upon in the Paris Agreement, will be necessary for bolstering North Korea's mitigation measures.

According to INDC, North Korea set its Business-as-Usual (BAU) scenario for GHG emissions at 187.73 million tCO_2eq by 2030, and suggested conditional and unconditional contributions to GHG emissions. First, the unconditional contribution considers the implementation of measures and policies by utilizing internal resources only, without support from the international community. Using the BAU scenario, North Korea promised to unconditionally reduce emissions by 8.0 percent by 2030. The conditional contribution, on the other hand, does consider support from the international community. As a member of the UNFCCC, North Korea is classified as a developing country that can receive support from the international community. If there is international cooperation in the form of financial support, technology transfer, and capacity building programs, North Korea could achieve 32.25 percent in additional GHG emissions reduction by 2030. Compared to the BAU scenario, the conditional contribution is an ambitious voluntary GHG reduction plan that could reduce GHG emissions by 40.25 percent by 2030 (DPRK 2016).

North Korea suggested ten specific measures to achieve the GHG emissions reduction targets of INDC, as seen in Table 10.2.

To achieve the conditional contribution, North Korea selected and prioritized nineteen mitigation measures. On the supply-side, North Korea emphasized the expansion of generation facilities, the improvement of energy efficiency, and the expansion of renewable energy capacity. On the demand-side, North Korea highlighted measures for retrofitting and improving the efficiency of household and rural communities' energy equipment and facilities. Moreover, the mitigation measures consider that agroforestry and sustainable forest management will absorb GHG emissions, and eventually achieve GHG emissions reduction. These measures imply North Korea's plan for establishing a low-carbon economy through financial support and technology transfer from the international community.

As stated in North Korea's INDC, North Korea intends to establish its long-term economic development plan with the consideration of climate change issues. This intention is meaningful in that North Korea is heading toward sustainable development goals as a member of the international community.

Table 10.2 Measures for achieving North Korea's conditional contribution

No.	*Measures*
1	Strengthen the national framework on climate change
2	Improve energy use efficiency and reduce energy consumption
3	Improve energy efficiency and encourage the use of alternative energy in electric power industry
4	Scale up the utilization of renewable energy development
5	Manage and develop forest in the sustainable manner
6	Introduce advanced technologies and methodologies for sustainable agriculture development
7	Introduce sustainable waste management
8	Raise public awareness and accelerate participatory process for responding climate change
9	Enhance international cooperation for mitigation of climate change
10	Increase financial support for mitigation measures

Source: Adapted from DRP Korea 2016

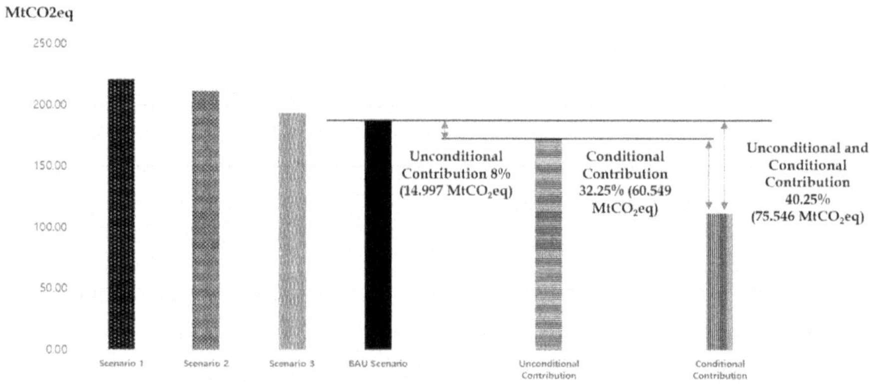

Figure 10.9 North Korea's GHG emissions projections (2030)

Source: Adapted from DPR Korea 2016

This section compares the 2030 CO_2 emissions projections in the previous section to North Korea's conditional and unconditional contributions stated in INDC (see Figure 10.9). The study suggests that North Korea's GHG emissions are expected to reach 210–220 million tCO_2eq, however, North Korea's INDC suggested 187 million tCO_2eq of GHG emissions as its BAU scenario. In the INDC (compared to the BAU scenario), North Korea announced its plan to reduce emissions using domestic resources by 8 percent, and reduce emissions by over 40 percent with international support, by 2030.

5 Conclusion

Establishing climate adaptation plans for mitigating impacts from climate change should be considered when expanding North Korea's social overhead capital (SOC) for economic development. A massive investment is necessary for the establishment and implementation of North Korea's climate change adaptation plan. It is also meaningful that North Korea submitted their INDC to participate in the international efforts on GHG mitigation as a member of the international community. In addition to its economic development, establishing a long-term development strategy that addresses climate change issues is an important step that simultaneously considers domestic economic issues and international matters. Enforcement is a more important matter, however. It is difficult to expect North Korea to prepare sufficient conditions for its long-term, ambitious economic plan within the near future. In order to implement its INDC effectively, therefore, the most urgent matter is to establish concrete financial and technical support programs to create the necessary conditions for success.

At the same time, it is necessary to establish a support system for North Korea in order to implement and evaluate GHG mitigation efforts effectively through a concrete capacity development program. Above all, it is imperative to increase North Korea's understanding of international practices. The transition from a socialist economic system that restricts international trade, toward an open market economic system that cooperates with the international community, is the way to realize North Korea's long-term economic development plan. Through efforts to tackle the climate change issue, North Korea can realize its long-term development plan and achieve a sustainable economy in the long run. As a member of international community, North Korea needs to develop its capacity to address international issues, such as climate change, and to participate in international affairs.

Along with North Korea's own economic and international efforts it will eventually be essential to alleviate and eliminate the economic sanctions imposed on it by the international community, which are the largest obstacles to North Korea's economic development. The prerequisite is that North Korea establishes and implements sincere efforts and concrete programs for denuclearization with the international community. Through this process, North Korea's financial and technical support as a member of the international community will be the fastest way to realize the various policies and concrete measures that North Korea has proposed in their INDC.

Note

1 The last sample period is six years (2011–2016).

References

Congressional Research Service. 2019. "North Korea: Legislative Basis for U.S. Economic Sanctions." Accessed February 2. https://fas.org/sgp/crs/row/R41438.pdf.

Democratic People's Republic of Korea. 2016. "Intended Nationally Determined Contribution of Democratic People's Republic of Korea." https://www4.unfccc.int/sites/ndcstaging/PublishedDocuments/Democratic%20People%27s%20Republic%20of%20Korea%20First/DPRK-INDC%20by%202030.pdf.

International Energy Agency (IEA). 2019. "IEA World Energy Statistics and Balances 2018 Database." Accessed March 20. www.iea.org/classicstats/relateddatabases/worldenergystatisticsandbalances/.

Kang, Sung Jin, Tae Yong Jung, and Sang Hak Son. 2018. "A Study on Necessary Investment in North Korea for Economic Transition and Economic Growth." *Korean Unification Studies* 22 (2): 5–48.

Kaya, Yoichi, and Keiichi Yokobori. 1997. *Environment, Energy, and Economy: Strategies for Sustainable Development*. Tokyo, New York and Paris: United Nations University Press.

Peters, Glen, Robbie Andrew, Josep Canadell, Sabine Fuss, Robert Jackson, Korsbakken, Jan Ivar Korsbakken, Le Quéré Corinne, and Nebojsa Nakicenovic. 2017. "Key

Indicators to Track Current Progress and Future Ambition of the Paris Agreement." *Nature Climate Change*. www.nature.com/articles/nclimate3202.
United Nations. 2019. "World Population Prospects 2019." Accessed March 17. https://population.un.org/wpp/Download/Standard/Population/.
World Bank. 2019. "Population, total [Data]." Accessed March 20. https://data.worldbank.org/indicator/sp.pop.totl.

11 The Paris Agreement and North Korea's sustainable development

Yoonhee Ha

1 Introduction

Climate change, which has emerged as one of the most urgent issues of the world, has had a great impact on the economy and society of each country.

North Korea is also experiencing serious economic and social problems due to climate change. Economic and social phenomena caused by warming and economic sanctions are influencing each other, and this situation is getting worse. North Korea recognizes that a response to climate change is a most important task for economic and social development, and has actively participated in related international climate conventions and governance. North Korea is actively participating in the Paris Agreement (PA). The PA has various support systems that can contribute to the sustainable development of developing countries such as North Korea.

This chapter aims to examine opportunities for economic and social development and inter-Korea cooperation that can be secured through North Korea's response to climate change under the Paris climate regime. Section 2 discusses the connection between the PA and sustainable development. Section 3 reviews the current status of the international cooperation activities to cope with North Korea's climate change and the clean development project under the Kyoto system. Section 4 examines opportunities for North Korea's sustainable development through actions against climate change. To this end, it reviews mechanisms the PA can utilize to support developing countries. Lastly, the PA's cooperative mechanism provides an opportunity to discuss the integration of North and South Koreas' carbon markets.

2 The Paris Agreement and sustainable development

The significance of the PA is that it has secured promises from almost every nation on the planet, both developed and developing, that translate into actions designed to stop climate change. As an introductory step, most parties of the United Nations Framework Convention on Climate Change (UNFCCC) create a nationally determined contribution (NDC) based on different historical responsibilities, capacities, and respective situations before starting to take climate actions. In this sense, the PA can be said to be a paradigm shift, expanding climate responsibilities to the past, present and future; that all humanity would commonly respond to climate change, unlike the Kyoto regime, in which only developed countries with the greatest responsibility for the past have an obligation.

To achieve the ambitious global temperature mitigation goals (<2°C) set by the active participation by countries in Asia and Africa, where rapid industrialization and population growth is occurring, is urgently needed.

Industrialization has presented tremendous material abundance to humanity, but at the same time it has been accompanied by inequality between classes and regions, environmental catastrophe, and poverty (Heilbroner 1991; Mumford and Winner 2010). Developing countries that are experiencing rapid economic growth have shown path-dependent industrialization (Fouquet 2016). As developed countries have done, they consume massive amounts of energy and resources, and the resulting carbon and waste has a huge adverse impact on the Earth's ecosystem. Asia is currently contributing 40 percent of the world's carbon footprint and this is projected to increase to 67 percent by 2030 if the current trend continues. In addition, carbon emissions in Africa, historically not responsible for climate change, have been increasing rapidly in recent years (Gomez-Echeverri 2018). In the third world, which has a high dependence on nature, the destruction of the environment plays a major role in strengthening poverty and inequality and increasing economic and social instability. Natural disasters, which have become more frequent and extreme due to climate change, are also driving citizens of the third world into a more vulnerable state (Dolan and Walker 2006).

In order to prevent apocalyptic climate change and address the challenges facing human society, it is urgent to change the development path. This is why the United Nations (UN) adopted the 2030 Agenda for Sustainable Development in 2015.

The sustainable development goals (SDGs), which are the core of the 2030 agenda, offer an action plan for humanity, the planet, and prosperity. It is composed of seventeen high-level goals and 169 sub targets. Most of the seventeen goals are closely related to climate change actions. This is because sustainable development is based on the recognition that socioeconomic development is impossible if the viability of the environment is undermined.

A significant portion of the sustainable development goals can be achieved through carbon reduction and implementation of climate change adaptation actions to achieve the targets of NDCs. Goal #13 of the SDGs' climate action calls for urgent actions to fight against climate change and to address its impacts. Goals #6 (clean water and sanitation), #7 (affordable and clean energy), #8 (decent work and economic growth), #9 (innovation and infrastructure), #11 (sustainable cities and communities), #12 (responsible consumption), #14 (life below water), and #15 (life on land) are directly linked to the PA.

Goals #1 (no poverty), #2 (zero hunger), #3 (good health and well-being), #4 (quality education), #5 (gender equality), #10 (reduced inequalities), and #16 (peace, justice, and strong institutions), represent the ultimate objectives of sustainable development (SD). These objectives can only be realized when directly linked to the PA, however, thus creating a strong interdependence between SD and the PA.

It should be noted that the various mechanisms created by SD to support the developing world's climate actions and governances contributed to the birth of the PA, which unites all of humanity in the fight against climate change. For developing countries suffering from a significant lack of basic infrastructure, as well as financial, technological, structural policy, and institutional deficiencies, calls for climate actions (especially carbon reduction) can be interpreted as forcing such nations to remain in perpetual poverty and underdevelopment. Thankfully, the PA's supporting mechanisms, including the financial support mechanism (Article 9), technical support mechanism (Article 10), cooperative mechanism between parties (Article 6), and capacity building (Article 11) have played crucial roles in turning doubts about the agreement into hopes for sustainable development through climate actions.

Developing countries vulnerable to climate change also strongly argued in the negotiation process that adaptation measures to reduce the negative impacts of climate change are as important as carbon reduction. As a result, the PA promises support and international cooperation for adaptation actions in developing countries, stating in Article 7, "recognize that greater adaptation needs can involve greater adaptation cost," Article 9 went even further with the following statement: "developed country Parties shall provide financial resources to assist developing country Parties with respect to both mitigation and adaptation."

With these measures, the PA can provide the fundamental and crucial means by which developing countries' actions against climate change can lead to balanced development of the economy, society and the environment.

Climate change is also challenging North Korea's economic and social development. North Korea's climate change trend is clear, and its impact is also serious. According to the 2012 report of Germanwatch that annually publishes each country's Climate Risk Index (CRI), North Korea was ranked at 7th in long-term CRI from 1992–2011 (Harmeling and Eckstein 2012). North Korea's climate change has worsened as forests have been damaged due to large-scale logging for food production domestically, which has increased the country's vulnerability to natural disasters. Responses to climate change, therefore, are of the utmost importance for North Korea's economic and social stability, and continued development. Under the dire circumstances, North Korea, one of the most private nations on the planet, has actively participated in international negotiations and global governances on climate change, contrary to general expectations. North Korea signed on with the PA and submitted the country's NDC to the UNFCCC in September 2016.

As shown in Figure 11.1, North Korea holds the lowest annual per capita income among developing countries at just $1,165 in 2016. Despite having the world's lowest economic level, North Korea underachieved, with an ecological deficit of 0.3, consuming ecosystem services beyond its ecological capacity.

Considering that Mongolia, a neighboring country with similar income levels, achieved an ecological surplus (+6.5) with a per capita income of $ 3,903, the ecological crisis in North Korea is considerable. The establishment of a low-carbon,

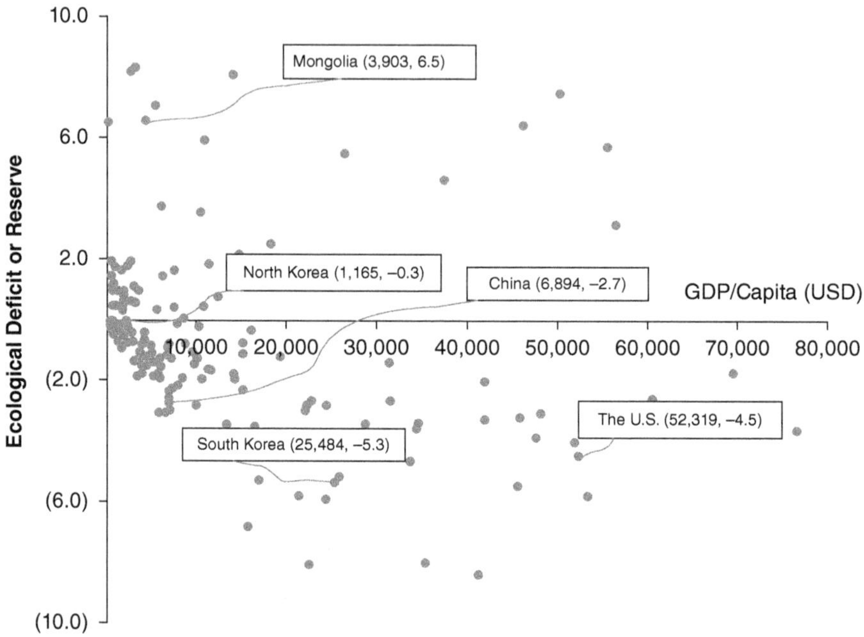

Figure 11.1 Ecological balance sheet

Source: Adapted from International Ecological Footprint 2020 and North Korea Economy Watch 2019

environmentally friendly development strategy and its successful implementation can be a fundamental solution to the socioeconomic problems facing North Korea. North Korea's NDC states that "integrating climate change considerations into relevant socioeconomic development strategies and plans is one of the most important means of ensuring the country's sustainable development" (United Nations Framework Convention on Climate Change 2016, 2).

3 North Korea's response to climate change

North Korea is aware of the seriousness of climate change and is seeking concrete ways to cope with it. Referring to North Korea's international cooperation activities to address climate change, North Korea's NDC, and their second national report on climate change, North Korea is prioritizing the establishment of a national response system, plus energy and forest restoration projects through the expansion of international investments.

3.1 North Korea's international cooperation in the environmental sector

North Korea is more flexible and open to international cooperation for climate actions compared to political and economic issues, such as diplomacy, military, and trade. The international community has continued to provide humanitarian aid to North Korea since the mid-1990s, when North Korea faced severe economic difficulties.

Organizations under the UN, government agencies of donor countries, and international NGOs such as Red Cross, have provided aid in the form of health and medical services. The United Nations Development Program (UNDP) has been promoting international technology transfer, and funding in the environmental sector. Due to North Korea's continued development of nuclear weapons, however, worldwide public opinion of North Korea has seen a negative trajectory, causing most projects to be reduced in size or suspended.

North Korea joined the UNFCCC in December 1994, ratified the Kyoto Protocol (KP) in April 2005, and, most recently, signed the PA for the second time in 2016. In recent years, the country has met the requirements of the Clean Development Mechanism (CDM) under the Kyoto regime. The CDM allows emission-reduction projects in developing countries to earn certified emission reduction (CER) credits, each equivalent to one tonne of CO2. These CERs can be traded and sold and used by industrialized countries to a meet a part of their emission reduction targets under the KP. The mechanism stimulates sustainable development and emission reduction, while giving industrialized countries some flexibility in how they meet their emission reduction targets.[1] With the United Nations Security Council's economic sanctions on North Korea greatly strengthened, North Korean authorities have actively promoted the CDM project by recognizing the sale of carbon credits as a means to attract foreign investment.

In an article titled "A Way to Expand Carbon Trade Focusing on Emissions Trading," published in Kim Il-sung University's bulletin (No. 3, 2017), released in September 2017, the merits of carbon credits trading for North Korea's development through the CDM projects were explained: "The main purpose of the

Table 11.1 Environmental conventions/protocols signed by North Korea

Conventions/Protocols	*Date*
United Nations Convention on Biodiversity	Oct. 26, 1994
United Nations Framework Convention on Climate Change	Dec. 5, 1994
Vienna Convention on the Protection of Ozone Layer	May 5, 1995
Montreal Protocol on Substances that Deplete the Ozone Layer	May 6, 1995
Stockholm Convention on Persistent Organic Pollutants	Aug. 19, 2002
Cartagena Protocol on Biosafety	July 29, 2003
United Nations Convention on Combating Desertification	Mar. 28, 2004
Kyoto Protocol to the United Nations Framework Convention on Climate Change	Apr. 27, 2005
Basel Convention on Trans-boundary Movements of Hazardous Wastes and their Disposal	July 10, 2008
Paris Agreement	Sep. 1, 2016

Source: Adapted from Ministry of Land and Environment Protection 2012

transaction is to attract investment from other countries and protect the country's environment while trying to build an economic powerhouse." This article emphasized, "If we make good public relations with the achievements and experiences obtained in the struggle process to create a clean environment, we will be able to further stimulate our investors' desire to invest" (Kim 2017). It shows North Korea's intention to draw technological and financial support from abroad to strengthen their country's capacity for economic recovery and sustainable development based on the understanding of the global agenda of GHG reduction and global warming prevention.

North Korea and UN agencies have conducted joint research on climate change and the environment. In 1999, under the financial support of the Global Environment Fund (GEF), North Korea and the UNDP established a "strategy for minimum cost greenhouse gas reduction." Also, North Korea conducted research across all fields, including forests, land, water quality, and biodiversity North Korea did this in cooperation with the United Nations Environment Program (UNEP), and subsequently published "DPR KOREA'S Environment and Climate Change Outlook 2012."

The UNDP has implemented projects to improve North Korea's environment through the Agricultural Recovery and Environment Protection (AREP) program from 1999. Various international and nongovernmental organizations have also carried out environmental improvement and environmental protection projects for the most vulnerable in North Korea.

Along with the external supports, the environmental regulation framework has been established. Since the mid-1990s, North Korea has enacted the "Environmental Protection Act," "Sea Pollution Prevention Act," and "Homeland Environment Protection and Enforcement Act," and continuously modified and supplemented internal regulations to meet international standards. Also, in order to facilitate cooperation with international organizations related to the environment, North Korea has joined or been ratified into more than ten international environmental agreements.

3.2 North Korea's clean development mechanism (CDM) under the Kyoto Protocol

The KP operated a flexible mechanism through which Annex I countries[2] could achieve greenhouse gas reduction through international cooperation as an auxiliary means of their reduction activities. The flexibility mechanism includes Joint Implementation (JI), Clean Development Mechanism (CDM), and Emission Trading (ET). CDMs offer developed countries the opportunity to create carbon credits by conducting greenhouse gas reduction projects in developing countries, thereby providing cost-effective reduction measures in developed countries, and environmental soundness and sustainable development in developing countries. As of June 4, 2019, North Korea had eleven CDM projects registered with the UNFCCC. Significantly, North Korean authorities have carried out the entire process of those projects in compliance with international regulations and standards.

Table 11.2 North Korea's international cooperation projects related to climate change

No	*Project title*	*GEF, **USD***	*Duration*	*Supporting **organization***
1	Enabling DPR Korea to Prepare its First National Communication in Response to its Commitments to UNFCCC	154,200	1997–2001	UNDP
2	National Biodiversity Strategy & Action Plan and Report to the COP	299,250	1998–2000	UNDP
3	Conservation of Biodiversity at Mount Myohyang in the DPR Korea	750,000	2000–2004	UNDP
4	Strengthening Environmental Assessment and Reporting in DPR of Korea	16,890	2001–2003	UNDP/UNEP
5	Coastal Biodiversity Management of DPR Korea's West Sea	774,523	2003–2006	UNDP
6	Enhanced National Capacity for Disaster Mitigation and Preparedness through GIS/RIS	504,822	2003–2006	UNDP
7	Strengthening Information Technology & Environment Monitoring Capability in DPR Korea Toward Sustainable Decision Making	344,830	2003–2006	UNDP/UNEP
8	National Capacity Needs Self-Assessment for the Global Environment Management (NCSA)	200,000	2004–2005	UNEP
9	Enabling Activity for the Preparation of the Second National Communication of Democratic Peoples' Republic of Korea to the UNFCCC (SNC)	405,000	2006–2012	UNEP
10	Capacity Building in Statistics Related to MDGs (MDG project)	734,770	2010–2011	UNDP
11	Sustainable Rural Energy Development (SRED)	5,076,205	2010–2012	UNDP
12	Small Wind Energy Development and Promotion in Rural Areas (SWEDPRA)	725,000	2010–2013	UNDP
13	Improved Seed Production for Sustainable Agriculture (ISPSA)	1,822,455	2011–2014	UNDP/FAO
14	Reduction of Post-Harvest Losses for Food Security (RPHLFS)	1,798,686	2011–2014	UNDP/FAO
15	Strengthening of Food and Agriculture Information System (SFAIS)	1,575,062	2011–2014	UNDP/FAO

Source: Adapted from Ministry of Land and Ministry of Land and Environment Protection 2012 and National Center on Education and the Economy (NCEE) and United Nations Environment Programme (UNEP) 2012.

North Korea's first CDM project was the Hamhung Youth No. 1 hydroelectric power plant. The project was registered with the UNFCCC in May 2012. Since then, a total of seven general CDM projects and four program CDM projects have been started.

From five CDM projects, North Korea earned a total of 392,199 tCO2eq of carbon credits from 2016 to 2018. The first project to be issued carbon credits was the hydroelectric development of Seongun Youth No. 2 in Baekdu, from which North Korea obtained 158,000 tCO2eq of carbon credits on September 23, 2016. Most of the general CDM projects in North Korea are small-scale reservoir-type hydroelectric power plant construction projects, yet there hasn't been any technology transferred from foreign companies, since the North Korean authorities invest directly in their own CDM projects. The Czech Topic Energo, which participates as an overseas operator, is only responsible for transferring and selling carbon credits issued by those projects.

Initially, the annual reduction amount from each project was expected to range from 20,000 tCO2eq to 480,000 tCO2eq. North Korea went further, achieving a total reduction from about 2.4 million tCO2, down to just 850,000 tCO2.

The project with the largest performance is the Yeseong River No. 5 hydroelectric power plant, which received a carbon credit of 850,000 tCO2eq in November 2017.

The program CDM projects related to wastewater treatment and methane gas utilization are evaluated based on their reduction outcomes. To initiate the program CDM means to register a group of individual projects promoted to achieve greenhouse gas reduction policies or goals.

4 Opportunities for North Korea's sustainable development and climate change actions

North Korea's poor environment has been pointed out as one of the major obstacles to North Korea's economic and social development. The response to climate change under the PA can be an important channel for solving the environmental, economic, and social problems facing North Korea. This section introduces the PA support mechanisms for developing countries to respond to climate change and boost economic and social development. In addition, we examine the possibility of inter-Korean cooperation on climate change using the carbon market.

4.1 Mechanisms of the PA for supporting climate actions in developing countries

The PA includes various mechanisms to support developing countries' greenhouse gas reduction and climate change adaptation activities. As shown in Figure 11.2, UNFCCC's developing country support mechanism consists of three types: technology, finance, and international cooperation. The technology and finance mechanisms support actions for reduction, adaptation, and capacity building, and the

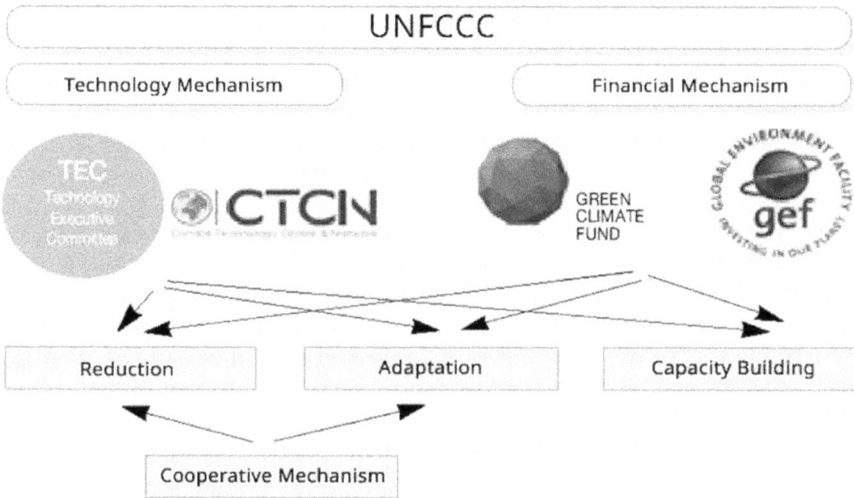

Figure 11.2 Supporting mechanisms of the PA for developing countries

Source: Author created

cooperative mechanism is for discretionary emissions reduction actions between the Parties to achieve the NDCs of the Parties.

The main bodies for the technology mechanism are the Technology Executive Committee (TEC) of the UNFCCC and the Climate Technology and Center Network (CTCN). The TEC is the policy arm of the technology mechanism. Its key role is to identify climate technology policies that support countries to achieve the PA's objectives. CTCN is the operational arm of the technology mechanism and provides technical assistance to developing countries. Technical support is provided at the request of developing countries and can include education/training, as well as action plans for technology evaluation and policy establishment.

The financial mechanism is implemented by the Global Environment Fund (GEF) and the Green Climate Fund (GCF). GEF was founded in 1991 on the eve of the 1992 Rio Earth Summit. Since its establishment, the GEF has provided over 17 billion USD in grants, and mobilized an additional 88 billion USD in financing for more than 4000 projects in 170 countries. Those projects cover all environmental issues, including biodiversity, climate change, international waters, land degradation, the ozone layer, persistent organic pollutants (POPs), mercury, sustainable forest management, food security, and sustainable cities. Since 1994, the GEF has been playing a key role in the implementation of the UNFCCC's financial mechanisms.

The GCF was founded by the UNFCCC in 2010 as a determination of the COP (Conference of Parties) 16, held in Cancun, Mexico. It is the implementation body of the UNFCCC's financial mechanism. Unlike the GEF, which is simultaneously responsible for the implementation of five environmentally relevant organizations and agreements, including the UNFCCC and finance projects across the environment, the GCF is dedicated to financial support for the UNFCCC's climate projects. The GCF seeks to provide equal funding for reduction and adaptation. In the first four years of its fundraising period, (2015 to 2018), forty-eight countries pledged to contribute 1.3 billion USD, of which 500 million USD was donated. This is far less than the 10 billion USD that developed countries had agreed to donate by 2020. While developed countries are the main contributors, small contributions are also being made by developing countries such as Indonesia, Vietnam, Peru, and Colombia. Investments are made in the form of grants, loans, capital, and guarantees. When 60 percent of the funds are exhausted, the process for replenishing the funds begins. To date, $200 million has been invested in 102 projects.

Article 6 defines the cooperative mechanism of the PA. The cooperative mechanism is comprised of the following two pillars: the Internationally Transferred Mitigation Outcomes (ITMOs), and the sustainable development mechanism. ITMOs were recently introduced as an avenue to support countries' NDC target achievements based on emissions trading. Projects targeting ITMOs should be promoted on the principles of sustainable development, environmental soundness, and transparency. ITMOs have a clear difference from the flexibility mechanism of the KP in that the reduction cooperation between the Parties is voluntary. Specifically, if the CDM under the KP is a top-down approach that is promoted and credited in accordance with the methods and procedures established by the UNFCCC, ITMOs of the PA take a bottom-up approach, in which methods and procedures are set by the discretion of involving parties. In the latter scheme, an official body of the UNFCCC is only involved in the verification of emissions reduction.

The Sustainable Development Mechanism (SDM) is the other pillar of the PA's cooperative mechanism. The PA's article 6.4 stipulates SDM. According to this article, it is expected that this mechanism will be operated in a similar manner as the KP's flexibility mechanism.

Although the market is not mentioned in Article 6, it is often referred to as a carbon market mechanism, with the expectation that carbon credits created by the cooperative mechanism will mainly be traded through the carbon market.

NDCs from 83 countries around the world refer to the international carbon market as a means to achieve their reduction targets (World Bank Group 2018). In the case of developed countries, reduction efforts have been carried out continuously, but there are many cases where the reduction capacity is insufficient and high costs are required.

For this reason, reduction projects in developing countries, where cost-effective reduction methods are still available can be easily implemented. It can bring great opportunities for developing countries' sustainable development, because those reduction projects should be promoted following the principles of sustainable development and environmental soundness.

4.2 Climate change response cooperation between the two Koreas through a cooperative approach and carbon market integration

According to the aforementioned article in the bulletin from Kim Il-sung University, North Korea's CDM projects aim to "protect the environment and achieve economic growth by attracting investment from outside." This means that North Korea, which maintains a closed economic system, can take a more open attitude toward attracting external capital to address climate change. North Korea can take advantage of the various opportunities, provided by the PA, for its sustainable development. In particular, the link between the cooperative mechanism of the PA and the carbon market can pave the way for cooperation between North and South Korea in coping with climate change, and be a starting point for discussion Koreas' unification. South Korea proposed a reduction target of "37% compared to BAU in 2030" through the country's NDC.

Initially, the South Korean government announced the 37 percent reduction target, of which 25.7 percent would be achieved domestically and 11.3 percent would be achieved overseas. With the Moon government's eco-friendly energy policy, however, a significant portion of the overseas reduction target was moved to the domestic reduction target in 2018. This resulted in the share of domestic reduction increasing to 37 percent, 4.5 percent of which would be reduced overseas or through forest absorption. This means that overseas reduction actions will be promoted by the overseas greenhouse gas reduction projects of the Korean government and/or companies. Overseas outcomes will be used to supplement South Korea's reduction contribution.

Despite the ambition and efforts of the South Korean government, it is concerned that Korea's geographical conditions are unfavorable to renewable energy production, and the energy-intensive industrial structure can be a major obstacle to achieving the domestic reduction target. In this situation, the high emissions reduction potential of North Korea could provide cost-effective reduction opportunities to the South Korean government, along with companies subject to reduction obligation, which are ultimately responsible for achieving the NDC. For South Korea, North Korea can be an attractive investment destination. The two countries have the same climate and natural conditions, so it is possible to apply the existing technologies without a demonstration or transformation for local application. Also, communication in the same language and close proximity can facilitate relatively simple operation and management.

For North Korea, active cooperation with South Korea, especially in green energy, can be an important avenue to restore the destroyed ecological environment, achieve economic growth, and improve the quality of life of its people by solving the energy shortage that is the root of low growth and environmental destruction. If North Korea wants to actively engage in climate actions through international cooperation, South Korea's carbon market and linked carbon market in Northeast Asia will provide North Korea with greater opportunities for economic and social development. The merit of carbon market linkage is reduced reduction cost by increasing market liquidity and providing flexibility to the reduction activities of entities subject to emission regulations. In terms of industrial competition, industries can prevent decreases in their competitiveness, and mitigate carbon leakage.[3] As of June 2019, eleven of the twenty carbon markets are operated in China, Japan, and South Korea. With its launch in December 2017, China's national emission trading scheme has emerged as the world's largest market in terms of regulated carbon. Korea's national emissions market is the third largest in the world. In terms of economy, emissions, and carbon market size, the impact of Northeast Asia on the international carbon market mechanism is profound. Even with the recent creation of the California-Quebec-Ontario emission market linkage and the EU-Swiss market linkage, the carbon market linkage joining the three countries in Northeast Asia is getting more attention. There has been particular excitement surrounding the possibility of linking the carbon markets between China and South Korea. The likelihood of this happening has increased due to the birth of China's national credit market.

Korea's Emission Trading Scheme (K-ETS) was launched in 2015 with the purpose of providing cost-effective means to achieve the reduction targets through emission trading between entities with insufficient credits and surplus credits. K-ETS is designed to be settled after three stages of planning. Currently, K-ETS is passing the phase 2 planning period (2018 – 2020).

Until now, the biggest problem facing K-ETS in operation has been the shortage of carbon credits. During the first planning period, the transaction of credits was only 0.3 percent and 2.3 percent in 2015 and 2016, respectively. This gave suppliers an absolute advantage in the market, and the price of emissions was maintained at the highest level in the world (World Bank and Ecofys 2018; Kim and Sim 2017). In 2015, the average price of the credits was USD 10.40, but more than doubled to USD 23.45 on February 7, 2017 (Kim and Sim 2017). In this situation, if North and South Korea's carbon markets had been integrated or linked, North Korea would have secured a stable credit demand market, and South Korea would have secured a stable supplier of credits. Furthermore, if the Korean Peninsula were to be recognized as a "single carbon reduction area" in the international community, such as by the International Olympic Committee and the World Cup's organizer, FIFA, then the two nations could integrate teams for these events and the reduction outcomes in North Korea would be counted as domestic reduction, making it easier for South Korea to achieve its emissions target.

Referring to the link between Norway-ETS and EU-ETS, and between California-ETS and Quebec-ETS, a long negotiation process will be necessary to harmonize key parts for market operation, such as technical cooperation and related rules. The inter-Korean carbon market linkage, or integrated operation, should also go through this process. South Korea is still in the process of developing the carbon market system, and North Korea has not yet been introduced to the market. It means that there are not many differences that need to be narrowed between the two parties, which can serve as a favorable environment for market linkage or integrated operation of the two markets. In addition, discussions on carbon market linkage may be easier than other political negotiations, in that they exclude issues of ideology between the two Koreas, and focus on mutual economic benefits.

In a linked carbon market, or integrated operation between the two Koreas, there can be an advantage in discussion on the linkage of Northeast Asia carbon markets. Linked or integrated K-ETS on the Korean Peninsula is expected to make a bigger voice in the discussion of linking the Northeast Asian carbon market, based on the expanded market size and enhanced price competitiveness. Of course, the establishment of the Northeast Asian carbon market will be neither smooth nor quick. The political and economic connection and geographical proximity of China, Japan, and Korea may be facilitating factors, but these conditions do not guarantee carbon market linkage. Rather, the differences in the market design in each country, climate change policies, and methods for setting reduction targets indicate that the journey toward a Northeast Asian carbon market will be a bumpy road. To be specific, China's ETS, unlike Japan's or South Korea's, is not based on an absolute reduction target, but on the energy intensity of entities subject to reduction obligation. Different designs of carbon markets will be the biggest roadblock to launching a linked Northeast Asia carbon market (Stowe 2017). In Japan, regional emission trading schemes are operated in Tokyo and Saitama. The introduction of national emission trading schemes has been discussed, but progress has not been made. Rather, it is expected that Northeast Asia will take a considerable amount of time to achieve national level carbon market linkage, because Japan is focusing more on expanding the Joint Crediting Mechanism (JCM)[4] than on carbon market linkage (Ewing 2017).

Despite these various obstacles, each country recognizes a linked Northeast Asian carbon market as an important avenue for regional cooperation. In 2018, the Ambassador for Climate Change in South Korea and the Special Representative for Climate Change in China agreed to strengthen cooperation between China, Japan, and South Korea.

As the regional and international carbon markets are currently being formed, if North and South Korea draw close cooperation in the carbon market, it will become the cornerstone of the birth of the Northeast Asian carbon market, secure economic benefits, and contribute to peace in Northeast Asia.

5 Conclusion

As discussed earlier, North Korea, despite its closed-state operating stance, has been actively participating in the international community's cooperative governance to cope with global environmental issues. This is due to the fact that the deteriorated environment in North Korea is putting its economy and society at risk, making its participation a crucial national task. To solve the environmental crisis in developing countries, the international community is setting various support measures, and North Korea recognizes that such a support system can be an important means for North Korea's sustainable development. In this context, North Korea has been trying to solve environmental and energy problems by attracting external investments using climate change response mechanisms. The new climate regime, which was launched with the enforcement of the PA, is highlighting the importance of international cooperation for achieving the NDC of each country, compared to the KP. Collaborative reduction actions between parties will become more active as all parties share common responsibility for reduction, and the cooperative mechanism governed by the UNFCCC has been expanded to a bottom-up method, driven by the discretion of the parties. This is because developing countries lack their own capacity to conduct climate actions, and developed countries can use cost-effective means to achieve reduction targets through international cooperation. This setting will provide North Korea important opportunities to attract external investment to solve its chronic energy shortage, and to promote economic growth and improve the quality of life of its people.

This chapter examined North Korea's current climate change response, the PA's support mechanism for North Korea's sustainable development, and the cooperation possibility existing in the carbon market between the two Koreas.

There are also various means for cooperation between the two Koreas in the field of environment and energy. Cooperation for a Renewable Energy Portfolio, which is a core policy for the deployment of clean energy, is one example. In order for these initiatives to be materialized, however, the instability of politics, institutions, and market opacity must be overcome, as was made clear by the events at the Kaesong Industrial Park.[5] Also, shortages of basic infrastructure, such as data on greenhouse gas inventories, must be resolved. Nevertheless, the viability of cooperation is high, in that cooperation between the two Koreas to stop climate change is based on mutual benefits, rather than the unilateral support for one party by the other party. In addition, the mutual understanding, trust, and the experience of successful cooperation that can be learned in the process of establishing a climate cooperation system, will provide important momentum for expanding the horizon of inter-Korean relations in the future.

Notes

1 See https://cdm.unfccc.int/about/index.html.
2 Parties include the industrialized countries that were members of the OECD (Organisation for Economic Co-operation and Development) in 1992, plus countries with economies in transition (the EIT Parties), including the Russian Federation, the Baltic States, and several Central and Eastern European States (Source: https://unfccc.int/parties-observers).
3 Carbon leakage refers to the situation that may occur if, for reasons of costs related to climate policies, businesses were to transfer production to other countries with laxer emission constraints.
4 The JCM is a mechanism to cooperate with developing countries for reducing carbon emissions, in which reduction outcomes are assessed as contribution by both partner countries and Japan.
5 The Kaesong Industrial Park is a special industrial region of North Korea for economic cooperation between two Koreas. It was formed in 2002 from part of the Kaesong Directly Governed City. It has repeatedly closed and opened depending on political and military issues of the Korean Peninsula.

References

Dolan, A. Holly, and Ian James Walker. 2006. "Understanding Vulnerability of Coastal Communities to Climate Change Related Risks." *Journal of Coastal Research* 39: 1316–1323.

Ewing, Jackson. 2017. "Incentives and Impediments to Carbon Market Cooperation in Northeast Asia." *Asia Society Policy Institute*. https://asiasociety.org/policy-institute.

Fouquet, Roger. 2016. "Path Dependence in Energy Systems and Economic Development." *Nature Energy* 1 (8): 16098. https://doi.org/10.1038/nenergy.2016.98.

Harmeling, Sven, and David Eckstein. 2012. *Global Climate Risk Index 2013: Who Suffers Most from Extreme Weather Events? Weather-Related Loss Events in 2011 and 1992 to 2011*. Berlin: Germanwatch E.V. Bonn.

Heilbroner, Robert. 1991. *An Inquiry into the Human Prospect: Looked at Again for the 1990s*. New York: W.W. Norton & Company.

International Ecological Footprint. 2020. "Ecological Footprint Explorer." Accessed March 2. http://data.footprintnetwork.org.

Kim, Hyo Jung. 2017. "North Korea Put a Focus on the Sales of Carbon Credits; Attract Investment and Protect the Environment." *Yonhap News*, October 22. www.yna.co.kr/view/AKR20171020130300014.

Kim, Kyung Hwan, and Seong Hee Sim. 2017. *Review on K-ETS and Its Reform Plan*. Ulsan: KEEI.

Luis, Gomez-Echeverri. 2018. "Climate and Development: Enhancing Impact Through Stronger Linkages in the Implementation of the Paris Agreement and the Sustainable Development Goals (SDGs)." *Philosophical Transactions of the Royal Society A: Mathematical, Physical and Engineering Sciences* 376 (2119): 20160444. http://doi.org/10.1098/rsta.2016.0444.

Ministry of Land and Ministry of Land and Environment Protection. 2012. "Democratic People's Republic of Korea Environment and Climate Change Outlook." https://wedocs.unep.org/handle/20.500.11822/9679.

Mumford, Lewis, and Langdon Winner. 2010. *Technics and Civilization*. Chicago: The University of Chicago Press.

National Center on Education and the Economy (NCEE) and United Nations Environment Programme (UNEP). 2012. "DPR Korea's Second National Communication on Climate Change."

North Korea Economy Watch. 2019. "New and Analysis of the North Korean Economy." Accessed June 14. www.nkeconwatch.com/category/statistics/gdpstatistics/.

Stowe, Robert C. 2017. "The Paris Agreement's Article 6 and Cooperation in Northeast Asia to Address Climate Change." In *Carbon Market Cooperation in Northeast Asia: Assessing Challenges and Overcoming Barriers*. New York: Asia Society Policy Institute.

United Nations Framework Convention on Climate Change. 2016. *Intended Nationally Determined Contribution of Democratic People's Republic of Korea*. INDCs as Communicated by Parties: DPR Korea. https://www4.unfccc.int/sites/submissions/INDC/Published%20Documents/Democratic%20People's%20Republic%20of%20Korea/1/DPRK-INDC%20by%202030.pdf.

World Bank, and Ecofys. 2018. *State and Trends of Carbon Pricing 2018*. Washington, DC: World Bank. https://openknowledge.worldbank.org/handle/10986/29687.

12 Impact of forest degradation in North Korea and restoration methodology

Woo-Kyun Lee, Sle-gee Lee, and Hyun-Ah Choi

1 Introduction

The impact of forest degradation in North Korea is widely known. Domestic and international organizations publishing on this issue have stated that North Korea needs to take immediate political action to begin the act of restoration. North Korea enacted the forest law in 1992, which emphasizes forest recovery actions and management. In April of 2012, North Korea issued a special announcement that the forests should be greened within the next ten years, showing that it considers forest restoration as one of its main objectives.

Forest degradation in North Korea is on such a serious level that it requires the solution to problems that are nearly insurmountable by themselves in terms of finances, technique, equipment, and labor force. It will take both international cooperation and inter-Korean cooperation to overcome these problems, in order to clear the way forward to restoring the forests. It is necessary that international issues like cause, effect, restoration method for degraded forest and climate change, sustainable development goals (SDGs), ecosystem services, water-food-energy stability, and degraded forests be taken care of at the same time. The application of international cooperation needs to be started carefully because it might trigger confusion, trial and error. Any possible political confrontation needs to be prevented before it comes to a cooperation agreement. Nevertheless, South Korea has wide knowledge on how to successfully accomplish this, as it has been restoring barren forest since the 1970s. This activity has aligned with economic development that has presented as the highest level for forest restoration in the world. In addition, the forest in North Korea is a pathway for the continuity of both ecology and environment. For that reason, the restoration plan should be imposed through international institutions and by cooperation led by North Korea and South Korea.

In view of these points, this chapter focuses on the current status of the ecosystem services and international issues as well as the current status, cause, and effect of degraded forest in North Korea. Also, it suggests methods to make stable food-water-energy balance and to solve the consequences resulting from forest degradation. Finally, methods for attaining and maintaining an inter-Korean led international cooperation are discussed.

2 Current Status of forest and degraded land in North Korea

Forest area in North Korea was 8.76 million ha at 1910 investigated by the Japanese government. The data for forest and degraded areas depends on the institution, type of image, and method of imagery interpretation, however, the temporal trend shows that the forest area gradually decreases over time, while the degraded area has increased. The range of total forest area has decreased from 9.85 million ha in the 1970s to 7.55 – 8.93 million ha by the early 2000s.

The degraded forest in North Korea could be classified as several types; the definitions are as follows (Korea Forestry Promotion institute 2016).

- Denuded land: a kind of grassland made by such human activities as firewood collection, domestic animals grazing, and forest fires
- Cultivated forest: marginal farmland that generally appears on the upper side of mountains cultivated from forest to agricultural land
- Barren forest: barren land or bare mountain influenced from forest degradation

There are various reports for recent degraded forest area in North Korea according to multiple institutions. The National Institute of Forest Science released that 1.63 million ha in 1999 and 2.84 million ha in 2008 have become degraded (Korea Forest Research Institute 2010; Park 2013). On the other hand, a study of the Korea Forestry Promotion Agency (2015) analyzed that the degraded forest area was almost 3.03 million ha in 2015. Moreover, an international report through diverse pathways states that degraded forest is from 1.60 million ha to 3.00 million ha in North Korea, which should be restored. This is 16–30 percent of the land area of South Korea. Fortunately, South Korea has experience in afforestation of massive areas: 1.08 million ha for the first afforestation plan (1973–1978), 1.07 million ha for the second afforestation plan (1988–1997), and 0.32 million ha for the third afforestation plan in South Korea (Korea Forest Service 1997).

3 Cases and impact of degraded forest in North Korea

3.1 Denuded land increasing by energy scarcity

A main cause of deforestation in North Korea is a deficiency in the energy supply, a shortage caused by the state's economy being unable to escape from the poverty trap (Kim 2005). The energy supply has dramatically decreased year after year from the 1990s (Kim 2018). The energy consumption of North Korea in 2016 was less than even that of the 1960s in South Korea. This energy shortage has only grown more severe since the middle of the first decade of the 21st century, remarkably continuing to intensify in more recent years.

The distribution system for household energy has collapsed to the degree that a regular citizen must get fuel at the market or self-obtain through other means, despite the political ideology of North Korea being based on communism (Kim 2013). Therefore, it is understood that household energy acquisition already exists outside the scope of governmental management, and that this energy demand relies on provision from the forest to fulfill. This phenomenon explains the huge amount of denuded land that has existed since the 1990s. Comparing 1979 to 2010, the denuded land increased 397 percent (Byeon 2014), which agrees with individual wood collection trends in the period.

3.2 Cultivated forest growth resulting from food shortage

The difficulty of food supply in North Korea is proved through various international reports. The government of North Korea has requested that residents supply food for themselves since the 1990s when the food shortage was deepened. During the Arduous March, large amounts of forest were cultivated. Unfortunately, however, this did not lead to food growth because they did not consider sustainable management planning (Park and Park 2012). Therefore, the food problem got worse due to environmental deterioration. Although North Korea has continued efforts to restore food supplies, it has not yet obtained good results. These problems resulted from a shortage of food and energy that caused forest degradation due to human activities.

3.3 Impact for forest ecosystem services according to deforestation

A forest provides provisioning, regulating, supporting, and cultural services through its ecosystem functions. An economic recession and forest degradation in North Korea mean the loss of various benefits from the forest resulting in damage to human well-being.

Forests change according to a nation's development level. With extreme poverty, the forest is rapidly deforested to get energy, commodities, and food for the residents. That is the current status of forests in North Korea. This same status also manifested in South Korea during the 1950s–1960s, and some of the more recent developing countries in Southeast Asia and Africa have experienced a similar phenomenon. The rapid increase in poverty that accompanies forest degradation demands new supplies of raw material, and the spatial range of settlement is expanded, as is wide-scale converting of forest area into resources. Thus, the forest, which is degraded for provisioning, negatively affects its supporting function. One piece of evidence of this relationship is well shown within the relationship between gross domestic product (GDP) and forest stock growth in South Korea and North Korea (see Figure 12.1). In the case of South Korea, an increased GDP is aligned with a growth trend for forest stock; inversely, GDP and forest stock simultaneously decreased in North Korea since 1987 (Song et al. 2017). This means that forest degradation not only is environmental desolation but is also tied to a poor economy. Forest degradation fundamentally affects local residents and their need to secure various services, but the truth is that degrading leads to poor provisioning, regulating, supporting, and cultural service on a nationwide scope. This in turn causes the need for more degradation, and repeats in a pattern, as it does at present in North Korea.

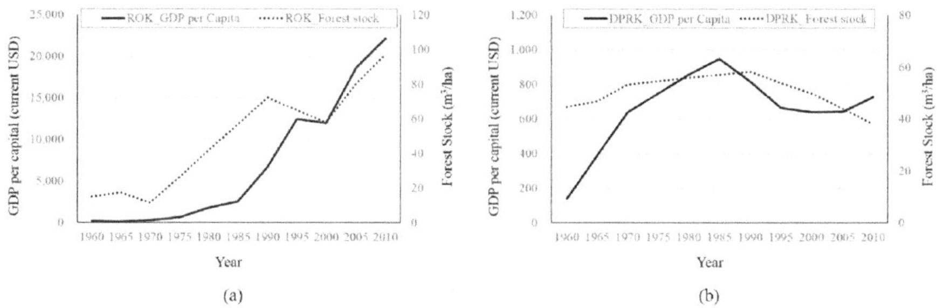

Figure 12.1 Relationship between GDP per capita and forest stock on the Korean Peninsula: (a) South Korea; (b) North Korea

Source: Song et al. 2017

One of the main provisioning services of forest is timber production. The forest stock curve of North Korea shows gradually increased and sharply decreased supply since the 1990s, which implies that the decline of timber production and associated ecosystem services is linked. The North Korean government has managed forests to prevent deforestation and wildfires by controlling residents in the past. However, they amended the forest law in 1992 so that citizens could cut timber as needed to support their livelihood without any plans for reforestation (Park, Bang, and Lee 2008). This signaled the fall of governmental ability to manage the forest, and it also brought a corresponding decrease in timber production.

The most important function of supporting services in the forest is building the fundamental structures and processes of the ecosystem cycle. It maintains balance between water, forest, and other ecosystems. Clean water from the forest promotes stable cultivation and life environments. Forest degradation disrupts this water cycle and the water balance of cropland (Lim et al. 2018, 2019). Assessment for the agricultural water equilibrium of South Korea over the past thirty years shows that water balance in North Korea is sharply negative relative to that of South Korea (see Figure 12.2). As converted cropland – which is considered one of the main causes of forest degradation – needs more water, the total water balance in North Korea worsened with expanded converted cropland. In particular, the gravest time for water imbalance for cropland was in the 1990s. The water supply decreased and water demand rapidly increased according to a comparative analysis for this deforestation period. Converted cropland entails a large number of handicaps concerning agriculture, environment, factors for soil and topography influences, increased runoff, and soil loss (Lim et al. 2017). It leads to a qualitative deterioration of crop productivity, which is the main reason that food output did not increase proportionately with cropland expansion.

Forest degradation in North Korea appears to be severe (see Figure 12.3). Forested land is recognized as both carbon storage and sink, and its carbon dioxide absorbing function will be utilized in each country's efforts to adapt to climate

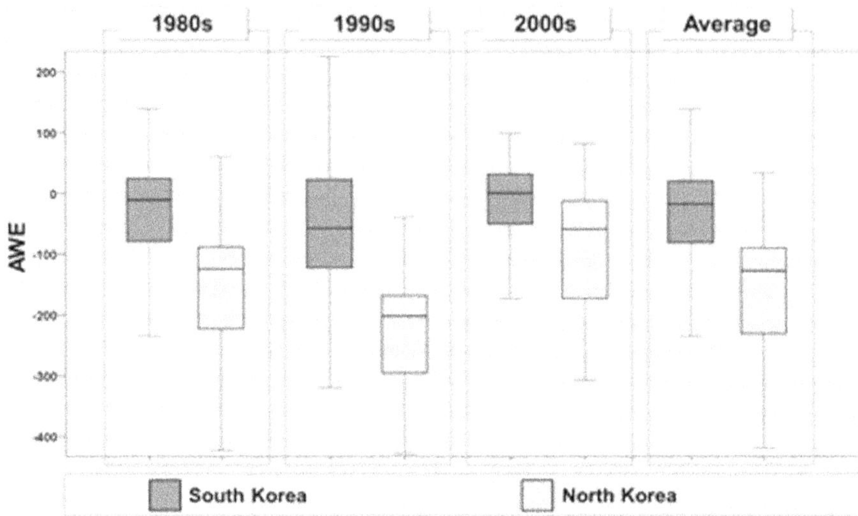

Figure 12.2 Comparison of the agricultural water equilibrium (AWE) between South and North Korea over the decades

Source: Lim et al. 2018

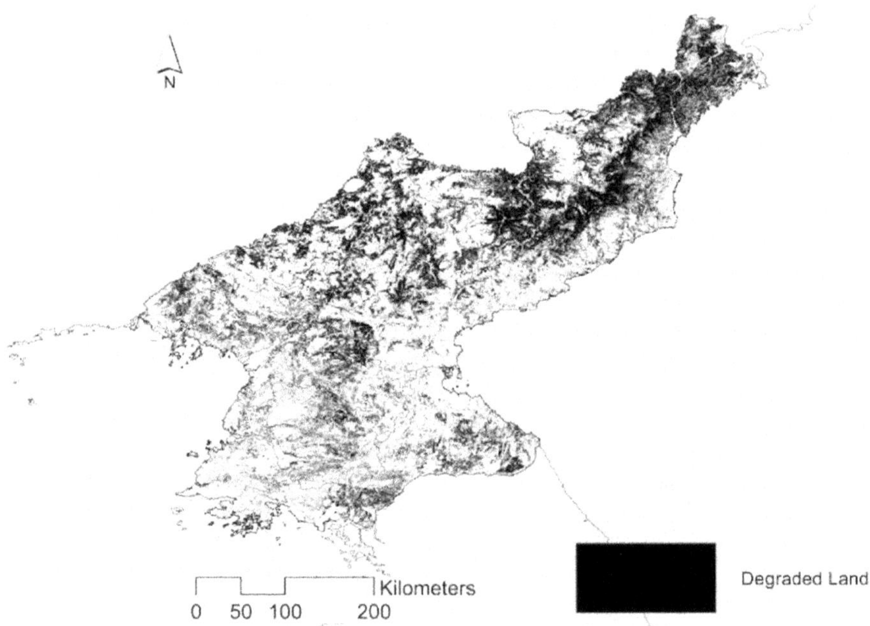

Figure 12.3 Classification map of degraded forest types in North Korea

Source: Lee et al. 2018

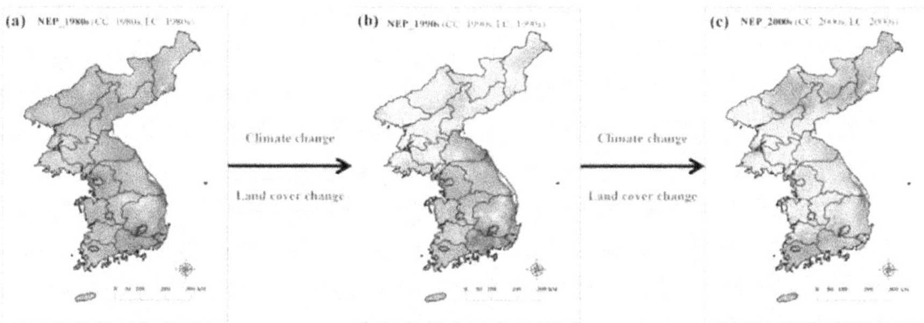

Figure 12.4 Spatial distribution variation of net ecosystem production (NEP)

Source: Cui et al. 2014

change. South Korea's established climate change adaptation plan requires that the absorption for the forest sector is twenty-two million tons per year by 2030. Forest management would contribute to national greenhouse gas reduction. Forest degradation continues to lessen the ability of forests to act as carbon storage. Climate change and forest degradation have made effective carbon capture by North Korea forest a thing of the past (see Figure 12.4).

The cultural ecosystem service the forest provides includes landscape and recreation functions, and it carries immaterial benefits that come along with supporting a forest environment. In North Korea, offering these cultural services stemming from forested land is impossible because of severe degradation, except for in some parts of the protected zones. On the other hand, the International Union for Conservation of Nature and Natural Resources (IUCN) biosphere reserve in North Korea has advantages; were it to be connected by railroad and thoroughfare, it would provide cultural services for attracting tourists from neighboring countries.

4 Restoration methods for degraded forest in North Korea

4.1 Restoration of degraded forest and ecosystem services (water-food-energy stability)

Efforts to restore degraded forest in North Korea should consider improving ecosystem services not simply planting. In particular, forest restoration precedes a healthy environment able to provide water-food-energy stably (see Figure 12.5). Therefore, the nexus approach would be an alternative method by which to transform problems in order to improve sustainably (Ringler et al. 2013). More specifically, it would fulfill the need to understand and improve required services immediately in North Korea according to the land development phases (degradation-restoration-sustainability).

The first ten years of the plan for forest restoration within the thirty-year Forest Master Plan (2013–2042) commenced in 2013 (Choi 2018). The main objective

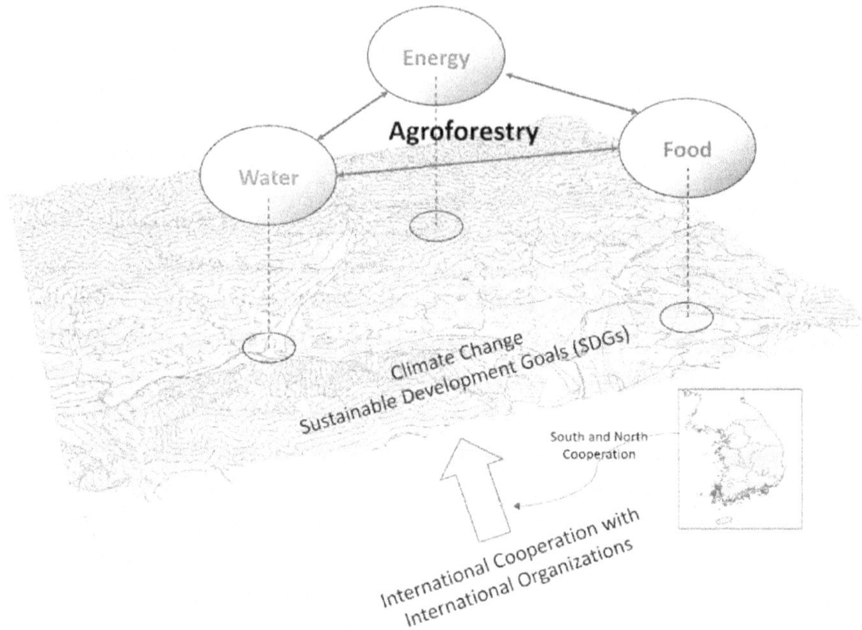

Figure 12.5 Food-water-energy nexus diagram to restore the degraded forest in North Korea

Source: Author created

of this plan overlaps with the ecosystem services category. While it would be achieved immediately by forest restoration, however, it only happens gradually in reality. Therefore, the first ten years of the North Korean plan needs a phased strategy in order to reach its goals. The forest in North Korea is considered to be in the degradation phase, and so it needs an urgent and effective short-term reconstruction plan. For the medium- and long term, it demands a plan suitable for later restoration and sustainability phases (see Figure 12.6).

4.1.1 Degradation phase

The degradation phase basically occurs when a populace attempts to solve a deficiency of food, water, and energy supply themselves using the forest without governmental support. It leads that forest area and forest stock to continuously decrease by using resources, and that degraded forest, in turn, affects the frequency of natural disasters and destroys the capability for greenhouse gas absorption. In this phase, the most urgent task is identifying and removing causes. In the degradation phase, provisioning service is absolutely needed to secure food, water, and energy, but it is impossible to achieve immediately by afforestation.

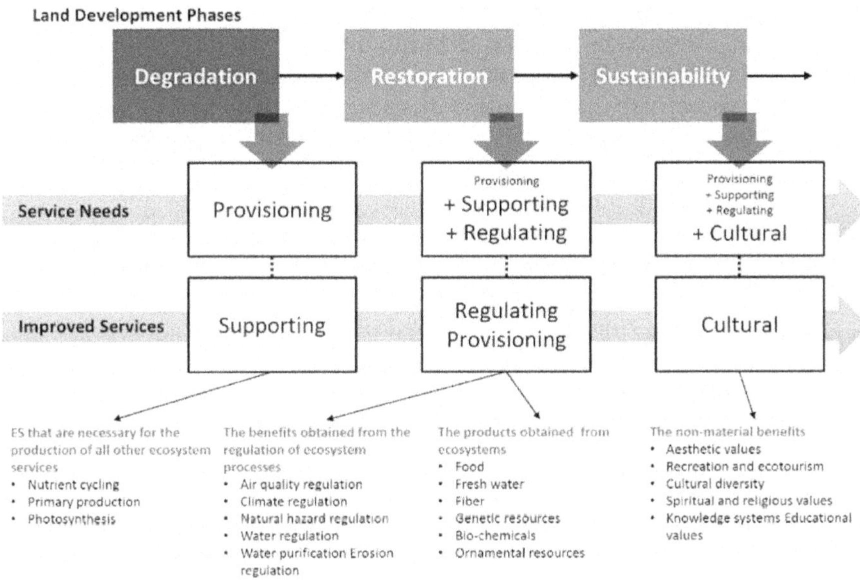

Figure 12.6 Promotion direction of ecosystem services demanding at each phase

Source: Lee 2018

The most needed service is provisioning, and so it should be facilitated by a supporting service that provides for the most basic ecosystem functions. Therefore, a basic forest environment foothold should be prepared through improving the structure of the forest ecosystem and through a carbon-nitrogen-water cycling process, an urgent problem which involves food and energy supply can be solved from outside such as with REDD+.

In order to prevent further erosion, erosion control should be carried out on damaged areas, as it is an essential task to protect cropland under the restored forest and also enhance the recovery rate of reforestation. In addition, the deteriorated soil should be fertilized. The erosion control and fertilization carried out with afforestation lay the foundation for forest supporting services. The food, water, and energy supplies, however, should come from sources other than the recovered forests. In other words, it is necessary to simultaneously supply food and energy to the forest restoration workers as well as to improve the water supply service in the recovery sub-region along with the agriculture and living sectors.

4.1.2 Restoration phase

The restoration phase can be regarded as a phase in which the forest area and forest stock are no longer reduced and where, at the state-level, food, energy, and water supply systems are in place. In most countries, the recovery period after devastation begins with a certain level of economic growth. The desperate need for food and energy to be supplied from the forest can be seen as having been overcome. It is a stage in which the restored forest takes over to overcome the degradation phase, and it can be regarded as a stage that would take more than ten years after the recovery begins. It is seen as a time when regulating and supporting services are strengthened.

Therefore, in the restoration phase, a strategy is needed to strengthen the supporting service from the restored forests so that the supply of water and nutrients to the forests for agricultural and agroforestry for food production is well achieved. In order to prevent natural disasters that frequently occurred during the degradation phase, a strategy is also needed to ensure that the services are presented from the restored forest. Soil improvement and restoration for other sites should be continued.

4.1.3 Sustainability phase

The sustainability phase of land development is a stage in which forest stock is steadily increasing while the forest area is maintained, and it can be seen as a stage supported by a national system that is well equipped to supply food, water, and energy. In this stage, provisioning services are available, such as the stable supply of timber; supporting services such as agriculture and domestic water based on stable ecological circulation processes are prepared with significant economic growth; and cultural services such as ecological education and recreation are strongly recommended. It can be considered as the next step after a long recovery period, after clearing the degradation and restoration phases.

The thirty-year Forest Master Plan seems to have presented a relatively good goal that can be achieved in the recovery phase (see Table 12.1). The goal for the first ten years of this plan can be considered a goal of escaping the degradation phase, and the target for the second stage, of twenty years, corresponds to the restoration phase. However, the targets proposed by North Korea are still mixed, with various targets without distinction of the aforementioned ecosystem services. Further details should be improved or be systematically established. It is easy to see from the experience of forest restoration in South Korea that if the ecosystem services are impossible to provide due to serious degradation, there is a high possibility that it will become a plan to rapidly fill in the achievement of detailed goals without setting clear targets for major ecosystem services. Considering the political system of North Korea, this plan could instead reduce sustainability once implemented, and there is a valid concern that current negative practices will remain the same.

4.2 Prior preparation for a forest restoration project in North Korea

In order to recover the degraded forest in North Korea, it is necessary to identify the monetary amount required for restoration. When that amount is figured out, timelines, materials, budgets, and work force estimates can be prepared. The first step in the recovery is to identify the distribution of degraded area that can be

Table 12.1 Phase goals and detail of forest restoration battle in the thirty-year Forest Master Plan (2013–2042)

Phase	*Goals*	*Detailed Contents*
1st phase (10 years)	Restoring forest ecosystem from degraded, decreasing lumber dependence, converting non-timber forest products to forest resources	1 Developing forest near the main road, railroad, village, and ecological basins 2 Increased seedling production for double 3 Improving lumber dependence from foreign countries by 20 percent 4 Establishing wildfire monitoring and extinguishment plan and completing the notification system 5 Building a physical foundation for disease, insect pest, and biotic pesticide control
2nd phase (20 years)	Transferring from pure forest to mixed forest, remodeling forest to achieve multipurpose forest management	1 Developing forest for degraded area 2 Increasing seedling production 3 Decreasing lumber dependence by 50 percent 4 Normalizing wildfire extinguishing facility and slope recovery 5 Controlling disease and insect pest and producing biotic pesticide

Source: Choi 2018

artificially recovered, followed by restoration methods and selection of suitable species. Through these steps, erosion control for degraded regions and nursery plans for supplying seedlings would be established.

The Korea Forestry Promotion Agency (2016) has selected suitable species for restoration by region in consideration of climate, topography, soil, and socioeconomic conditions in North Korea (see Figure 12.7). These species are as follows: *Picea jezoensis*, *Quercus mongolica*, *Larix gmelinii*, *Pinus koraiensis*, *Pinus densiflora*, and *Quercus actissima*, which are viewed as suitable species for 3.9 million ha; Looking at the suitable restoration species for the recoverable area of 1.77 million ha, the recommended species are *P. jezoensis*, *Q. mongolica*, *P. densiflora*, *Q. actissima*, *P. koraiensis*, and *L. gmelinii*.

The forest restoration should occur in each region under a national recovery strategy. In order to restore forests by region, it is important to spatially identify both the deforested areas in North Korea and suitable species for those areas. Figure 12.7 shows suitable restoration species by region. In the cases of *P. jezoensis, A. nephrolepis, P. koraiensis, L. gmelinii, Q. mongolica*, these species are suitable in northern high-altitude mountainous areas, unlike *Q. actissima, or P. thunbergii*, which are matched to the western lowlands. On the other hand, *P. densiflora* is found to be suitable throughout the country.

4.3 Methods of restoration in North Korea

The forest restoration of North Korea is not a project that can produce results in a short period. South Korea was able to achieve visible greening success through

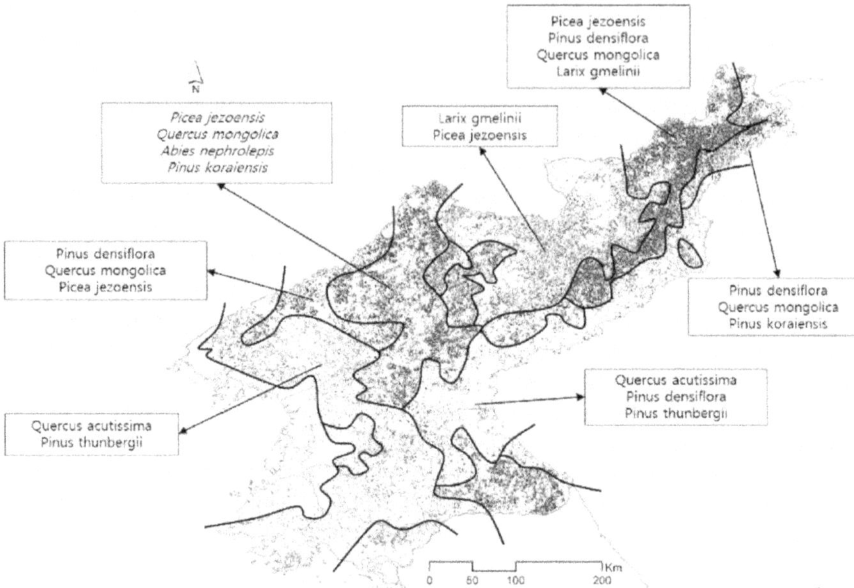

Figure 12.7 Suitable restoration map for degraded forest in North Korea

Source: Lee et al. 2018

the thirty-year plan comprising three stages, which began in 1972. And now, as it enters the sustainability phase, the forest is managed by the national forest basic plan, the regional forest plan at regional level, the regional plan for basic municipality, and the forest management plan system at the implementation level. Similarly, a basic restoration plan that includes a national restoration strategy (general plan), a detailed restoration plan at a regional level (detailed plan), and a restoration plan at a site level (implementation plan) should be established with linkage. Table 12.1 published by North Korea would consider a national restoration strategy. To succeed in implementation, a detailed plan must be prepared that is matched with the ten-year plan for forest restoration in North Korea.

The step-wise plan needs spatial information corresponding to the stage, which could be identified by fitting spatial scale for planning units. Lee et al. (2018) made suitable restoration maps with a spatial resolution of 12.5 km^2 for the general plan, 5 km^2 for the detailed plan, and 1 km^2 for the implementation plan level (see Figure 12.8). For the general plan at the national level, watershed-level information should be used as one of the criteria for forest management, and the detailed plan at the regional level should be able to support any decision-making necessary for restoration. In case of the site-level implementation plan, the most circumstantial information required for restoration should be provided for each restoration location.

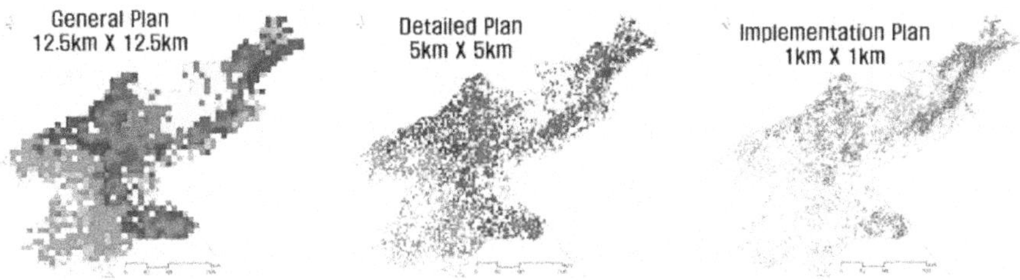

Figure 12.8 Resolution of general, detailed, and implementation plans by suitable unit in North Korea

Source: Lee et al. 2018

The national-local-site planning method requires not only spatially different amounts of information but also different planning periods in time. The general plan at the national level needs a long-term plan of more than ten years, the detailed planning at the regional level demands a medium-term plan of about five years. The site-level implementation plan should be a short-term plan with a specific schedule for restoration work.

The degradation problem in North Korea has been carried out over a long period, and the degree of deforestation is so severe that many places need to do erosion control. In particular, the steeper the slope, the higher the need for erosion control. Erosion control is defined as a project for planting and creating structure to prevent the collapse of mountainous areas, soil loss, and desertification (Park, Bang, and Lee 2008). The Korea Forestry Promotion Agency proposed a restoration plan for each type of degradation forest according to the terrain factoring in conditions such as altitude, slope, and aspect (see Table 12.2).

As shown in Table 12.3, the reforestation area of lower than 1,000 m in altitude and less than a 10° slope is 1.7 million ha. Thus, seedlings corresponding to the reforestation area for each species should be produced. Considering the transportation of seedlings, it is necessary to develop a nursery plan for each region where seedlings are produced in areas where restoration will take place. Recalling the species selection shown in Figure 12.7, nurseries should be established locally according to region to produce seedlings of suitable species.

One of the reasons to consider restoring North Korea forest is to solve the food and energy shortages with restoration at the same time. In North Korea, agroforestry is emphasized to solve forest recovery and food problems simultaneously. North Korea's Ministry of Land, Infrastructure and Transport presented implementation details, evaluation methods, indicators, and the persons in charge to achieve the goals by National Agroforestry Strategy and Action Plan for the next ten years (2015–2024). As defined by North Korea, agroforestry management is a continuous integrated management of trees, crops, and livestock in the same land area, and more specific forms of agroforestry have been introduced since the

Table 12.2 Restoration method for types of degraded forest according to topographical condition

Degraded Type	*Elevation*	*Slope*	*Aspect*	*Restoration Method*
Cultivated Forest	All possible	≥ 20°	All possible	General Erosion Control
		< 20°		Fundamental Erosion Control
Denuded Land, Barren Forest	< 1,000 m	≥ 30°	W, SW, S, SE	Special Erosion Control
			E, NE, N, NW	General Erosion Control
		< 30°	W, SW, S, SE	General Erosion Control
			E, NE, N, NW	Fundamental Erosion Control
	≥ 1,000 m	All possible		Afforestation for Erosion Control

Source: Adapted from Korea Forestry Promotion Institute 2015

Table 12.3 Erosion control types for forest restoration

Types of Erosion Control	*Detailed Contents*
Fundamental Erosion Control	• Restoration is possible to apply general afforestation that surface erosion has not shown in cultivated forest
General Erosion Control	• More than 20 percent slope is presented in cultivated forest, or both above 30° and below 1,000 m for degraded land in case of denuded and barren forest. It has relatively vulnerable for erosion and landslide.
Special Erosion Control	• Surface erosion and landslide could easily occur that is located below 1,000 m and more than 30° in denuded and cultivated forest. When a restoration implies this region, protecting structure should be accompanied.
Afforestation for Erosion Control	• Barren or denuded forest near mountain top above 1,000 m could restore by effective plant for erosion control without protecting structure.

Source: Adapted from Korea Forestry Promotion Institute (2015).

2000s (Ministry of Land and Environment Protection 2015). Agroforestry was actively adopted in North Korea to meet food production and forest management goals. The Korea Forestry Promotion Institute (2016) presented the appropriate planting of tree species for agroforestry management adopted by North Korea.

5 International cooperation to restore degraded forest in North Korea

5.1 International cooperation connecting global issues with forest restoration in North Korea

The degraded forest in North Korea is linked through issues of interest to international organizations such as poverty due to food shortages, threats to basic living conditions due to water and energy shortages, and destruction of environmental resilience. Therefore, it is essential to find various issues related to the degraded forest in North Korea and to promote cooperation projects in various forms with international organizations suitable for the issues. For example, the project to improve the international carbon balance through the restoration of degraded land can be promoted as an international organization project related to climate change, such as the Green Climate Fund (GCF) and Global Environment Facilities (GEF) (Choi and Seliger 2017).

The Paris Climate Agreement and the SDGs of the United Nations did not end in a declarative character, and so the implementation of each country is required at a mandate level. Additionally, considering the situation in which various international cooperation projects are required to contribute to the Paris Climate Change Convention and SDGs, the restoration of degraded forest in North Korea will contribute to such international issues.

5.2 Multilateral cooperation between North Korea, South Korea, and international organizations

North Korea and South Korea have common affiliations with many international organizations, so they will be able to multilaterally cooperate. Recently, it has been made known that North Korea is actively pursuing international cooperation projects to restore through cooperation with the United Nations Convention to Combat Desertification (UNCCD). Since South Korea joined FAO in 1949 and North Korea joined in 1977, respectively, FAO actively promotes the GCF project with North Korea government such as Ministry of Land and Environment Protection. This is a good chance to approach multilateral cooperation through international organizations.

The United Nations and North Korea have written a strategic framework for cooperation (Son et al. 2017). This framework provides a comprehensive plan for UN agencies to consider when working in North Korea (Jeong 2018). UN organizations will consider this framework and promote international cooperation with North Korea. It is fundamental to derive an international cooperation plan that actively introduces the priorities and strategic results of the strategic framework for cooperation (see Table 12.4).

5.3 International cooperation project led by an inter-Korean cooperation

International cooperation with the United Nations and other international organizations is a clear way to provide an opportunity to resolve the deforestation in North Korea by linking the problems with various international issues. However, if connected with too many agendas, it is possible to lose sight of the original goal of restoring the degraded forest, ecosystem and environmental aspects. Therefore, it should be established that the master plan is for restoration of degraded forest in North Korea and that seeking international cooperation for the success for restoration is only a guideline.

Table 12.4 Priority and strategic results in the strategic framework for cooperation between the UN and North Korea

Year	*Priority*	*Strategic Results*
2017–2021	Food and Nutrition Security	– Sustainable food production and strengthen productivity in agriculture, horticulture, fishery, and livestock industry – Strengthen food accessibility of the weak group – Improvement nutritive conditions for infants and female
	Social Development Service	– Sustainable and equal healthcare – Reinforcement health service for treatment of disease – Strengthen health crisis response ability – Supply equal benefit for drinking water, health, and hygiene by household unit – Improvement vocational education and training level at the state education system
	Resilience and Sustainability	– Enhance for climate change and disaster response for the weak group including female – Strengthen accessibility to energy resources – Applying an equal approach to manage the environment, energy, climate change, and disaster risk
	Data and Development Management	– Reinforcement accessibility for developed data and detailed humanitarian assistance – Empowerment of the DPRK for applying international criterion and technique – Strengthen implementation and reporting structure of the DPRK about an international treaty

Source: Author created

Inter-Korean cooperation starts from the stage of preparing the restoration plan and project guidelines. The first step in this inter-Korean cooperation project is to form a joint investigation and planning team for the identification of degraded forest in North Korea and the collaborative establishment of a restoration plan. The mission of this organization is identifying the current status, establishing a general – but detailed – implementation plan, and to develop policies to follow that plan. In addition, that organization would be responsible for the acquisition of budgets, labor, and applied technology. Through the initial inter-Korean cooperation, we believe that a successful path is can be forged, while minimizing trial and error and avoiding losing sight of the goal to restore the degraded forest in North Korea.

6 Conclusion

Data show that North Korea was covered by 80 percent forest until the 1970s. However, deforestation and conversion have led to a significant decrease in forest area due to food and fuel shortages. Those factors caused the collapse of forest functions and ecosystem services that ultimately worsened the lives of residents. In North Korea, forest restoration efforts are being made to resolve this damage, but the current outlook is not good.

Forest restoration in North Korea should be directed toward restoring forest ecosystem services so that food-water-energy can be supplied stably in connection with food and energy issues that are the cause of forest degradation. Under these goals, a restoration strategy for each stage of the degradation-restoration-sustainability phase should be established. In other words, restoration is carried out in the form of agroforestry management to solve food problems along with erosion control that can reduce damage such as soil loss, flooding, and drought in the current degradation phase. The spatio-temporal restoration plan should be established so that the long-term general plan at the national level, the mid-term detailed plan at the regional level, and the short-term implementation plan at the site level can be interlinked. Based on the spatial distribution of the degraded land and the restoration suitability for each region in North Korea by remote sensing technique, it is possible to establish a restoration plan for each phase. This can lead to a restoration in inter-Korean cooperation.

From an international point of view, deforestation in North Korea exacerbates various global issues such as reducing carbon sinks and deteriorating carbon balance in terms of climate change and the associated issues surrounding food, water, energy, health, and the environment relating to SDGs. In this regard, forest restoration in North Korea is seen through the lens of various international issues and can lead to or attract international cooperation. To prevent any confusion that can be caused from international partnerships, the restoration in North Korea should be carried out by inter-Korean leadership.

References

Byeon, Jeong Kyun. 2014. *Forest Change in the DPRK Strengthen Ability for Recovery*. Korean Academy of Science and Technology, South Korea.

Choi, Hyeon Ah. 2018. "Prospect and Implementation Strategy of the Inter-Korean Forest Cooperation." *Unification Policy Study* 27 (2): 1–20.

Choi, Hyun-Ah, and Bernhard Seliger. 2017. "International Cooperation to Solve Environmental Problems in DPRK." *Unification Policy Study* 21 (1): 47–73.

Cui, Guishan, Woo Kyun Lee, Da Min Kim, Eun Jung Lee, Han Bin Kwak, Hyun Ah Choi, and Seong Woo Jeon. 2014. "Estimation of Forest Carbon Budget from Land Cover Change in South and North Korea Between 1981 and 2010." *Journal of Plant Biology* 57 (4): 225–238.

Jeong, Koo Yeon. 2018. "Status and Evaluation for Aid of North Korea by UN." In *Understanding Development Cooperation in North Korea: Theory and Practice*, 125–149. Seoul: Oreum Press.

Kim, Kyeong Sool. 2013. "Research and Analysis of Energy Consumption form in the DPRK." *Korea Energy Economics Institute Research Paper* 13 (23).

Kim, Kyung Sool. 2018. "South-North Energy Status and Energy Cooperation Outlook." Presentation at the Seminar with Korean Nuclear Society and Korean Society for Nuclear Policy, Press Center Breifing Room, Seoul, July 6.

Kim, Yong Hwan. 2005. "A Study on Ecological Restoration Measures for the Degraded Land in North Korea (Focusing on South Korea's Restoration Policy)." *Journal of the Institute of North Korea Studies* 9 (2): 21–50.

Korea Forest Research Institute. 2010. "Cooperation Direction and Assignment for Restoration of Degraded Forest in the DPRK." *Research Report of Korea Forest Research Institute*: 10–11.

Korea Forest Service. 1997. *Outcome and Introspection for Mountain Area Resource Development Plan*. Korean Society for the Study of the Provisional Government.

Korea Forestry Promotion Institute. 2015. "Analyzing Forest Condition in the DPRK Utilized Satellite Data." www.kofpi.or.kr/intro/bizGuide_09_05.do.

Korea Forestry Promotion Institute. 2016. "Selecting Suitable Afforestation Species and Upgrading Mountainous Soil in the DPRK." www.kofpi.or.kr/index.do.

Lee, Sle Gee, Hyun Ah Choi, Hye Ji Yoo, Chol Ho Song, Sung Eun Cha, Sang Won Bae, and Woo Kyun Lee. 2018. "Restoration Plan for Degraded Forest in the Democratic People's Republic of Korea Considering Suitable Tree Species and Spatial Distribution." *Sustainability* 10 (3): 856.

Lee, Woo Kyun. 2018. "Forestation Plan for Climate Change Adaptation in the DPRK." Paper Presented at the Climate Change Center Conference: DPRK Achieving the SDGs Through Action to Climate Change, Press Center International Conference Room, Seoul, March 14.

Lim, Chul Hee, Chol Ho Song, Yu Young Choi, Seong Woo Jeon, and Woo Kyun Lee. 2019. "Decoupling of Forest Water Supply and Agricultural Water Demand Attributable to Deforestation in North Korea." *Journal of Environmental Management* 248.

Lim, Chul Hee, Yu Young Choi, Moon Il Kim, Seong Woo Jeon, and Woo Kyun Lee. 2017. "Impact of Deforestation on Agroenvironmental Variables in Cropland, North Korea." *Sustainability* 9 (8): 1354.

Lim, Chul Hee, Yu Young Choi, Moon Il Kim, Soo Jeong Lee, Christian Folberth, and Woo Kyun Lee. 2018. "Spatially Explicit Assessment of Agricultural Water Equilibrium in the Korean Peninsula." *Sustainability* 10 (1): 201.

Ministry of Land and Environment Protection. 2015. *DPRK National Agroforestry Strategy and Action Plan (2015–2024)*. Swiss Cooperation Office DPR Korea.

Park, Kyung Seok. 2013. "Forest Present Condition and Forest Policy in the DPRK." *North Korean Agricultural Trend* 15 (3): 1–21.

Park, Kyung Seok, and So Yeong Park. 2012. "The Rehabilitation of North Korea's Devastated Forest." *Research on North Korean Studies* 8 (1): 133–159.

Park, So Yeong, Kyung Seok Bang, and Seong Yeon Lee. 2008. "Forest Administrative Organization of North Korea and -Characteristics of Forest Work." *Research on North Korean Studies* 4 (2): 75–101.

Ringler, Claudia, Anik Bharduri, and Richard Lawford. 2013. "The Nexus Across Water, Energy, Land and Food(WELF): Potential for Improved Resorce Use Efficiency?" *Current Opinion in Environmental Sustainability* 5 (6): 617–624.

Son, Hyuk Sang, Eung Jo Yoo, Ji Young Kim, Ji Yeon Park, Ji Hwan Hwang, Yool Kwon, Sangki Kim, Taekyun Kim, Kyung Yeon Moon, and Gooyeon Jeong. 2017. *Understanding for Cooperative Development in the DPRK*. Seoul: Oreum press.

Song, Chol Ho, Sea Jin Kim, Joo Yeon Moon, Soo Jeong Lee, Wona Lee, Nahui Kim, and Woo Kyun Lee. 2017. "Classification of Global Land Development Phases by Forest and GDP Changes for Appropriate Land Management in the Mid-latitude." *Sustainability* 9 (8): 1342.

Index

Note: Page numbers in *italics* indicate figures; numbers in **bold** refer to tables.

For Product Safety Concerns and Information please contact our EU representative GPSR@taylorandfrancis.com
Taylor & Francis Verlag GmbH, Kaufingerstraße 24, 80331 München, Germany

www.ingramcontent.com/pod-product-compliance
Ingram Content Group UK Ltd.
Pitfield, Milton Keynes, MK11 3LW, UK
UKHW022130190926
475702UK00013B/1719
9780367569440